In the Footsteps of Thoreau

In the Footsteps of Thoreau

25 HISTORIC & NATURE WALKS ON Cape Cod

by
Adam Gamble

With Illustrations by
Matthew Gamble

On Cape Publications
Yarmouth Port, Massachusetts

10 9 8 7 6 5 4 3 2

All illustrations are by Matthew Gamble, except where otherwise noted.
Cover/book design and production by Joseph Gallante.
Cover photo of Nauset Light Beach by Adam Gamble.
Portrait of Henry David Thoreau in 1854 by Samuel Worcester Rowse, courtesy
of the Concord Free Public Library.

ISBN 0-9653283-0-9
Library of Congress Catalog Card Number 96-068256

Additional Copies of *In the Footsteps of Thoreau* may be ordered by
sending $14.95, plus $3 postage and handling to: On Cape Publications,
P.O. Box 218, Yarmouth Port MA 02675.
For further information:
http://www.capecod.net/oncape/

TABLE OF CONTENTS

THE ADDITIONAL HIKES #1 & #2

THE SITES

LIST OF MAPS

LIST OF ILLUSTRATIONS

Acknowledgements

In the Footsteps of Thoreau is the product of the contributions, small and large, of more people than can conveniently be listed here. Nevertheless, the author would like to express his sincere gratitude and deepest appreciation to some of the most important individuals and groups.

First and foremost is my wife, Rachel Gamble, who has influenced every aspect of this book. From hiking the trails to editing the text, from patiently listening to actively pushing, she has been there each and every step of the way. No one has ever had a better walking companion.

Next, Dennis Clark and the Provincetown Recreation Department need to be recognized, not only for inspiring this project, but for proving just how much fun it could be. Also, I salute all the men and women "out on the trail" at the Stephen L. French Youth Forestry Camp in Brewster, where lives are routinely transformed through the experience of hiking Cape Cod.

The efforts of Bill Steere, Chuck Stanko and Chip Hughes have also been crucial. Bill, for helping to keep this book focused on the nobility of Thoreau and the "spectacular!" beauty of the Cape; Chuck, for his valued friendship and assistance with the illustrations; and Chip, for dragging me out of the Stone Age and into the magical world of computers.

I'd also like to thank Mary Sicchio, Special Collections Librarian at the William Brewster Nickerson Room at Cape Cod Community College, for freely sharing her deep understanding of Cape Cod history. Also, Jim Owens, the miller at Eastham Windmill, for his keen insights into many subjects covered by this book. And Chief Ranger Rick Obernesser and Supervisory Ranger Bill Burke at the Cape Cod National Seashore for pointing me in the right direction.

The illustrations of Matthew Gamble and the design and production work of Joe Gallante speak for themselves.

Finally, I want to recognize Daisaku Ikeda for his inspirational example. And last but not least, my editor, Stuard Derrick, who has made the process of being edited both educational and pleasurable.●

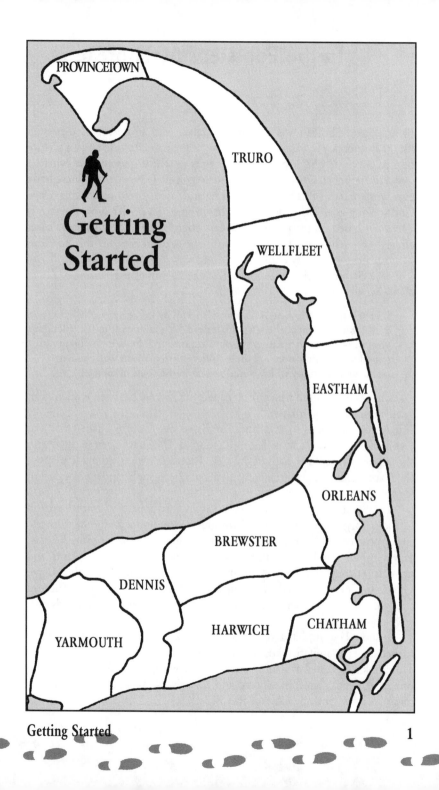

Getting
Started

PROVINCETOWN

TRURO

WELLFLEET

EASTHAM

ORLEANS

BREWSTER

DENNIS

YARMOUTH

HARWICH

CHATHAM

In the Footsteps of Thoreau

Henry David Thoreau was a dedicated walker with an unsurpassed passion for the outdoors. He was a gifted observer of the natural world and an accomplished surveyor who kept detailed records of where he went and what he saw. His nature classic *Cape Cod* is widely considered to be the finest book ever written about this part of New England. Who could be a better Cape Cod walking guide and companion than Thoreau himself? *In the Footsteps of Thoreau* is based on the premise that by better understanding Thoreau's legendary experiences on Cape Cod, our own experiences on this precious peninsula can be greatly enriched.

In 1854, one reviewer of Thoreau's recently-published *Walden, or Life in the Woods*, wrote:

> If men were to follow in Mr. Thoreau's steps, by being more obedient to their loftiest instincts, there would, indeed, be a falling off in the splendour of our houses, in the richness of our furniture and dress, in the luxury of our tables, but how poor are these things in comparison with the new grandeur and beauty which would appear in the souls of men...[1]

Such is the spirit in which *In the Footsteps of Thoreau* has been written nearly a century and a half later.

All of the routes in this guide are based on Thoreau's actual walks as recorded in *Cape Cod* and in Thoreau's journal. They have been selected with the aid of 19th-century maps of the area, Thoreau's own hand-made maps of the Cape, recent topographical maps, aerial photographs and a great deal of legwork in the field.

In addition to the twenty-five walks in this book, the "Sites" section includes fifty-five roads, rivers, lighthouses, windmills and other historic sites, most of which Thoreau wrote about and can still be visited today. Furthermore, this book features many illustrations of places, plants and animals encountered by Thoreau that are still found on the Cape. Quotations are also used throughout this book as examples of what Thoreau thought while he was here, and to serve as inspirations for each walker's own adventures.

It should be emphasized that *In the Footsteps of Thoreau* was not conceived to help walkers imitate Thoreau or to re-enact his Cape Cod experiences. This book is designed as a tool to provide a new approach for understanding one of America's greatest writers, and to assist walkers in discovering the many wonders of Cape Cod for themselves.

Thoreau once wrote:

I desire that there be as many different persons in the world as possible; but I would have each one be very careful to find out and pursue his own way and not his father's or his mother's or his neighbor's instead.[2]

With this in mind, it is hoped that those who follow *In the Footsteps of Thoreau* will come away with an enhanced appreciation of not only Thoreau's *Cape Cod*, but of their own Cape Cod.●

Following *In the Footsteps of Thoreau*

Organization

In the Footsteps of Thoreau is divided into seven sections:

Section 1, **Getting Started**, which you are now reading, serves as the introduction to this book. It offers basic information about the purpose of this book, how to use this book, and safe walking.

Section 2, **Our Guide Thoreau**, includes a brief biography of Henry David Thoreau, an account of Thoreau's visits to the Cape, and an essay about Thoreau's book, *Cape Cod*.

Section 3, **The Individual Walks**, contains fifteen separate short walks, each of which are related to Thoreau's visits to the Cape.

Section 4, **The Great Thoreau Hike, Parts I-VIII**, contains eight challenging hikes that can be followed separately, combined to make one very long hike, or mixed and matched in a variety of ways. It is based specifically on Thoreau's initial Cape Cod walk of 1849 that forms the narrative structure of *Cape Cod*.

Section 5, **The Additional Hikes #1 & #2**, consists of two separate hikes that are also based on Thoreau's 1849 Cape walk.

Section 6, **The Sites**, contains fifty-five historically interesting sites located along the routes of the hikes in this book.

Section 7, **Finishing Up**, includes notes, a bibliography, and an index.

What Thoreau Saw and Words to Walk by

This book includes two components that appear in various places throughout the text. **What Thoreau Saw** consists of more than thirty illustrations and photographs of subjects that Thoreau actually saw on Cape Cod and includes quotations from Thoreau about these subjects. **Words to Walk by**, on the other hand, consists of inspirational quotations from Thoreau that deal specifically with the subject of walking.

Customizing This Book to Fit Your Needs

This guide has been designed so that individual hikes and sites can be enjoyed independently from the rest of the book, allowing each reader to follow *In the Footsteps of Thoreau* in his or her own unique manner.

For instance, this book is designed to be used even by readers who are not interested in walking but who may simply wish to drive to historic sites on Cape Cod. Each site in this book includes directions on how to reach it by car, a description of its historical background and pertinent information about Thoreau. Readers can skip the walks in this book entirely and go directly to the "Sites" section to plan a great guide to driving around historic Cape Cod.

Similarly, this book is set up to be used easily by walkers who are not interested in historic information but who simply want to follow some of the best hiking routes on Cape Cod. Each walk includes detailed directions and information needed to accurately follow it, how to get to the walk by car, a map of the route, and pertinent information about Thoreau. Readers can simply skip the historical information in the "Sites" section.

In fact, this book can even be easily used by those who are uninterested in Thoreau, simply by skipping the subsections of each hike and site entitled "THOREAU." (Of course, hikers who pass up the chance to learn about Thoreau don't know what they are missing!)

But these are extreme examples. Most people have preferences that are less absolute. Some may want to choose a walk based on its location, some are more interested in the lengths of the walks, while others have keen interests in certain historic sites such as windmills or lighthouses. Whatever your needs or inclinations, this book has been designed to allow you the maximum flexibility in using it.

And if you are unsure of what interests you the most, simply follow the hikes in this book in the order that they are listed—and enjoy! This way you'll encounter all of the historic sites and there will be no reason to pick and choose if you don't want to.

Bold Type

To make using this book even easier, a simple method for cross-referencing related hikes and sites using bold-face type has been adopted throughout. The first time any hike or site in this book appears beneath a heading (such as "Location," "Description" or "Thoreau") it is set in bold type to signify that it is a hike or site and can be referenced elsewhere for further information.

For instance, under the "Description" part of the Fort Hill & Red Maple Swamp Trail, the route is described as running past "the grounds of one of the most famous captain's homes on Cape Cod, the **Penniman House**." Bold type is used here to signify that the Penniman House is a historic site listed in this book and that further information about it may be found in the "Sites" section. If you are interested in the Penniman House, you can simply flip to the "Sites" section and read about it. All of the hikes and sites in this book are listed with their page numbers in the Index and the Table of Contents.

Bold type is also used throughout this book to highlight special notes and warnings in the text, such as recommendations to pay particular attention to a direction or a hazard. Also, the title of the "Safe

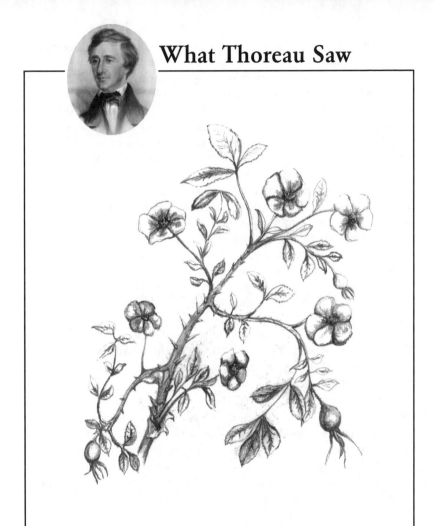

Salt Spray Rose or Rosa Rugosa

When the roses were in bloom, these patches in the midst of the sand displayed such a profusion of blossoms, mingled with the aroma of the bayberry, that no Italian or other artificial rose-garden could equal them. They were perfectly Elysian, and realized my idea of an oasis in the desert.

Walking" subsection is highlighted.

Maps

Another way to cross-reference the hikes and the sites in this book is by using the maps. For instance, Map #6, which describes the Fort Hill & Red Maple Swamp Trail, includes the words "Penniman House" next to a circle with the #5 in it: ❺

This circled #5 signifies that the Penniman House is Site #5 in the "Sites" section of this book and that additional information about it is located there.

Likewise, the individual entry for each site in this book has the map numbers on which it is included in parenthesis directly below its name. Page numbers for all of the maps are listed in the List of Maps that appears after the Table of Contents.●

Safe Walking

Planning Your Walk

There are dangers involved in any outdoor activity, and walking is no exception. Smart, informed planning is one of the best defenses against these dangers, so be sure to read through each walk in this book carefully before heading out onto the trail. Although Cape Cod is not often thought of as a dangerous wilderness, some of the hikes in this book cover significant distances and run through genuinely remote areas. This Safe Walking entry offers a variety of recommendations on a host of different safe walking topics, so please take the time to read it carefully.

Bringing along water is always a good idea no matter how far you are hiking, but especially on routes of 2 miles or more. Furthermore, every hiker should wear thick-soled, comfortable shoes, preferably with good ankle supports.

Cape Cod is fortunate to have four relatively mild seasons, and enjoyable hiking conditions are common every month of the year. Still, dressing for the season is of the utmost importance. In winter be sure to dress in layers. In summer a wide-brimmed hat and sunscreen lotion ought to be kept handy. Rain gear should be considered year-round, and insect repellent is indispensable from spring through autumn.

Distances, Times & Ratings

The total distance, the estimated completion time and the difficulty rating are posted at the top of the first page of each hike in this guide. Use this information to help you gauge your water, food and clothing needs, as well as to allow yourself enough time to complete the walk before nightfall.

All of the walking times in this book are based on the formula of 1 mile per 30 minutes of regular walking with an additional 15 minutes per mile allotted for walking in thick sand. This formula yields a conservative estimate of the time required for an experienced hiker to complete a given route, not including breaks. **NOTE: Do not assume that the estimated printed times will reflect the actual amount of time you will require to complete any given hike until you ascertain how your own pace compares with the above formula.** Every walker proceeds according to his or her own abilities and interests.

As for the rating system, a subjective scale is used. Walks are rated as being either very easy, easy, moderate, difficult, very difficult or extremely difficult. Like the estimated walking times, do not rely on the difficulty ratings in this book until you have learned how they compare with your own abilities.

In the Footsteps of Thoreau

What Thoreau Saw

Tern

Mackerel-gulls were all the while flying over our heads and amid the breakers, sometimes two white ones pursuing a black one; quite at home in the storm, though they are as delicate organizations as sea-jellies and mosses; and we saw that they were adapted to their circumstances rather by their spirits than their bodies. Theirs must be an essentially wilder, that is, less human, nature than that of larks and robins. Their note was like the sound of some vibrating metal, and harmonized well with the scenery and the roar of the surf, as if one had rudely touched the strings of the lyre, which ever lies on the shore; a ragged shred of ocean music tossed aloft on the spray.

Thoreau called terns "mackerel gulls." Depicted here is a roseate tern, currently an endangered species.

Poison Ivy

Poison ivy grows abundantly in many of the dunes and wooded areas described in this guide. The rhyme "leaves of three/let it be" is used by many people to remember what poison ivy looks like. Unfortunately, while poison ivy leaves do grow in groups of three, the plant can appear as a trailing vine, a climbing vine or as an erect shrub. Its leaves can also be green or red, shiny or dull. Learn what poison ivy looks like and be sure to avoid it.

Ticks

See "What Thoreau Saw" illustration on opposite page.

Walking on the Beach

Walking on the beach can be a joyous experience, but at the wrong time it can also be extremely dangerous. This is true of all the beach walking included in the hikes in this guide, but it is particularly true of the beach walking in **The Great Thoreau Hike**. Every part of The Great Thoreau Hike includes a substantial walk along the **Great Beach**, which lies between the Atlantic Ocean and the high, sandy cliffs that run the length of the Outer Cape. Thoreau recorded the observation in Cape Cod that it "was sometimes inconvenient and even dangerous walking under the bank, when there was a great tide, with an easterly wind, which caused the sand to cave." And as usual, he was right.

During very high tides and severe storms the ocean washes right up to the base of the cliff and erodes it. At these times the entire beach can become submerged and can be a perilous place. The distance between "hollows," where one can easily climb off the beach, can be as much as five miles; and climbing up the steep sandy cliff-face–in places as high as 170 feet!–can be impossible. **Do not walk on the beach during very high tides or severe storms.**

Tops of the Cliffs

The top of the marine scarp, or cliff, that runs the length of the **Great Beach** is an unsafe place to stand or walk. While the footing there may appear to be solid, the cliff-face below the edge may have eroded away, leaving it on the verge of collapsing.

Hunting

Most of the hikes in this guide run through areas where hunting is strictly prohibited at all times. This includes all fifteen of the hikes in the "Individual Walks" section, both of the hikes in the "Additional Walks"

In the Footsteps of Thoreau

What Thoreau Saw

Deer Tick & American Dog Tick

But it must be added, that this kind of shrubbery swarmed with wood-ticks, sometimes very troublesome parasites, and which it takes very horny fingers to crack.

As Thoreau discovered, ticks are common on Cape Cod. This is a particular problem for outdoor enthusiasts, as various species can carry diseases. Deer ticks may transmit Lyme Disease, and the American Dog tick may carry Rocky Mountain Spotted Fever and other diseases. In order to avoid being bitten by ticks be sure to tuck the bottom of your pants into your socks, and your shirt into your pants, to help keep ticks on the outside of your clothing. Various sources also recommend wearing light colors, so that ticks can be seen more easily. You should also check yourself frequently, wear insect repellent (especially on pants, shoes and legs), and have someone check you after you complete each walk.

section, and Part I of **The Great Thoreau Hike**. Furthermore, no hunting is allowed anywhere in Massachusetts on Sundays.

Nevertheless, some stretches of The Great Thoreau Hike Parts II-VIII pass through areas where hunting is permitted from September 1 through March 31, excluding Sundays. **NOTE: During these times walkers are advised to wear a hunter-orange hat or other hunter-orange clothing while on the "Initial Routes" of Parts II-VIII of The Great Thoreau Hike. Walkers should also avoid wearing predominantly black, brown or tan clothing during hunting season, or clothing with patches of white that could be mistaken for the white tail of a deer.**

Throughout the annual hunting season various dates are legally designated for hunting specific game and for using various weapons. The most dangerous of these times for hikers on Cape Cod is "Deer Week" (usually the first week of December), when shotgun hunting for deer is permitted. **NOTE: The author of this book strongly discourages walking any of the "Initial Routes" of Parts II-VIII of The Great Thoreau Hike during Deer Week.**

Hiking along the "Initial Routes" of The Great Thoreau Hike, Parts II-VIII during other parts of hunting season is left to each individual's discretion. (Walkers should be safe year-round from hunters on the "Return Routes" of The Great Thoreau Hike that run along the **Great Beach**.) A free hunter information pamphlet that includes maps of hunting areas within the **Cape Cod National Seashore** is available at the **Park Headquarters**, the **Salt Pond Visitor Center** and the **Province Lands Visitor Center**. Call the Park Headquarters at (508) 349-3785 for further information. Also, the Massachusetts Division of Fisheries & Wildlife puts out a pamphlet with abstracts of the hunting rules and regulations and other information. A copy of these abstracts can be obtained at most sporting goods stores and may also be requested directly from the Division of Fisheries & Wildlife by calling (617) 727-3151.

Avoid Getting Lost

As stated elsewhere in this guide, walkers should find it fairly easy to avoid getting lost on all fifteen of the routes in the "Individual Walks" section of this book, and on both of the routes in the "Additional Walks" section. However, all eight parts of **The Great Thoreau Hike** include routes that are not officially marked, and which can be challenging to follow. (See the Introduction to The Great Thoreau Hike for further information.) **To avoid getting lost, walkers are recommended to thoroughly read through each hike *before* going out and to carry a compass at all times.** Some walkers may even want to supplement the maps included in this book with U.S. topographical maps which are available at various local sporting goods stores, and at the **Salt Pond Visitor Center**, the **Cape Cod National Seashore Park Headquarters** and at the **Province Lands Visitor Center**. The maps entitled "Orleans Quadrangle," "Wellfleet Quadrangle," "North Truro Quadrangle" and "Provincetown Quadrangle" together cover all eight parts of The Great Thoreau Hike, and both routes in the Additional Walks section.

If you do get lost (which all hikers inevitably do at one time or another), the best course of action is to backtrack immediately to the last known landmark that you passed. Once you have returned to this landmark, continue ahead again. You should thus be able to find your way through a steady process of elimination. By closely reading the map and directions, and by paying close attention to their surroundings, most walkers should be able to find their way.

Of course, there is no substitute for experience. The more one hikes, the better one will become at staying on the trails. Inexperienced hikers should follow the shorter walks in this guide before attempting the longer trails.

Walking Plans

While most of the hikes in this guide, particularly those listed in the "Individual Walks" section, tend to follow well-marked and frequently-followed trails, the use of a walking plan can be a prudent precaution when following longer hikes, especially those in **The Great Thoreau Hike** section of this book. Your plan should include your route, what time you are leaving and what time you are expected back. Leave your walking plan with a responsible person who is not coming along. This person should be directed to call the appropriate authorities (police or Park Rangers) if you do not return by a mutually agreed-upon time.

Low Impact Hiking

In order to insure that other walkers may continue to enjoy the natural settings of these hikes, certain rules of etiquette must be followed by all. **It is each individual walker's personal responsibility to keep his or her impact on the trail and the surrounding environment to a minimum.** Thoreau has often been quoted as asserting, "In wildness is the preservation of the world"[1]; and in following in his footsteps we should all remember to:

- Carry out everything we bring in.
- Stay on marked trails.
- Keep noise levels low.
- Avoid disturbing natural features such as animals or plants.

- Avoid disturbing cultural features such as historic structures, monuments, etc.
- Avoid walking on beach grass and other plants, especially in the dunes.
- Stay off the "foredune" area, which is designated as the first row of dunes back from the beach.
- Refrain from climbing on the cliff-face of the marine scarp that runs along the **Great Beach**.
- Stay back from cliff edges.
- Keep all pets on leashes and avoid bringing them into areas where pets are prohibited.
- Stay away from designated bird nesting areas.
- Obey all posted rules and regulations.●

In the Footsteps of Thoreau

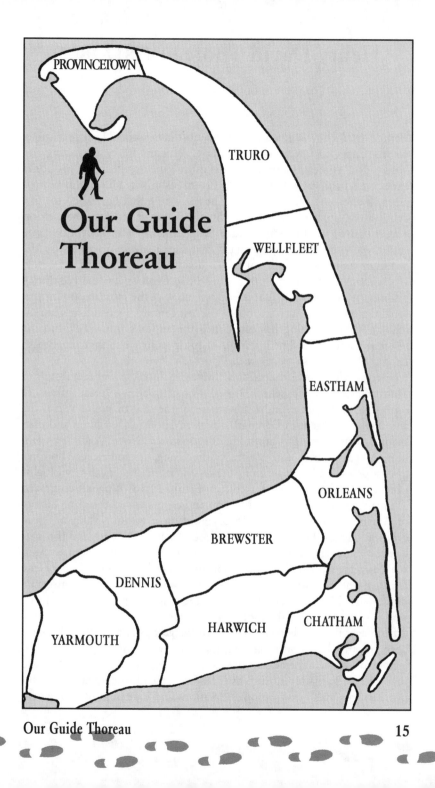

Our Guide Thoreau

Henry David Thoreau (1817-1862)

Henry David Thoreau lived one of the most inspirational lives of all time. As his Cape Cod walking companion, William Ellery Channing, Jr., observed in Thoreau's very first biography, "The excellence of his books and style is identical with the excellence of his private life." In his master-piece, *Walden, or Life in the Woods*, Thoreau wrote that he wished to "live deliberately"–and live deliberately he did. Thoreau dedicated himself on a daily basis to what he identified as "Higher Laws," the concept that one "must get your living by loving,"[1] that living life to its fullest is the birthright and responsibility of each individual.

Although Thoreau did not receive the recognition he deserved during his lifetime, he has nevertheless inspired many of the most important personalities and social movements of the last century. Preeminent Thoreau scholar Walter Harding has catalogued the author's influence[2], and the result is astounding. For instance, Harding points out that the British Labour Party was so taken with Thoreau's views that for a time they referred to their local chapters as "Walden Clubs." Another example is Mahatma Gandhi, who cited Thoreau as having been a "great influence" on his life and work in India. Elsewhere, at the start of World War II the anti-Nazi movement in Denmark espoused Thoreau's teachings and used them in their campaign against Hitler's supporters. Nobel Peace Prize-winning American hero Dr. Martin Luther King, Jr. embraced Thoreau's philosophies as a key tenet in his leadership of the American Civil Rights Movement. Revolutionary architect Frank Lloyd Wright recognized Thoreau's influence on his profession and even asserted that "the history of American architecture would be incomplete without Thoreau's wise observations on the subject." Jack Kerouac, Allen Ginsberg and the Beat Generation revered Thoreau, as did many members of the Vietnam Anti-war Movement. What's more, Thoreau is largely considered to be the father, if not the patron saint, of the all-pervasive modern environmental movement. His declaration, "In Wildness is the preservation of the world," for instance, is the motto of the Sierra Club.

Indeed, the numbers and names of the groups and leaders who have been inspired by Thoreau are impressive; however, it is the uncounted legions of individual readers whose values have been shaped by Thoreau that are sure to matter most in the grand scheme of things. Even with his penchant for making sweeping declarations and his oftentimes judgmental attitudes, Thoreau has a way of connecting with people on a deeply personal, even intimate level. Whether explaining his method of cleaning his hut, railing against the inhumanities of slavery, observing the colors and patterns of bird plumage, or describing the roar of the ocean, Thoreau bespeaks an eloquence and earnestness that does not fail to reach his readers. So strong is his voice that many of his readers view their first reading of *Walden* as major turning points in their lives.

Although he is today recognized as a truly world-class writer, and is read by a world-wide audience*, Thoreau was anything but a world traveller. Born in Concord, Massachusetts, he lived there his entire life and made no excursions farther than Canada and Minnesota. Instead of combing the globe for subjects, he believed that his native New England provided more than enough writing material. "I will not talk about people a thousand miles off, but come as near home as I can," he once declared.[3]

While Thoreau is often misunderstood as an ivory-tower dreamer, he actually kept his feet planted firmly on the ground. In fact, for such a prodigious and erudite writer, he was exceedingly handy when it came to practical matters. Partially out of economic necessity, and partially because he was naturally adept at getting things done, he worked a variety of jobs during his lifetime. In 1847, he responded to a questionnaire sent to him by his alma mater, Harvard College, as follows:

> I know not whether mine is a profession, or a trade, or whatnot. It is not yet learned, and in every instance has been practiced before being studied....I am a Schoolmaster—a private Tutor, a Surveyor—a Gardener, a Farmer—a Painter, I mean a House Painter, a Carpenter, a Mason, a Day-Laborer, a Pencil-Maker, a Glass-paper Maker, a Writer, and some times a Poetaster.

At a time when a college education virtually assured one of a professional career with significant social status and wealth, Thoreau was one Harvard graduate who did not mind getting his hands dirty.

As for his literary career, Thoreau was fortunate to come into contact with some of the foremost writers of his day. He knew Nathaniel Hawthorne, Henry Wadsworth Longfellow, Margaret Fuller, and even met Walt Whitman, to name just a few. However, it was Thoreau's association with Ralph Waldo Emerson that was most important, not only for Thoreau but for American literature in general. The relationship between Thoreau and Emerson proved to be one of the most intriguing and influential in the history of American letters.

---

* Harding claims that copies of Walden are even more common today in Japanese bookstores than they are in the U.S.!

Emerson, who was 14 years older than Thoreau, not only wrote Thoreau a letter of recommendation for a scholarship to Harvard, but also presented the Phi Beta Kappa oration* at Thoreau's graduation ceremony. After college Thoreau returned to Concord, where he and Emerson developed a deep friendship, particularly through their activities with a group of like-minded thinkers known as Transcendentalists. As their relationship progressed, Thoreau eventually moved into Emerson's home and became a close friend to the entire Emerson family. While there, he earned his keep in a variety of the occupations listed above, including laborer, gardener, and writer and assistant editor for the Transcendentalist magazine, *The Dial*. Although their friendship later deteriorated, Thoreau spent about three years as part of the Emerson household; and this period of time does not include the two years that Thoreau lived on Emerson's land at Walden Pond, yet another example of the extent of their historic literary connection.

Thoreau's experience at Walden Pond was one of the most important events of his life. It was there that he developed his skills as a farmer, a mason, a carpenter and, of course, a writer. Most importantly, his experiences at the pond inspired what novelist Sinclair Lewis has described as "one of three or four unquestionable classics of American Literature,"[4] *Walden, or Life in the Woods*.

Like all great books, *Walden* has meant many things to many people. Thoreau wrote that he "went to the woods to front the essential facts of life," and his attempt to do so is at the heart of the book. Unfortunately, various myths have sprung up around Thoreau's life at Walden that need to be debunked. The primary misconception is that Thoreau advocated living like a hermit. The fact is that *Walden* is not so much about moving away from people, as it is about moving closer to nature.

Although Thoreau was a free-thinker and no slave to society, he was hardly a hermit. As we know, he was very close with the Emerson family and participated extensively in New England Transcendentalist circles. But he was also extremely dedicated to his own family. In addition, he developed a number of important friendships, like the one he had with Channing; and he also dutifully maintained correspondences with a wide variety of friends and acquaintances. Furthermore, he served as a "conductor" for the underground railroad, aiding runaway slaves on their flights to freedom in Canada. And he even became an active lecturer who was paid to address large audiences from different communities around New England. Furthermore, Thoreau was a much-respected surveyor who

*Emerson's address was later released in essay form as "The American Scholar" and has since been recognized as a major turning point in the development of American literature.

dealt with numerous clients from across the Concord area. Despite his life-long bachelorhood and his famously independent nature, he was a very active member of his community.

As to Thoreau's life at Walden Pond, the esteemed scholar Robert D. Richardson, Jr. has written, "Thoreau was very aware that what he was doing was not braving wildness.... It was clear to him at the very outset that what he was doing could be done by anyone. It did not require a retreat from society. Thoreau's venture was in no sense a retreat or withdrawal."[5] In Thoreau's own words, he strove "to live deep and suck the marrow out of life" and "to rout all that was not life, to cut a broad swath and shave close, to drive life into a corner." This attitude is one of the key reasons that *Walden* is such an enduring treasure. It is about much more than mere thoughts and theories; it is about living well, living "deliberately."

While Thoreau wrote many respected works–including *A Week on the Concord and Merrimack Rivers*, *The Maine Woods* and *Cape Cod*–two other relevant literary works are the essay "Civil Disobedience" and his journal. "Civil Disobedience" is without a doubt Thoreau's most important political tract. In it he explains why he allowed himself to be arrested and jailed for non-payment of taxes, as a protest against the U.S. Government's support of slavery and its involvement in the Mexican War of 1846-1848. In "Civil Disobedience" he champions the idea that the laws of the state are subservient to the laws of right and wrong to which each individual must hold himself accountable. Thoreau presents many intelligent and persuasive arguments in "Civil Disobedience," but what makes it such a powerful document is that he uses his own experiences to illustrate his points. Thoreau actually lived up to the lofty ideals he espouses in "Civil Disobedience" and even chose to be incarcerated rather than compromise his beliefs.

Although *Walden* is generally celebrated as Thoreau's greatest work, his journal may well prove in time to be equally important. Thoreau's journal is massive–over two million words, or about 7,000 printed pages! But it is not the mere quantity of the writing in his journal that makes it such an invaluable resource; it is the quality of that writing. Thoreau began his journal at the age of 20, at the suggestion of Emerson, and used it throughout his lifetime to record his daily activities, and as a breeding ground for many of the ideas he later developed in his more formal works.

In his journal, Thoreau's ingenious intellect and intense passion for life are given free reign; and through its copious pages, he emerges as someone who not only wrote about how he lived, but who lived in a manner that was worthy of being written about.

In simple, contemporary terms, Thoreau walked his talk. It is hoped that *In the Footsteps of Thoreau* will enhance the appreciation of both his walk and his talk.●

Thoreau on Cape Cod

Thoreau outlined his visits to the Cape on the very first page of *Cape Cod*:

> I made a visit to Cape Cod in October, 1849, another the succeeding June, and another to Truro, 1855; the first and last time with a single companion, the second time alone. I have spent, in all, about three weeks on the Cape; walked from Eastham to Provincetown twice on the Atlantic side, and once on the Bay side also, excepting four or five miles, and crossed the Cape half a dozen times on my way; but, having come so fresh to the sea, I have got but little salted.

While Thoreau's account is accurate as far as it goes, it does not include his fourth Cape excursion of June 1857, by which time the majority of his book had been written. This fourth visit, which Thoreau made alone, brought the total number of nights he spent "on Cape" to thirty. Thoreau's friend, the poet William Ellery Channing, Jr., served as the "single companion" who accompanied him in October of 1849 and July of 1855.

As to the writing of *Cape Cod*, Thoreau appears to have laid down the framework for the book within the first few months after returning to Concord in 1849. In fact, he was able to present four well-received lectures about Cape Cod in the early months of 1850, prior to making his second visit to the Cape that June. Thus, Thoreau's 1849 trip established the narrative structure of the book to which various passages, impressions and anecdotes were added from his subsequent Cape sojourns, experiences elsewhere and ongoing research.

By 1855 Thoreau had arranged to have *Cape Cod* serialized in the literary magazine *Putnam's Monthly*, which had already published his travelogue known today as "A Yankee in Canada." The first four chapters of *Cape Cod* appeared in 1855 in the summer issues of *Putnam's*; however, the series was abruptly dropped by the magazine without explanation.

Although it is uncertain why *Putnam's* discontinued *Cape Cod*, scholar Joseph J. Moldenhauer has made a persuasive case that the magazine's editors "took umbrage" at Thoreau's relatively raw and often irreverent

What Thoreau Saw

Thoreau's Map of Cape Cod

Cape Cod is the bared and bended arm of Massachusetts; the shoulder is at Buzzard's Bay, the elbow, or crazy-bone, at Cape Mallebarre, the wrist at Truro, and the sandy fist at Provincetown—behind which the State stands on her guard, with her back to the Green Mountains, and her feet planted on the floor of the ocean, like an athlete protecting her bay—boxing with the north-east storms, and, ever and anon, heaving up her Atlantic adversary from the lap of earth; ready to thrust forward her other fist, which keeps guard the while upon her breast at Cape Ann.

Shown here is a map of Cape Cod in Thoreau's own hand, probably traced or copied from another source. Thoreau may have carried this map with him on one or more of his visits to Cape Cod. Permission to reprint it here was given by the Concord Free Public Library.

humor, especially that of Chapter 5, "The Wellfleet Oysterman."* Given Thoreau's staunch resistance to censorship, it is believed that the editors chose to simply stop printing *Cape Cod*, rather than engage its author in a lengthy debate about those aspects of the book they considered offensive.

Apparently Thoreau did not bother to submit *Cape Cod* for publication elsewhere during his lifetime. No portions of it appeared in print again until two chapters were run in the *Atlantic Monthly* in the autumn of 1864, and the complete ten-chapter book was finally released by Ticknor & Fields early in 1865.

Interestingly enough, it does not appear that Thoreau ever really stopped working on *Cape Cod*. Moldenhauer has found evidence that Thoreau added bits and pieces to the text as late as 1860 and probably even as late as 1861, by which time he had contracted the cold that would lead to his prolonged illness and subsequent death on May 6, 1862.

Given Thoreau's lack of enthusiasm for travel, it is noteworthy that he visited Cape Cod a total of four times, and that he even returned to the Cape after his book about it had essentially been written. The fact that he was still making additions to *Cape Cod* a dozen years after he began it says as much about his passion for his book as it does about his attitude toward the Cape. Thoreau may have only "got but a little salted" while on Cape Cod, but it is clear that both his imagination and his heart were captured by it.●

* Moldenhauer served as the editor of the superb Princeton University Press 1988 edition of *Cape Cod*. His outstanding scholarship, particularly in his "Historical Introduction" and "Textual Introduction" to the Princeton text, has been invaluable to the writing of *In the Footsteps of Thoreau*, especially this section.

In the Footsteps of Thoreau

What Thoreau Saw

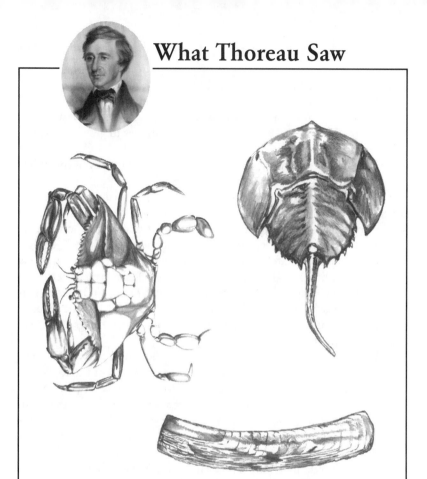

Crabs, Horse-shoes & Razor Clams

The sea-shore is a sort of neutral ground, a most advantageous point from which to contemplate this world. It is even a trivial place. The waves forever rolling to the land are too far-travelled and untamable to be familiar. Creeping along the endless beach amid the sun-squall and the foam, it occurs to us that we, too, are the product of sea-slime. It is a wild, rank place, and there is no flattery in it. Strewn with crabs, horse-shoes, and razor-clams, and whatever the sea casts up...

Thoreau's *Cape Cod*

Thoreau's *Cape Cod* is unquestionably the best book ever written about the place. Its influence in forming the world's opinions of Cape Cod, and for that matter Cape Cod's opinions of itself can not be overestimated. Since its publication in 1865, its popularity continues to grow. It is generally accepted as the standard by which all other books on Cape Cod are measured, and has been paraphrased and quoted by virtually every author who has written about the Cape since Thoreau's time.

One reason for *Cape Cod*'s importance is that virtually no interesting aspect of the place escaped Thoreau's eyes. Although he only visited Cape Cod four times, and spent a total of only about one month "on Cape," Thoreau's range of subjects include the peninsula's history, geology, botany, zoology, climate, characters, religions, leaders and legends. As Cape Cod anthologist and nature writer Robert Finch has written, "No better writer has ever written so extensively of it."[6] From windmills to saltworks, from beach fleas to blackfish, from lighthouses to Humane Houses, like no writer before or since, Thoreau wrote of those things that have made the Cape truly unique.

Another aspect of *Cape Cod* that has made it such a favorite is the sense one gets that Thoreau truly enjoyed the time he spent here. For all of the wonderful poems, stories, novels, histories, guidebooks, and natural and scientific studies that have been written with Cape Cod as their subject, none is as humorous as Thoreau's. Where else in all of Cape Cod literature, can one find a chapter more humorous than Thoreau's "Wellfleet Oysterman?"

Thoreau's walking partner and dear friend, William Ellery Channing, Jr., put it simply: "I think Thoreau loved Cape Cod."[7] Likewise, the great Thoreau scholar Walter Harding has been quoted many times for his observation that "*Cape Cod* is Thoreau's sunniest happiest book. It bubbles over with jokes, puns, tall tales, and genial good humor."[8] Indeed, in *Cape Cod* Thoreau not only has fun, he pokes fun—at preachers, politicians, fishermen, sea captains, the Pilgrims, the soil, the trees, the roads and more. As *Cape Cod*'s recent editor, Joseph J. Moldenhauer has pointed out, it may well have been *Cape Cod*'s irreverent humor that prevented it from being published in its entirety during Thoreau's lifetime. In fact, there are still Cape Codders around who have not entirely forgiven Thoreau for his description of Cape Cod women:

> A strict regard for the truth obliges us to say that the women we saw that day looked exceedingly pinched up. They had prominent chins and noses, having lost all their teeth, and a sharp W would represent their

profile. They were not so well preserved as their husbands; or perchance they were well preserved as dried specimens. (Their husbands, however, were pickled.)

Despite his many good-natured jabs at them, the truth is that Thoreau displayed much more respect for Cape Codders than he is given credit for. He once wrote, "The deeper you penetrate into the woods, the more intelligent, and, in one sense, less countrified do you find the inhabitants; for always the pioneer has been a traveler, and, to some extent, a man of the world."[9] And although Thoreau did not consider Cape Codders to be woodsmen, he certainly thought them to be pioneers of a sort—and men of the world. He writes:

> A great proportion of the inhabitants of the Cape are always thus abroad about their teaming on some ocean highway or other, and the history of one of their ordinary trips would cast the Argonautic expedition into the shade.

Thoreau recounts his 1849 stagecoach journey from Sandwich to Orleans: "I was struck by the pleasant equality which reigned among the stage company, and their broad and invulnerable good humor. They were what is called free and easy, and met one another to advantage, as men who had, at length, learned how to live." Similarly, despite his knee-slappingly funny repartee with the cantankerous Wellfleet Oysterman, it is clear that the Concordian had a genuine affection and respect for the Cape Codder.

Cape Codders were fascinating to Thoreau, not so much because they were plain-spoken, or because many of them were provincial, but because of their ability to coexist with the fierce and unpredictable Atlantic. Thoreau visited the Truro Shipwreck Monument, a memorial for 57 fishermen lost in a single storm in 1841, and wrote, "Their graveyard is the ocean." He contemplated a so-called **Humane House** and concluded that it was only "a stage to the grave." He passed by homes with only widows for residents. He even spoke with a man who disliked the sound of the ocean because it reminded him of the son he lost to it. "It would not do to talk of shipwrecks there, for almost every family has lost some of its members at sea," Thoreau realized. And with this knowledge of the integral role the Atlantic played in the lives, and deaths, of Cape Codders he wrote:

> Yet this same placid Ocean, as civil now as a city's harbor, a place for ships and commerce, will erelong be lashed into sudden fury, and all its caves and cliffs, will resound with tumult. It will ruthlessly heave these vessels to and fro, break them in pieces in its sandy or stony jaws, and deliver their crews to sea-monsters. It will play with them like sea-weed,

distend them like dead frogs, and carry them about, now high, now low, to show to the fishes, giving them a nibble. This gentle Ocean will toss and tear the rags of a man's body like the father of mad bulls and his relatives may be seen seeking the remnants for weeks along the strand.

Throughout his life Thoreau searched for an understanding of what he called "wildness"–that ultimate quality of nature that he considered superior to the artificiality of civilization. He once declared, "Life consists with wildness. The most alive is the wildest. Not yet subdued to man, its presence refreshes him."[10] In *Walden*, he found such "wildness" at a pond. In his first book, *A Week on the Concord and Merrimack Rivers*, he discovered it along waterways. In *The Maine Woods*, he realized it on a mountaintop. But in *Cape Cod*, he encountered a wildness the presence of which does more than "refresh." He found a "wilderness reaching around the globe, wilder than a Bengal jungle, and fuller of monsters…"

Thus, it is no accident that Thoreau opens *Cape Cod* with a scene of carnage as powerful as anything he has ever written. When he reports on the remains of the shipwreck of the *Saint John* in Cohasset, he is reporting on the ultimate consequences of wildness. There he saw the "marble feet and matted heads" of the dead, including one "swollen and mangled body of a drowned girl…to which some rags still adhered, with a string, half concealed by the flesh, about its swollen neck." And from this first grim chapter, Thoreau continues throughout his text to expound on the realities of the wildness he encountered on the Cape. In addition to the *Saint John*, there are the wrecks of the British man-of-war **Somerset**, the pirate ship **Whydah**, the Franklin, the Brutus, and even a lumber-laden schooner at Wood End. There are descriptions of human corpses, of slaughtered whales, of a "vast morgue… strewn with crabs, horse-shoes and razor clams."

In *Cape Cod* Thoreau grapples with far more than any merely intellectual or philosophical concept of wildness. He deals with what became for him a very personal and physical understanding of it–personal not just because of his meticulous research, his discussions with locals or his vast experiences elsewhere with nature, but because of what he physically discovered along the beach.

Less than three weeks after having returned to Concord from his second *Cape Cod* excursion, and less than ten months after his first Cape visit, the tragedy of death at sea struck Thoreau's own life. On July 19, 1850 Margaret Fuller, her husband and their young son were lost off Fire Island, New York in the wreck of the *Elizabeth* en route from Italy to America.

Margaret Fuller had been an integral part of the close-knit Transcendentalist group to which Thoreau and Ralph Waldo Emerson belonged. Soon after the wreck, Thoreau was dispatched to Fire Island

What Thoreau Saw

Truro Shipwreck Monument

Truro was settled in the year 1700 as Dangerfield. This was a very appropriate name, for I afterward read on a monument in the graveyard, near Pamet River, the following inscription:

> Sacred to the memory of 57 citizens of Truro, who were lost in the seven vessels, which foundered at sea in the memorable gale of Oct. 3rd, 1841.

Their names and ages by families were recorded on different sides of the stone. They were said to have been lost on George's Bank, and I was told that only one vessel drifted ashore on the back side of the Cape, with the boys locked into the cabin and drowned. It is said that the homes of all were "within a circuit of two miles."

This monument is located in the cemetery of the First Congregational Parish of Truro.

with funds from Emerson and written documents from Channing (Fuller's brother-in-law) to act as a representative of Fuller's family in the recovery of the corpses and personal effects of the Fullers. Arriving at the scene some days later, Thoreau made an extensive but essentially fruitless search of the area around the wreck and questioned many locals before finally receiving word that a body had washed up on the beach some two miles away. After dutifully hiking up the beach, he found that the "body" was little more than a pile of bones with "flesh adhering to them." Incorporating the experience into *Cape Cod* he wrote:

> But as I stood there they grew more and more imposing. They were alone with the beach and the sea, whose hollow roar seemed addressed to them, and I was impressed as if there was an understanding between them and the ocean which necessarily left me out, with my snivelling sympathies. That dead body had taken possession of the shore, and reigned over it as no living one could, in the name of a certain majesty which belonged to it.

Although the bones were never identified, it is clear that their discovery impressed Thoreau deeply and greatly contributed to his understanding of his encounters with the wildness of Cape Cod. Thus, when he writes of the beach, he does so as more than just a well-read and perceptive landlubber. Speaking from his own experience, Thoreau can write, "There is naked Nature—inhumanely sincere, wasting no thought on man...." He knows it to be "a wild rank place" where "the carcasses of men and beasts together lie stately up upon its shelf, rotting and bleaching in the sun and waves."

Thoreau wrote that he perceived "a certain majesty" to the bones he found on the beach. It is this "certain majesty" that echoes throughout *Cape Cod* as loud as the sound of the surf, and which makes the walks in this book such powerful educational experiences. Shipwrecks are thankfully not as common as they once were, but one will still find "naked Nature" here. Thoreau's final words on Cape Cod remain as true as ever:

A man may stand there and put all America behind him.●

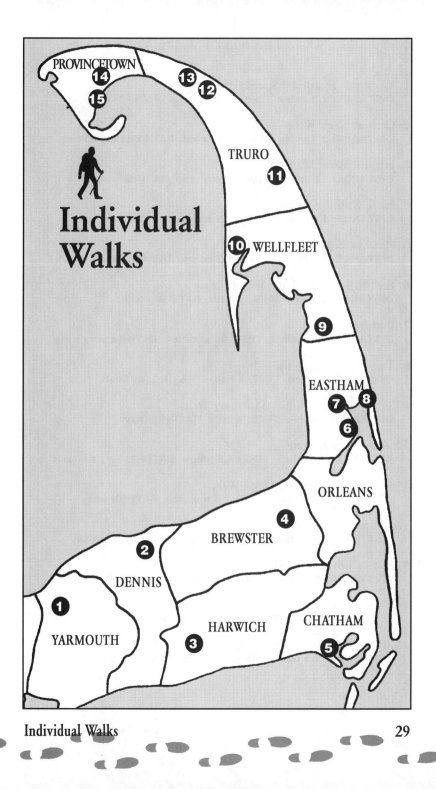

PROVINCETOWN

14

15

13
12

TRURO

11

10 WELLFLEET

9

EASTHAM

7 8

6

ORLEANS

4

BREWSTER

2

DENNIS

1

YARMOUTH

HARWICH

3

CHATHAM

5

Individual
Walks

Individual Walks

1. Yarmouth Historical Society Trails
   DISTANCE: 1.5 miles   TIME: 45 minutes   RATING: easy

2. Quivett Neck Walk
   DISTNACE: 3.8 miles   TIME: 2.5 hours   RATING: moderate

3. Herring River Walk
   DISTANCE: 1.6 miles   TIME 45 minutes   RATING: easy

4. Little Cliff Pond Trail
   DISTANCE: 1.6 MILES   TIME: 45 minutes   RATING: easy

5. Harding Beach & Lighthouse Walk
   DISTANCE: 1.8 miles   TIME: 1.5 hours   RATING: easy

6. Fort Hill & Red Maple Swamp Trail
   DISTANCE: 2 miles   TIME: 1 hour   RATING: easy

7. Buttonbush Trail
   DISTANCE: 0.25 miles   TIME: 20 minutes   RATING: very easy

8. The Outermost Walk
   DISTANCE: 5 miles   TIME: 4 hours   RATING: difficult

9. Wellfleet Bay Wildlife Sanctuary Trails
   DISTANCE: 2 miles   TIME: 1 hour   RATING: easy

10. Great Island Trail
   DISTANCE: 7.7 miles   TIME: 4.5 hours   RATING: very difficult

11. Pamet Cranberry & Dune Walk
   DISTANCE: 1.1 miles   TIME: 45 minutes   RATING: easy

12. Pilgrim Spring Trail
   DISTANCE: 0.75 miles   TIME: 30 minuites   RATING: easy

13. Small's Swamp Trail
   DISTANCE: 0.75 miles   TIME: 30 minutes   RATING: easy

14. Beech Forest Trail
   DISTANCE: 1 mile   TIME: 45 minutes   RATING: easy

15. Provincetown Center Walk
   DISTANCE: 1.3 miles   TIME: 1-2 hours   RATING: easy

In the Footsteps of Thoreau

Introduction to the Individual Walks

Unlike the eight parts of **The Great Thoreau Hike** in this guide, which can be very challenging and require substantial amounts of time and supplies, most of the fifteen walks described in this section can be followed with a minimum of supplies and preparation. In fact, only the 7.7-mile **Great Island Trail**, the 5-mile **Outermost Walk**, and the 3.8-mile **Quivett Neck Walk** have estimated walking times of more than 2 hours. In general, these walks include well-maintained trails and are recommended more as short and pleasant morning or afternoon strolls than as major treks.

All of the "Individual Walks" have been selected to provide followers of *In the Footsteps of Thoreau* with as many walking locations, challenges and terrain as possible. They do not attempt to duplicate the extensive walks Thoreau was famous for taking on his daily outings. These walks are spread across ten Cape towns, from the **Yarmouth Historical Society Trails** in Yarmouth Port, all the way to the **Beech Forest Trail** in Provincetown. They vary in terrain from Chatham's **Harding Beach & Lighthouse Walk**, which runs through sand dunes and along the beach, to the **Provincetown Center Walk**, which is situated in the center of the most densely populated village on the Cape.

These walks offer many exciting insights into both Thoreau and Cape Cod history. The **Little Cliff Pond Trail** in Brewster, for instance, runs around one of the kettle ponds that Thoreau encountered and commented on in 1857. The **Outermost Walk** in Eastham retraces the route that nature writer Henry Beston followed to and from his famous "Outermost House." The **Herring River Walk** in Harwich runs along the same river from which Thoreau's eel breakfast was caught when he stayed near its banks. And the **Pilgrim Spring Trail** runs past the spring from which the Pilgrims drank their first New World water.

From beach walks to woodland walks, from the Pilgrims to Thoreau, from the Mid-Cape to the Outer Cape, the routes in this section offer something for everyone.●

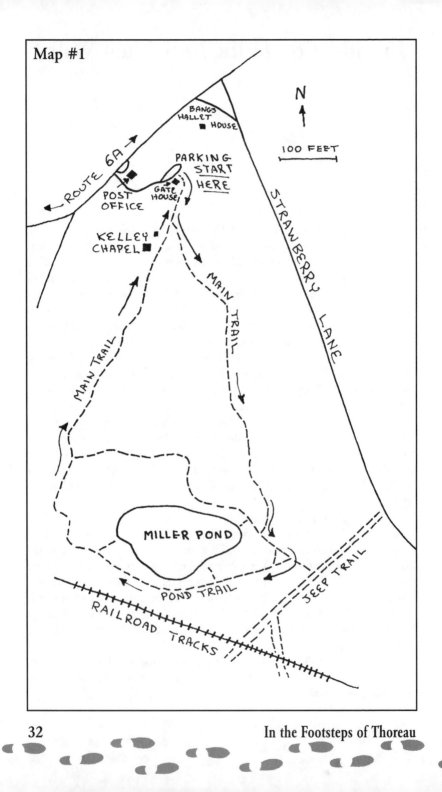

Map #1

N

100 FEET

ROUTE 6A

BANGS
HALLET
HOUSE

PARKING
START
HERE

POST
OFFICE

GATE
HOUSE

STRAWBERRY LANE

KELLEY
CHAPEL

MAIN TRAIL

MAIN TRAIL

MILLER POND

POND TRAIL

JEEP TRAIL

RAILROAD TRACKS

In the Footsteps of Thoreau

Yarmouth Historical Society Trails

No. 1

DISTANCE 1.5 miles
TIME 45 minutes
RATING easy

Location

This walk is located just south of the Yarmouth Port Post Office, off Route 6A. Follow Route 6 to Exit 7. At the end of the off-ramp turn right and follow Willow Street 1.2 miles to the t-junction with Route 6A. Turn right onto Route 6A and follow it 0.6 miles. Turn right just before the Yarmouth Port Post Office onto the paved driveway marked "Yarmouth Historical Society & Nature Trails" and park near the gatehouse.

Description

These lovely trails are located on land that was originally owned by Anthony Thacher, one of Yarmouth's first three European settlers who began cultivating the property as early as 1639. An easy walk, this route includes just a few hills and consists of two overlapping trails, the "Main Trail" and the "Pond Trail." The former runs past the quaint Kelley Chapel, while the latter offers scenic views of Miller Pond and skirts the Yarmouth railroad tracks and Woodside Cemetery. The trail also starts near the lovely Bangs Hallet House, home of the Yarmouth Historical Society.

Thoreau

When Thoreau came to Yarmouth in 1857, he stopped less than a mile from these trails at the Yarmouth Railroad Depot and asked for directions for walking to "Friends Village" (also called "Quaker Village"), which was then located in South Yarmouth near Bass River. The author was frustrated, however, when a stagecoach driver at the station provided him with directions along the **Old Kings Highway** (today's Route 6A), right through the center of Yarmouth Port. Thoreau complained in his journal:

> Thus it is commonly; the landlords and stage-drivers are bent on making you walk the whole length of their main street first wherever you are going. They know no road but such as is fit for a coach and four.
> I looked despairingly at this straggling village [Yarmouth Port] whose street I must run the gauntlet of—so much time and distance lost....
> I have found the compass and chart safer guides than the inhabitants, though the latter universally abuse the maps. I do not love to go

through a village street any more than a cottage yard. I feel that I am there only by sufferance; but I love to go by the villages by my own road, seeing them from one side, as I do theoretically. When I go through a village, my legs ache at the prospect of the hard gravelled walk. I go by the tavern with its porch full of gazers, and meet a miss taking a walk or the doctor in his sulky, and for half an hour I feel as strange as if I were in a town in China; but soon I am at home in the wide world again, and my feet rebound from the yielding turf.

According to his journal, Thoreau followed the Old Kings Highway just past the site of today's Yarmouth Port Post Office before heading south onto today's Strawberry Lane, which runs directly adjacent to the **Yarmouth Historical Society Trails.**

The Trail

The trailhead to this walk is located just behind the Historical Society gatehouse. The Society requests a 50-cent donation for adults and a 25-cent donation for children be placed in the slot by the gatehouse door. Trail guides are available and include a numbered plant identification system. Benches are also located along the trail for resting while enjoying the woods.

➜ Just a few hundred feet past the gatehouse the trail comes to a fork. Follow the arrow on the stone marker and take the path on the left.

➜ After turning left at the fork continue along the Main Trail. On your way you will encounter Eastern white pines, Eastern red cedars, apple trees, bayberry (see illustration opposite), cherry, sumac, honeysuckle, and, of course, pitch pine.

➜ When you arrive at the next fork, proceed to your left and continue onto the Pond Trail. **NOTE: Just after turning onto the Pond Trail, the path bends hard to the right.**

Words to Walk By

I have met with but one or two persons in the course of my life who understood the art of Walking, that is, of taking walks—who had a genius, so to speak, for sauntering, which word is beautifully derived "from idle people who roved about the country, in the Middle Ages, and asked charity, under pretense of going à la Sainte Terre," to the Holy Land, till the children exclaimed, "There goes a Sainte-Terrer," a Saunterer, a Holy-Lander. They who never go to the Holy Land in their walks, as they pretend, are indeed mere idlers and vagabonds; but they who do go there are saunterers in the good sense, such as I mean.

—*Walking*, 1862

In the Footsteps of Thoreau

What Thoreau Saw

Bayberry

Our way to the high sand-bank, which I have described as extending all along the coast, led, as usual, through patches of Bayberry bushes, which straggled into the sand. This, next to the Shrub-oak, was perhaps the most common shrub thereabouts. I was much attracted by its odoriferous leaves and small gray berries which are clustered about the short twigs, just below the last year's growth. I know of but two bushes in Concord, and they, being staminate plants, do not bear fruit. The berries gave it a venerable appearance, and they smelled quite spicy, like small confectionery.

Be sure to make this turn which is marked by a sign. If you miss this turn you'll know almost immediately, as you'll come to a jeep trail.

→Once on the Pond Trail, you will encounter various spur trails to your right that lead down to Miller Pond. These paths are worth following for the different perspectives they offer of the pond.

→A few hundred yards along the Pond Trail, you may be able to spot the Yarmouth railroad tracks through the woods to the left. These tracks were established in 1865, after Thoreau's visits.

→Just prior to returning to the Main Trail, you will also pass Woodside Cemetery on your left.

→Upon reaching the t-junction with the Main Trail, stay to the left and follow the path to Kelley Chapel, about 10 minutes farther. Keep an eye out for blueberry bushes, gray birch and English oak along this section of trail.

→Kelley Chapel is a restored non-denominational chapel that is occasionally used for weddings and other special functions. Don't be surprised if you encounter a furry creature somewhere on the grounds; in recent years a woodchuck has made his home nearby.

→From the chapel, the Society parking lot is just a few hundred feet straight ahead.

→Once back at the Historical Society parking lot take a minute to view the Bangs Hallet House, which is located just up the hill. Portions of this structure date from the 1740's, and it is furnished with authentic 19th-century period pieces. The house is open Sundays 1-4 p.m. from June through September. Tours can also be arranged by calling the Historical Society at (508) 362-3021.●

In the Footsteps of Thoreau

In short, Brewster with its noble ponds, its bare hills, gray with poverty grass and lichens, and its secluded cottages, is a very interesting town to an inlander.
—Henry David Thoreau, Cape Cod, 1865.

Thoreau walked right by this famous store, built in 1852 as a church. The Brewster Store is one of the most frequently photographed and painted landmarks on Cape Cod. Before heading out on the trail, start your day with the store's famous coffee and donuts; treat yourself to penny candy and roasted peanuts. Reserve your daily newspaper; pick up a gift, a necessary lamp part, or a book for yourself or a friend. Enjoy an ice cream cone from **The Brewster Scoop** during the summer months.

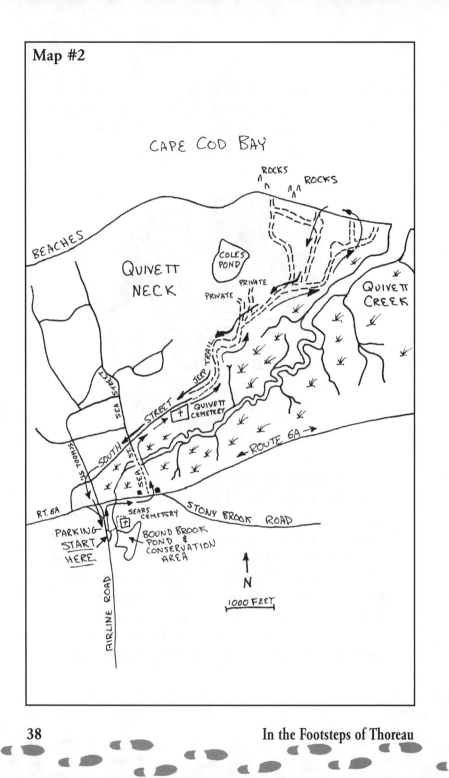

Map #2

CAPE COD BAY

ROCKS   ROCKS

BEACHES

QUIVETT NECK

COLES POND

PRIVATE
PRIVATE
PRIVATE

QUIVETT CREEK

JEEP TRAIL

SEA STREET

SOUTH STREET

QUIVETT CEMETERY

ROUTE 6A

SCHOOL ST.

RT. 6A

SEA ST.

PARKING
START HERE

SEARS CEMETERY

STONY BROOK ROAD

BOUND BROOK POND & CONSERVATION AREA

AIRLINE ROAD

N

1000 FEET

In the Footsteps of Thoreau

Quivett Neck Walk

No. 2

DISTANCE 3.8 miles
TIME 2.5 hours
RATING moderate

Location

This route runs along the northeast corner of the Town of Dennis, from the Bound Brook Conservation Area to Cape Cod Bay and back. Follow Route 6 to Exit 9. From the off-ramp turn north onto Route 134 and proceed 0.7 miles to Airline Road on the right. Follow Airline Road 1.6 miles to the three-way Stop sign. Proceed straight across at the Stop sign and continue 1.3 miles on Airline Road to the Bound Brook Conservation Area on the right, just before the junction with Route 6A.

Description

A moderately long walk, most of this route follows a flat dirt road, with some sections located along paved roads and a quarter-mile stretch along a thick sandy beach. The trail offers scenic views of a variety of aquatic environments including a pond, a brook, a saltwater marsh, and the seashore. The route can be especially fun in early spring when herring migrate up Quivett Creek and the Bound Brook herring run* to Bound Brook Pond. There are also a pair of secluded cemeteries along the way. Sears Cemetery is full of interesting 19th-century headstones and, with its picture-postcard view of Bound Brook Pond, is as quaint and quiet a spot as any on the Cape. Quivett Neck Cemetery, on the other hand, is not as old as the Sears Cemetery but presents a pleasing view of the marsh and Quivett Creek. An out-of-the-way section of Cape Cod Bay on the northern end of the walk provides a perfect place for beachcombing.

Words to Walk By

NOTE: Be aware that a 0.2-mile segment of this walk follows Route 6A where there is no sidewalk. Also, use cau-

The walking of which I speak has nothing in it akin to taking exercise, as it is called, as the sick take medicine at stated hours—as the swinging of dumbbells or chairs; but is itself the enterprise and adventure of the day.

–Walking, 1862

*John Hay's classic 1959 Cape Cod text, *The Run*, is highly recommended to anyone interested in herring runs, or, for that matter, nature in general.

tion in July and August when the jeep trail can be busy with traffic accessing the beach. Fortunately, during the rest of the year—and even on early summer mornings—walkers often have the area all to themselves.

Thoreau

Riding on the stagecoach through Dennis in 1849, Thoreau was impressed with what he saw:

> At Dennis, we ventured to put our heads out of the windows, to see where we were going, and saw rising before us, through the mist, singular barren hills, all stricken with poverty grass, looming up as if they were in the horizon though they were close to us, and we seemed to have got to the end of the land on that side, notwithstanding that the horses were still headed that way. Indeed, that part of Dennis which we saw was an exceedingly barren and desolate country, of a character which I can find no name for; such a surface, perhaps, as the bottom of the sea made dry land day before yesterday…. We passed through the village of Suet, in Dennis, on Suet and Quivett Necks, of which it is said, "when compared with Nobscusset… it may be denominated a pleasant village; but, in comparison with the village of Sandwich, there is little or no beauty in it." However, we liked Dennis well, better than any town we had seen on the Cape, it was so novel, and, in that stormy day, so sublimely dreary.

Founded in 1639, the village of Suet was one of the first to be settled in Dennis. Today there are many houses on Quivett Neck that proudly display their 18th-century construction dates on markers next to their doors. The area is also the birthplace of the American saltworks industry that once flourished on Cape Cod. (See illustration opposite.)

The Trail

➜After parking at the Bound Brook Conservation Area, take a brief walk to Sears Cemetery on the short trail that overlooks Bound Brook Pond and the Bound Brook herring run. From March to June keep your eyes open for alewives—members of the herring family—which migrate by the hundreds up the brook, jumping in the air from pool to pool. You will also likely encounter swans in Bound Brook Pond.

➜Once back at the conservation area parking lot, turn right onto Airline Road and proceed 0.1 miles north to Route 6A.

➜Turn right onto Route 6A, also known as the **Old Kings Highway**, the same road that Thoreau's stagecoach followed a century and a half ago. NOTE: Unfortunately, this part of the road is not as quiet as it was in Thoreau's day. Be sure to exercise caution, as there is no sidewalk here.

➜Follow Route 6A 0.2 miles east to a path on the left, between the first and second houses on the left-hand side of Route 6A. This path is actually the

In the Footsteps of Thoreau

What Thoreau Saw

Saltworks

Captain John Sears, of Suet, was the first person in this country who obtained pure marine salt by solar evaporation alone; though it had long been made in a similar way on the coast of France, and elsewhere. This was in the year 1776, at which time, on account of the war, salt was scarce and dear. The Historical Collections contain an interesting account of his experiments, which we read when we first saw the roofs of the salt-works. Barnstable county is the most favorable locality for these works on our northern coast, there is so little fresh water here emptying into the ocean. Quite recently there were about two millions of dollars invested in this business here. But now the Cape is unable to compete with the importers of salt and the manufacturers of it at the West, and accordingly, her salt-works are fast going to decay. From making salt they turn to fishing more than ever.

This illustration was taken from Deyo's History of Barnstable County, published in 1880.

Kelp Weed

This kelp, oar-weed, tangle, devil's-apron, sole-leather, or rib-bon-weed,—as various species are called—appeared to us a singularly marine and fabulous product, a fit invention for Neptune to adorn his car with, or a freak of Proteus. All that is told of the sea has a fabulous sound, to an inhabitant of the land, and all its products have a certain fabulous quality, as if they belonged to another planet, from sea-weed to a sailor's yarn, or a fish story. In this element the animal and vegetable kingdoms meet and are strangely mingled.

Illustration by Chuck Stanko

entrance to an abandoned road, Sea Street*, and is marked with a "Dead End" sign. If you mistakenly walk past Sea Street, you will come to Stony Brook Road on the right, at which point you will know you have gone too far. More than 100 years old, Sea Street was once the regular route between Quivett Neck and Brewster but became less and less travelled in the 20th century as demographic changes occurred. Sea Street was finally abandoned in the 1970's when damages caused by the frequent flooding of nearby Quivett Creek were deemed too costly to repair. (Notice the old town-line post, which seems so odd now in the middle of the salt marsh.)

➡Proceed 0.2 miles along the Sea Street path and turn right onto South Street.

➡Follow South Street 0.5 miles to the "Crow's Pasture, Dennis Conservation Lands" sign, where the road becomes a dirt track, just past the privately-owned Quivett Neck Cemetery on the right.

➡Proceed onto the unpaved Crow's Pasture road. This jeep trail winds 1.75 miles to the beach. **NOTE: Be sure to stay on the main path here and avoid the turn-offs to the left.**

➡Follow this jeep trail all the way out to the beach. The view from the shore here is something special, with Cape Cod Bay opening up to the north, Quivett Creek to the south, and acres of largely undeveloped conservation land in between.

➡Once out on the beach, turn left (west) and follow the shoreline 0.25 miles to the first off-road vehicle path. There are a number of large boulders along the shore here that serve as good resting places.

➡Follow the off-road vehicle path 0.35 miles to return to the junction with the jeep trail that you followed in.

➡Bear right and retrace your steps 0.5 miles to South Street.

➡Once back on South Street follow it 0.7 miles, past Sea Street, to the intersection with School Street.

➡Turn left onto School Street and follow it 0.1 miles back to Route 6A.

➡Proceed straight across Route 6A onto Airline Road and follow it 0.1 miles back to the conservation area parking lot to complete the walk.●

*There is an excellent essay about Sea Street in Robert Finch's 1986 collection of Cape Cod nature essays, *Outlands*, which offers a fascinating commentary on this little-known byway.

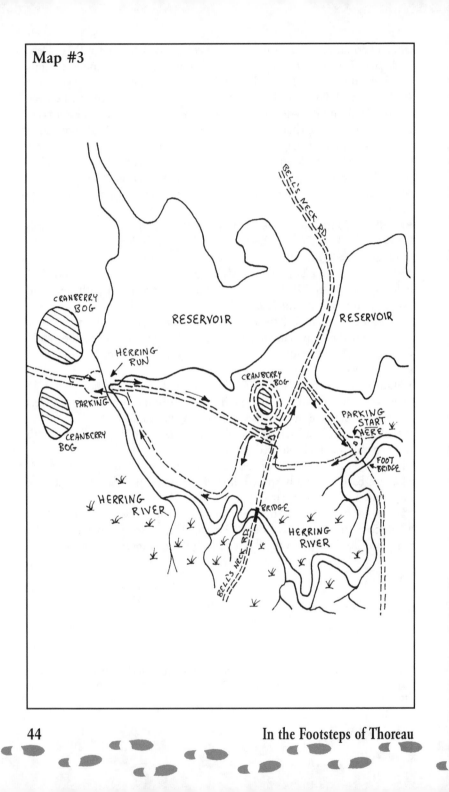

Map #3

In the Footsteps of Thoreau

Herring River Walk

No. 3

DISTANCE 1.6 miles
TIME 45 minutes
RATING easy

Location

This walk is located in West Harwich. Follow Route 6 to Exit 9. Turn south at the off-ramp onto Route 134 and follow it south 2 miles to the intersection with Route 28. Turn left onto Route 28 and follow it 1.8 miles east into Harwich to Depot Road West just before the First Baptist Church of Harwich on the left. Turn left onto Depot Road West and after just a couple hundred feet, bear right onto Bell's Neck Road, just at the end of the church cemetery. Follow Bell's Neck Road 0.6 miles north to where it crosses the Herring River by way of a small wooden bridge. (Just before the bridge, Bell's Neck Road changes from a paved road to a dirt road.) From the small bridge that crosses the Herring River, continue north on Bell's Neck Road 0.25 miles to the first unmarked dirt road on the right. Turn right onto this dirt road and follow it 0.2 miles to the small parking area near the footbridge that crosses the Herring River.

Description

This route runs through a beautiful section of the Town of Harwich's prized conservation lands, along shady walking paths and unpaved roads where it is not uncommon to encounter a variety of wildlife. The meandering Herring River, with its wide stretches of saltwater marsh, is a popular birding spot. Keep an eye out for great blue herons, snowy egrets, ducks, kingfishers, ospreys and hawks, to name just a few. Also, deer make their home in the surrounding woods. Watch for foxes, raccoons, skunks and owls; and don't be surprised if you encounter some of the horseback riders who frequent the area's trails. The large town reservoir is also home to many swans, snapping turtles, frogs, and even some otters. And at the juncture of the river and the reservoir there is a herring run which teems with alewives, a member of the herring family*, in the spring.

Bell's Neck was named for John Bell who owned a large tract of land in the area in the 1600's.

*See footnote on page 39.

Thoreau

> There are many Herring Rivers on the Cape; they will, perhaps, be more
> numerous than herrings soon.

So commented Thoreau in 1849 when he encountered the Herring River
in Wellfleet during his stay at the nearby Wellfleet Oysterman's house.
However, when Thoreau returned to the Cape in 1857 he spent a night in
Harwich near a completely different Herring River, where this walk is
located. During this trip Thoreau walked from the Bass River in the southern part of Dennis to West Harwich, where he passed the night at a house
owned by one Isaiah Baker near Harwich's own Herring River. Baker's
house was located at the southern end of today's Bell's Neck Road, adjacent to the First Baptist Church of Harwich.

At Baker's, Thoreau had a Cape Cod breakfast of "fresh eels from the
Herring River, caught with an eel-pot baited with horseshoe crabs cut up."
Although he only stayed in West Harwich for one night, his description
offers a colorful look at the area during the mid-19th-century. The road he
mentions below is today's Route 28:

> It was a sandy road, with small houses and small pine and oak wood
> close bordering the road, making the soil appear more fertile than in
> reality it is. As in Canada along the St. Lawrence, you never got out of
> the village, only came to a meeting-house now and then. And they told
> me there was another similar street parallel with this further north. But
> all this street had a peculiarly Sabbath-day appearance, for there was
> scarcely an inhabitant to be seen, and they were commonly women or
> young children, for the greater part of the able-bodied men were gone to
> sea, as usual. This makes them very quiet towns. Baker said that half or
> three quarters of the men were gone.... Herring River was near by, and
> Baker sent a little boy to set an eel-pot for breakfast. We had some of
> the herring for supper. He said that eels went down the river in the
> spring and up in the fall! That last winter many were found in holes
> under the ice, left dry by the tide. He said it was a consideration with
> poor men who talked of migrating West that here shellfish and eels were
> abundant and easily obtained.

The Trail

Before beginning this walk, take a short stroll from the parking area out
onto the footbridge for a look at the Herring River and its surrounding
marsh. The river winds its way through the salt marsh to the left (north)
before hooking around to the south, passing under Route 28 and continuing to Nantucket Sound.

→After viewing the river from the footbridge, turn around and walk back
to the parking area where you will find a well-worn walking path on the

left (west). This walking path is partially obstructed by a pair of large cement blocks which prevent motor vehicle traffic from entering it.

→Follow this path 0.2 miles to the intersection with Bell's Neck Road. Turn right onto Bell's Neck Road, and proceed a few hundred feet to the north before turning onto the first dirt road on the left (west), just before the small cranberry bog which is also on the left.

→Follow this dirt road a couple of hundred yards to the west and turn left onto the walking path that leads toward the river.

→This path follows the river for about 0.3 miles before coming to a t-junction near the reservoir.

→Turn left at the t-junction and you will arrive at the herring run where the river and the reservoir meet.

→Cross the herring run and proceed across the parking area and along the dirt road for a look at the large working cranberry bogs on both sides of the road. To add to this walk, follow one of the dirt roads that circle the bogs.

→From the bogs, retrace your steps back to the herring run.

→Cross the herring run and follow the walking path that leads east, straight back to Bell's Neck Road 0.4 miles away. You'll see glimpses of the reservoir through the trees to your left until you return to the small cranberry bog by Bell's Neck Road.

→Turn left onto Bell's Neck Road and follow it 0.1 miles (north) to the unmarked dirt road on the right.

→Turn right onto this road and proceed 0.2 miles back to the parking area and footbridge to complete this walk.●

Words to Walk By

Of course it is of no use to direct our steps to the woods, if they do not carry us thither. I am alarmed when it happens that I have walked a mile into the woods bodily, without getting there in spirit. In my afternoon walk I would fain forget all my morning occupations and my obligations to society. But it sometimes happens that I cannot easily shake off the village. The thought of some work will run in my head and I am not where my body is—I am out of my senses. In my walks I would fain return to my senses. What business have I in the woods, if I am thinking of some thing out of the woods.

–Walking, 1862

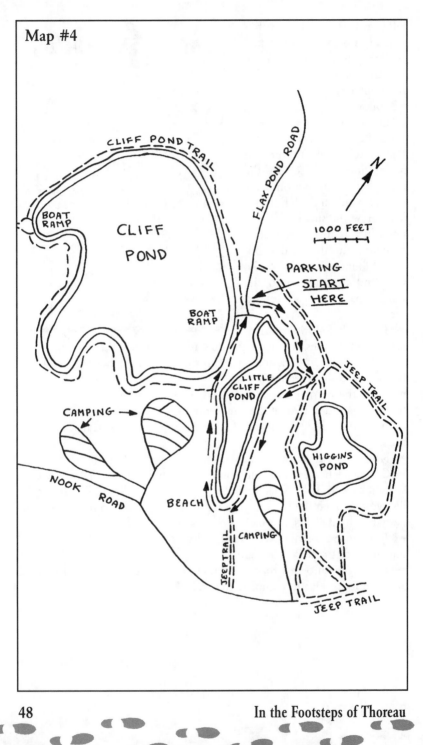

Map #4

CLIFF POND TRAIL

BOAT RAMP

CLIFF POND

FLAX POND ROAD

N

1000 FEET

PARKING
START
HERE

BOAT RAMP

JEEP TRAIL

LITTLE CLIFF POND

CAMPING

HIGGINS POND

NOOK ROAD

BEACH

JEEP TRAIL

CAMPING

JEEP TRAIL

In the Footsteps of Thoreau

Little Cliff Pond Trail

DISTANCE 1.6 miles
TIME 45 minutes
RATING easy

Location

This trail is located in Nickerson State Park in Brewster. From mid-Cape locations, follow Route 6 west to Exit 12. Turn left at the end of the off-ramp onto Route 6A and proceed 1.5 miles west to the entrance to the park on the left. Once in the park, continue 0.3 miles past the gatehouse to Flax Pond Road on the left which is marked with signs reading "Area 5" and "Boat Ramp." Follow Flax Pond Road 1.2 miles to the boat ramp where parking is located on both sides of the road.

Description

Nickerson State Park is the most popular state-run camping facility in Massachusetts. Donated to the Commonwealth in 1934 by Addie Nickerson in memory of her son, Roland C. Nickerson, Jr., the park encompasses more than 2,000 acres of woodlands that include seven ponds, seven camping areas, eight miles of bike paths, and plenty of great hiking.

This narrow and moderately hilly trail runs through scenic woods before descending to a soft sandy shoreline that separates Little Cliff Pond from neighboring Cliff Pond. Cliff Pond is the largest body of water in Nickerson State Park and one of the most popular recreation spots in the area. But while water-skiers, fishermen and swimmers all vie for space at Cliff Pond, Little Cliff Pond fortunately enjoys a lower profile next door. Little Cliff Pond is primarily used by canoeists and a few fisherman, and the beach at its southern tip is seldom crowded.

This walk can easily be extended by following the jeep trail around Higgins Pond to the east (1.6 miles/1 hour), or by following nearby Cliff Pond Trail to the west (3.25 miles/2 hours).

Tent sites are available in the park on a first-come, first-served basis for $6 per night. Call the park at (508) 896-3491 for further information.

Thoreau

On June 17, 1857 Thoreau made his way from Long Pond in Harwich to Orleans. On his way, he tramped through the woods of what now comprises Nickerson State Park, where he came across some ponds which

Words to Walk By

N o wealth can buy the requisite leisure, freedom, and independence which are the capital in this profession. It comes only by the grace of God. It requires a direct dispensation from Heaven to became a walker. You must be born into the family of the Walkers. "Ambulator nascitur, non fit."

–Walking, 1862

---

included what are today Little Cliff Pond, Higgins Pond and Cliff Pond.

All of the ponds in Nickerson are kettle ponds which were formed after the last Ice Age when massive sheets of ice as thick as two miles extended down from the north. When these glaciers receded, they left behind huge quantities of earth which formed land masses like Cape Cod. But the glaciers didn't just deposit earth; in some spots they also left considerable chunks of ice, sometimes as much as a mile or more across. Dirt was often piled up around these iceberg-sized blocks, so that when they melted they left cavities or pits in the sand surrounded by very steep walls. Those cavities that were deep enough to intersect the water table were flooded and formed kettle ponds. This method of geological formation has tended to give many kettle ponds common characteristics such as high hills around their edges sandy shorelines, as well as a general absence of streams feeding into them. Kettle ponds are also frequently found in clusters and are very often separated only by small spits of sand. Although the geological principles behind the formation of kettle ponds had not yet been articulated in Thoreau's day, his observations of the ponds in Brewster was characteristically keen. He writes in his journal:

> I soon came out on the open hills in the northeast part of Brewster, from which I overlooked the Bay, some two miles distant. This was a grand place to walk. There were two or three more of those peculiar ponds with high, shiny sand-banks, by which you detected them before you saw the water, as if freshly scooped out of the high plains or a table-land. The banks were like those of the sea on the Back Side, though on a smaller scale, and they had clear sandy shores. One pond would often be separated from another by low curving beaches or necks of land. The features of the surrounding landscape was simple and obvious.... In short, Brewster with its noble ponds, its bare hills, gray with poverty-grass and lichens, and its secluded cottages, is a very interesting town to an inlander.

The Trail

→The trailhead to Little Cliff Pond Trail is sign-posted to the left, on the eastern side of Flax Pond Road, as you face down the hill toward the boat ramp.

In the Footsteps of Thoreau

➡Follow the trail 0.3 miles along the hills above Little Cliff Pond until it curves off to the left and away from the pond, thereby avoiding the pond's marshy northeast corner. Here, the walking path intersects the jeep trail that runs between Little Cliff Pond and Higgins Pond.

➡At this junction, Little Cliff Pond Trail bends back to the right, toward Little Cliff Pond and away from the jeep trail. **NOTE: The path can be difficult to follow here, so look for the blue, plastic triangular trail-markers that have been attached to trees along the trail to point the way.** (For a brief detour, cross the jeep trail here and walk down to the shore of secluded Higgins Pond.)

➡Follow Little Cliff Pond Trail south as it makes its way up and down some steep hills before slowly descending to the southern end of the pond, 0.4 miles farther.

➡**NOTE: At the southern end of Little Cliff Pond, be sure to take the path down to the sandy beach, rather than following the jeep trail that continues south and away from the pond.**

➡The trial continues on the far side of the beach. After 0.3 miles you will reach the narrow strip of sand that separates Little Cliff Pond from Cliff Pond. Walk across to the shore of Cliff Pond for a change of scenery and continue north.

➡Just before returning to the parking area you will encounter a high knoll. Circle around to the left (west) of the knoll and return to the parking area to complete this walk.●

Map #5

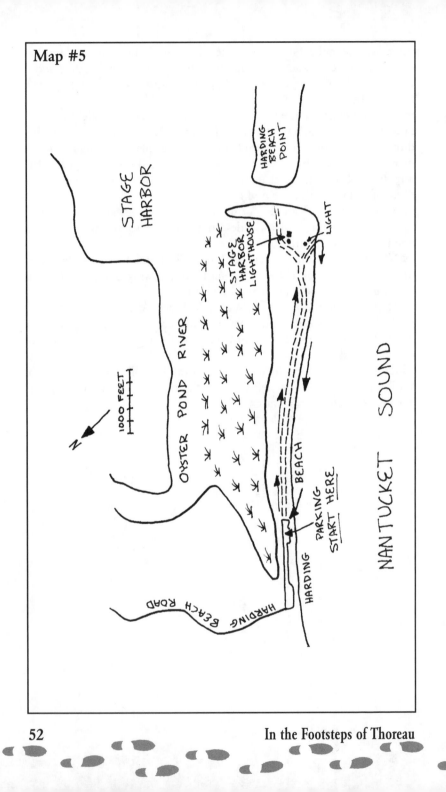

STAGE HARBOR

HARDING BEACH POINT

OYSTER POND RIVER

STAGE HARBOR LIGHTHOUSE

LIGHT

N

1000 FEET

BEACH

PARKING START HERE

HARDING

HARDING BEACH ROAD

NANTUCKET SOUND

In the Footsteps of Thoreau

Harding Beach & Lighthouse Walk

No. 5

DISTANCE 1.8 miles

TIME 1.5 hours

RATING easy

Location

This trail runs along the southern shore of the town of Chatham. Follow Route 6 to Exit 11. Turn left at the end of the off-ramp and follow Route 137 south 2.8 miles, to the t-junction with Route 28. Turn left onto Route 28 and proceed east 1.5 miles to Barn Hill Road on the right, which is marked with a sign to Harding Beach. Turn right onto Barn Hill Road and proceed 0.4 miles to the fork at Harding Beach Road. Bear right onto Harding Beach Road and continue 0.7 miles to the beach parking lot, where the Town of Chatham charges parking fees from July through Labor Day. This walk begins at the far left (eastern) end of the parking lot.

Description

This short, sandy walk is one of the most enjoyable in this guide. The route runs down a sandy jeep trail and then along Harding Beach, offering magnificent views of Oyster Pond River, Stage Harbor and Nantucket Sound, across which walkers can see the famous Monomoy National Wildlife Refuge.

Of course, the "highlight" of this walk is Stage Harbor Lighthouse, also called Harding Beach Lighthouse—the last lighthouse to have been established on Cape Cod, in 1880. Stage Harbor's cast-iron lighthouse tower is of similar design to the towers of the current Chatham Lighthouse and **Nauset Lighthouse**; but unlike these towers, which are still in use, Stage Harbor's tower was shut down in 1933, when an unmanned light was set up on a skeleton tower nearby as a replacement. A few years later, the Stage Harbor Lighthouse and keeper's house were sold by the government as surplus and were purchased by the Hoyt family, who have used it as a summer home.[1]

Thoreau

During Thoreau's last visit to Cape Cod in 1857, he walked for about a mile along the beach of Nantucket Sound and offered the following account in his journal of what he saw:

> This beach seems to be laid down too long on the map. The sea
> never runs very much here, since the shore is protected from the swell
> by Monomoy.... A fish hawk or eagle sailed low directly over my head

as I sat on the bank. The bank is quite low there. I could see Monomoy, very low and indistinct, stretching much further south than I expected. The wooded portions of this, and perhaps of Nauset Beach further to the north, looked like islets on the water. You could not distinguish much without a glass, but the lighthouse and fishermen's houses at the south end loomed very large to the naked eye.

When Thoreau walked to the west of the present-day Harding Beach (along stretches of the shoreline that are now privately owned), he would not have seen Stage Harbor Lighthouse, as it was not built until 23 years later. Still, the perspective from the beach across Nantucket Sound remains just as pleasing today as it was when it greeted Thoreau. Just as they seemed to Thoreau, Nauset Beach and Monomoy still appear "very low and indistinct," like "islets on the water." In fact, today's Monomoy consists of two separate islands, North and South Monomoy; and a significant stretch of Nauset Beach has recently separated from the mainland. These changes are not particularly remarkable, however, as Monomoy and Nauset Beach are anything but static geographic entities. For instance, at various times over the centuries Monomoy has been a peninsula, a single island and even multiple islands; and Nauset Beach is just as unstable*.

Other changes in the locale since Thoreau's time include the facts that there are no longer any "fishermen's houses" or "wooded portions" on Monomoy, and that Monomoy Lighthouse no longer "looms very large to the naked eye." Interestingly, when Monomoy Lighthouse was built in 1823 it was constructed at the southern tip of the island; but in the almost two centuries that have passed since that time, deposits of sand have lengthened Monomoy so that the lighthouse is now fairly well inland. Furthermore, although Monomoy was inhabited by colonists since at least the early 1700's—and probably for many centuries prior to that by Native Americans—there have not been any full-time human residents there for many years. Today, Monomoy is administered by the U.S. Fish and Wildlife Service as a National Wildlife Refuge and is home to various endangered birds, a substantial population of seals, and many other plants and animals.

The Trail
➜From the eastern end of the Harding Beach parking lot proceed onto the jeep trail and follow it 0.9 miles east to the lighthouse. Although this

*For further information on these changes see *Breakthrough: The Story of Chatham's North Beach*, by Timothy J. Wood, a Cape Cod Chronicle Publication, published in 1988 and updated in 1995.

jeep trail is open to "Authorized Vehicles Only," walking along its length is permitted. As you make your way toward the lighthouse, you will notice Oyster Pond River to the left (north) and may also encounter various numbered stone markers. These markers are from a nature trail (entirely different from the route described here) that was formerly maintained by the Chatham Conservation

Words to Walk By

In one half-hour I can walk off to some portion of the earth's surface where a man does not stand from one year's end to another, and there, consequently, politics are not, for they are but as the cigar-smoke of a man.

–Walking, 1862

Foundation. Unfortunately, much of that trail has been destroyed by storms and has subsequently been abandoned. **NOTE: Some walkers may enjoy exploring the remnants of the trail. But remember to avoid treading on plants.** (See "Safe Walking.")

➡When you reach Stage Harbor Lighthouse, you will notice the active, unmanned signal light that stands on a metal skeleton tower in front of the lighthouse to the southwest. Admont G. Clark, in his enjoyable and authoritative work, *Lighthouses of Cape Cod, Martha's Vineyard, Nantucket: Their History and Their Lore*, points out that although Stage Harbor Lighthouse remained active for only a short time, its history was rather colorful. Stage Harbor's lighthouse keepers participated in many rescue efforts and worked diligently to prevent maritime accidents. One of the keepers committed suicide by hanging himself in the shed behind the lighthouse. And, it seems that the passageway between the keeper's house and the tower was used by smugglers as a storage facility for bootlegged liquor during Prohibition!

➡The beach behind the lighthouse to the northeast offers an impressive view of Stage Harbor, across which you may be able to spot Chatham Lighthouse about two miles away on a hill. The two high wooded areas that border the right (eastern) side of the harbor are Stage Island and Morris Island.

➡Walk out to Harding Beach, which is in front of the lighthouse to the south. From there, depending on the visibility, you should be able to see the Monomoy Islands stretching across Nantucket Sound.

➡Follow the shoreline back to the parking lot to complete this walk.●

 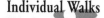

Map #6

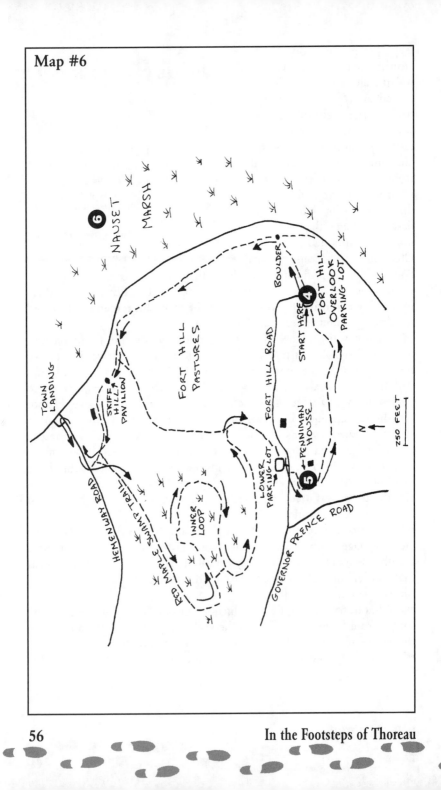

In the Footsteps of Thoreau

Fort Hill & Red Maple Swamp Trail

No. 6

DISTANCE 2 miles
TIME 1 hour
RATING easy

Location

This trail runs through the **Cape Cod National Seashore's Fort Hill Area** which is located on the banks of **Nauset Marsh** in Eastham. Follow Route 6 to the Orleans Rotary and then continue 1.3 miles north on Route 6 to Governor Prence Road on the right, which is marked with a sign for the Fort Hill Area. Turn right onto Governor Prence Road and follow it 0.25 miles to the small intersection. Turn right onto Fort Hill Road and proceed 0.2 miles, past the **Penniman House** on the right, to the overlook parking lot. Additional parking is located across from the Penniman House.

Description

While the **Cape Cod National Seashore** divides the Fort Hill and Red Maple Swamp trails into two separate but overlapping walks, combined they make one of the most scenic and varied short walks on Cape Cod. Walkers on this route will witness spectacular views of **Nauset Marsh** and enjoy exploring the unique recesses of Red Maple Swamp. The route runs past a boulder which Native Americans used to sharpen weapons and along the grounds of one of the most famous captain's homes on Cape Cod, the **Penniman House**.

The trail consists mainly of well-kept, easy-to-follow dirt and gravel paths, stretches of boardwalks through a swamp, and just a few easy hills.

Thoreau

In 1849 Thoreau walked directly along the western edge of today's **Fort Hill Area** via the **Old Kings Highway**, formerly the Cape's main stage route that included the eastern end of today's Governor Prence Road. At that time, the Fort Hill Area was owned by members of the Knowles family and by Daniel Penniman, father of Captain Edward Penniman who in 1868 built the **Penniman House**.

Thoreau wrote at length in *Cape Cod* about one of the Fort Hill Area's earliest European owners, the Reverend Samuel Treat. In his research, he also came across an early map of **Nauset Marsh** and the Fort Hill Area that he referred to in *Cape Cod*. (See the illustration on page 61.)

The Trail

The Fort Hill overlook parking lot provides a great view of **Nauset Marsh**, its barrier beach Nauset Spit, and the Atlantic Ocean beyond. Just off to the left in the distance is the **Eastham Coast Guard Station** building; beyond it, a sharp eye can sometimes catch glimpses of **Nauset Light**'s beacon. The bluffs on the far right-hand side of Nauset Marsh are Nauset Heights, part of the town of Orleans; and the body of water directly to the right of Fort Hill is the mouth of Town Cove, which separates Eastham and Orleans.

→From the parking lot, walk straight ahead down the white-shelled path toward the marsh where a massive glacier erratic boulder sits. Like the other boulders which dot the shoreline along this route, this rock was transported here during the last Ice Age by massive glaciers. (See Doane Rock for further information.) A spike embedded in its south side is speculated to have been inserted there as an anchor for a block-and-tackle, perhaps used to haul salt hay barges across the marsh.

→At the boulder turn left and follow the shoreline northward for about 0.25 miles. The path here is lined with bayberry, honeysuckle and salt-spray rose. The small boggy area to the left, just a couple hundred yards past the boulder, was formerly the site of a saltworks, where small windmills pumped marsh water into vats for evaporation and the extraction of salt.

→After reaching the third low stone wall on the left, follow the path into the thicket of cedars, where you will soon encounter Skiff Hill. The Park has built a pavilion here where you will find a rock which the Nauset Indians once used for sharpening their tools and weapons. A glacier boulder, "Sharpening Rock" was moved by the Park to its present location from the marsh below, where it had been in danger of being swallowed by the mud and overgrowth.

→Proceed along the paved way and you'll soon pass another overlook with benches where the skiffs of local shellfishermen and recreational boaters can be seen in the waters below.

→A couple hundred yards along the trail from this overlook are seasonal restrooms on the right, the start of the Red Maple Swamp Trail on the left, and Hemenway Road straight ahead.

→Follow Hemenway Road around to the right, and the town landing will be in plain sight, offering yet another perspective of the marsh.

→From Hemenway Landing, return to the Red Maple Swamp Trail. Step into its dank, freshwater shade and you may find it hard to imagine that the ocean is so nearby.

→Half a mile farther you will come to a fork. Turn left to follow the trail's

What Thoreau Saw

Nauset Marsh,
as represented by French explorer
Samuel de Champlain (1567-1635)

In Champlain's "Voyages," there is a plate representing the Indian cornfields hereabouts, with their wigwams in the midst, as they appeared in 1605, and it was here that the Pilgrims, to quote their own words, "bought eight or ten hogsheads of corn and beans," of the Nauset Indians, in 1622, to keep themselves from starving.

Champlain visited Nauset Marsh on July 20, 1605. Reprinted courtesy of the Cape Cod National Seashore.

inner loop.

→0.2 miles along the inner loop you will return to the main trail where there will be another fork. Turn left at this fork.

→From this second fork, follow the Red Maple Swamp Trail 0.1 miles up the hill to return to the Fort Hill pastures.

→Turn right at the pastures and a few hundred feet farther is the area's lower parking lot.

→From the lower parking lot, cross Fort Hill Road and walk to the right through the frequently photographed **Penniman House** whale-jawbone gate and continue up onto the Penniman House front lawn.

→Proceed past the Penniman House front porch, and pick up the Fort Hill Trail again behind the house.

→From the house, the path continues 0.2 miles, through a small thicket that is often filled with songbirds. It then crosses a field and ascends Fort Hill to the overlook parking lot.●

Words to Walk By

Some do not walk at all; others walk in the highways; a few walk across lots. Roads are made for horses and men of business. I do not travel in them much, comparatively, because I am not in a hurry to get to any tavern or grocery or livery-stable or depot to which they lead. I am a good horse to travel, but not from choice a roadster.

–Walking, 1862

What Thoreau Saw

Nauset Women

We saw one singularly masculine woman, however, in a house on this very plain, who did not look as if she was ever troubled with hysterics, or sympathized with those that were; or, perchance, life itself was to her a hysteric fit—a Nauset woman, of a hardness and coarseness such as no man ever possesses or suggests. It was enough to see the vertebrae and sinews of her neck, and her set jaws of iron, which would have bitten a board-nail in two in their ordinary action-braced against the world, talking like a man-of-war's-man in petticoats, or as if shouting to you through a breaker, who looked as if it made her head ache to live; hard enough for any enormity. I looked upon her as one who had committed infanticide; who never had a brother, unless it were some wee thing that died in infancy—for, what need of him?—and whose father must have died before she was born.

This contemporary photograph, taken at the Penniman House whale jawbone gate, shows that not all Nauset women are as imposing as the one Thoreau described.

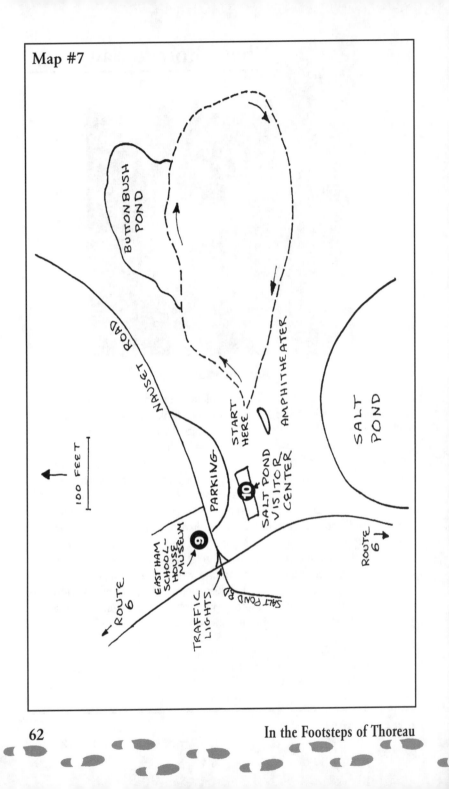

Map #7

BUTTON BUSH POND

NAUSET ROAD

ROUTE 6

100 FEET

START HERE

AMPHITHEATER

SALT POND

PARKING

EASTHAM SCHOOL-HOUSE MUSEUM

⑨

⑩

SALT POND VISITOR CENTER

TRAFFIC LIGHTS

SALT POND RD

ROUTE 6

In the Footsteps of Thoreau

Buttonbush Trail

No. 7

DISTANCE 0.25 miles
TIME 20 minutes
RATING very easy

Location

The Buttonbush Trail is located on the grounds of the **Cape Cod National Seashore's Salt Pond Visitor Center** in Eastham. Follow Route 6 to the Orleans Rotary and then proceed north on Route 6 for 3 miles to the traffic lights at the intersection with Nauset Road. Turn right, and the entrance to the parking lot is on the right.

Description

This short self-guided trail, designed specifically for the sight impaired, is a fine resource for all Cape Cod walkers. Its series of interpretive plaques identifies many common plants and serves as an excellent introduction to Cape Cod botany. Blue-stone gravel covers most of the wide trail pathway, except where a sturdy bridge crosses Buttonbush Pond; and with the exception of a few small steps, the trail offers flat, easy walking.

Established in the 1970's by various members of the sight-impaired community in conjunction with the National Park Service, the Buttonbush Trail is a short loop complete with a guide rope and text panels in both Braille and large Roman lettering. In addition to providing the sight impaired with interesting natural and historical information on a user-friendly walk, the plaques encourage all walkers to pay more attention to the natural world around them. And unlike the vague plaques that line so many other walking trails, these are clear and easy to follow.

The Buttonbush Trail is also conveniently located near a number of other sites and walks in this book. The **Eastham Schoolhouse Museum**, run by the Eastham Historical Society, is located just across Nauset Road from the trailhead. Take the time to explore the **Salt Pond Visitor Center** where you will find an educational movie theater, a museum and a great Cape Cod book shop. Furthermore, the Visitor Center is the starting point of **The Great Thoreau Hike**, as described in this guide.

Thoreau

Thoreau utilized all of his senses in his attempt to absorb and record everything he encountered on Cape Cod. In addition to his keen eye, he tasted such native delicacies as herring, sea clams and eels. He took the time to touch things—whether it was seaweed, whale blubber, or an old arrowhead buried in a tree. He made notes of many scents, such as that of bayberries, salt-spray roses and even the "rotting carcasses" of blackfish on the beach. And, of course, he listened attentively, making note of the many sounds he encountered: from the voices of individual sea birds, to the barks of dogs, to the roar of the Atlantic. Not far from the **Buttonbush Trail**, for instance, Thoreau walked with a local boy who took the sounds of the ocean for granted:

> All the morning we had heard the sea roar on the eastern shore, which was several miles distant; for it still felt the effects of the storm in which the *St. John* was wrecked—though a schoolboy, whom we overtook, hardly knew what we meant, his ears were so used to it. He would have more plainly heard the same sound in a shell. It was a very inspiriting sound to walk by, filling the whole air, that of the sea dashing against the land, heard several miles inland. Instead of having a dog before your door, to have an Atlantic Ocean to growl for a whole Cape!

Although the Atlantic is seldom audible from the Buttonbush Trail today, in Thoreau's time most of the woods in Eastham had been clear-cut, and the ocean could be heard much farther inland. Later in Cape Cod, Thoreau returns to his dog/ocean theme, but this time in a more jocular vein:

> Sometimes we met a wrecker with his cart and dog—and his dog's faint bark at us wayfarers, heard through the roaring of the surf, sounded ridiculously faint. To see a little trembling dainty-footed cur standing on the margin of the ocean, and ineffectually barking at a beach-bird, amid the roar of the Atlantic! Come with designs to bark at a whale perchance! That sound will do for farmyards. All the dogs looked out of place there, naked and as if shuddering at the vastness.

Of course, listening to the barking of dogs and the roar of the Atlantic were only a small part of Thoreau's Cape experience. He paid keen attention to as many aspects of the Cape's natural environment as he could, just as the Buttonbush Trail encourages us to do.

The Trail
The Buttonbush trailhead is located just to the left of the **Salt Pond Visitor Center** amphitheater.
➡Follow the guide rope around clockwise as directed by the signs.
➡Not far from the start of the walk you will cross Buttonbush Pond. Largely overgrown, it serves as a unique contrast to nearby Salt Pond. Although they are both kettle ponds, and were formed by the same glacial processes, over the years Salt Pond has become connected to ocean-fed

In the Footsteps of Thoreau

Nauset Marsh, while Buttonbush Pond has remained landlocked and is slowly being filled in by vegetation.

→On this trail, you will encounter a red cedar tree, a black alder tree, buttonbushes, a locust tree, an arrowwood shrub, grape vines, roses, an apple tree, a pitch pine, beach plums, a maple tree, a pear tree and more.

→Once back at the trailhead take the time to walk down to the shore of scenic Salt Pond.

The path to the pond is located on the far side of the amphitheater.●

Words to Walk By

You may safely say, "A penny for your thoughts, or a thousand pounds." When sometimes I am reminded that the mechanics and shopkeepers stay in their shops not only all the forenoon, but all the afternoon too, sitting with crossed legs, so many of them—as if the legs were made to sit upon, and not to stand or walk upon, I think that they deserve some credit for not having all committed suicide long ago.

–*Walking*, 1862

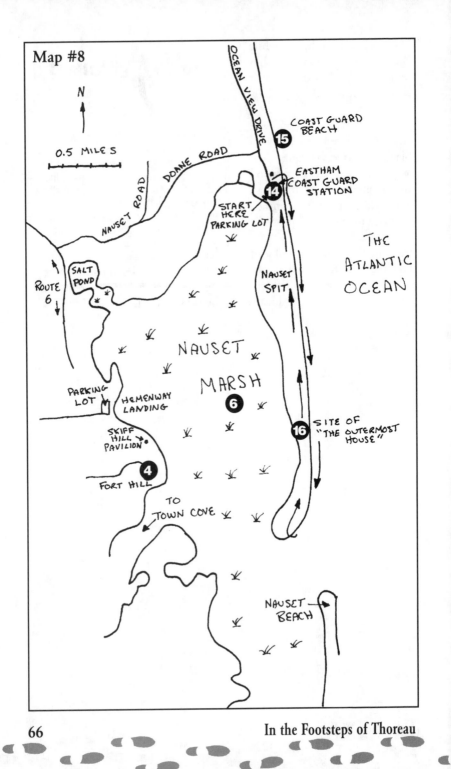

Map #8

N

0.5 MILES

OCEAN VIEW DRIVE

COAST GUARD BEACH

15

EASTHAM COAST GUARD STATION

14

DOANE ROAD

NAUSET ROAD

START HERE PARKING LOT

THE ATLANTIC OCEAN

ROUTE 6

SALT POND

NAUSET SPIT

NAUSET MARSH

6

PARKING LOT

HEMENWAY LANDING

SKIFF HILL PAVILION

16

SITE OF "THE OUTERMOST HOUSE"

4

FORT HILL

TO TOWN COVE

NAUSET BEACH

In the Footsteps of Thoreau

The Outermost Walk

DISTANCE 5 miles

TIME 4 hours

RATING difficult

Location

This hike begins at **Coast Guard Beach** on the eastern shore of Eastham. Follow Route 6 to the Orleans Rotary, and then proceed north on Route 6 for 3 miles to the second set of traffic lights. Turn right onto Nauset Road. After 0.7 miles Nauset Road bears off to the left and Doane Road continues straight ahead. Proceed straight ahead onto Doane Road, and 1.7 miles from Route 6 you will arrive at a junction. Turn right and continue 0.2 miles to the parking lot for Coast Guard Beach. A $7 daily fee or a $20 seasonal fee is charged for daytime summer parking at this and all other **Cape Cod National Seashore** managed beaches. However, the small parking lot here is often filled in the summer, at which times visitors are required to park at the Little Creek Staging Area and use the beach shuttle that runs between it and the Coast Guard Beach parking lot. The staging area is located 0.6 miles back up Doane Road on the right.

Description

> It is true that I could see the houses of Eastham village on the uplands across the marsh, and the passing ships and fishing boats, but these were the works of man rather than man himself. By the middle of February the sight of an unknown someone walking the beach near the Fo'castle would have been a historical event.[2]

So wrote Henry Beston of Nauset Spit in his nature classic *The Outermost House* some 70 years ago, and so Nauset Spit remains to this day.

Like all of Cape Cod's outer beaches, Nauset Spit consists of thick, soft sand and makes for moderately difficult walking. But for all its seeming simplicity, walking the spit can nevertheless be a powerful experience. Wedged between the scenic beauty of **Nauset Marsh** and the magnificent expanse of the Atlantic, it is a spectacular place from which to view the world.

Nauset Spit stretches approximately 2.5 miles south from the **Eastham Coast Guard Station**, and is made of detritus stripped by the ocean from the cliffs to the north. Serving as a bulwark between the ocean and the marsh, the spit is in a constant state of flux, with both its length and shape varying considerably from year to year.

Throughout most of this century, there were a number of hunting camps and cottages along Nauset Spit, all of which have since fallen victim to erosion. Today one can still encounter old water pipes, lumber, foundation slabs and other remnants of these dwellings along the spit. For decades a jeep trail wound along the marsh-side of Nauset Spit; but today that trail is long gone, and in the spring and summer most of this part of the beach is cordoned off for the protection of nesting shore birds. Although many bird species can be seen in and around the marsh, the endangered piping plover and the roseate tern are of special concern. **NOTE: Be careful not to walk too close to the terns, as they can be fiercely protective of their nests.**

In winter it is also common to encounter harbor seals sunning themselves along Nauset Spit, especially at low tide when they congregate on nearby sandbars.

Thoreau

In 1857, Henry David Thoreau made his last walk along Cape Cod's **Great Beach** at the age of 39. Coincidentally, 70 years later in 1927, Henry Beston finished his own Cape sojourn on the Great Beach, also at the age of 39. But this is not all that these two "Henrys" have in common: Both were natives of the Boston area. Both graduated from Harvard College. Both are celebrated American nature writers. Both are inspirations to the modern environmental movement. And both wrote books about their Cape Cod experiences that have become world-renowned classics—*Cape Cod* and *The Outermost House.*

A major difference between Thoreau and Beston, however, is the manner in which they approached their shared subject. Thoreau chose to "strike the beach" north of Nauset Spit at today's **Nauset Light Beach**, and wrote a traveler's account of the place. Beston, on the other hand, settled down on the beach and wrote from an essentially stationary perspective, framed by the course of a year. Today, no study of Cape Cod history, natural history or literature can be considered complete without reading both Thoreau and Beston. Walking Nauset Spit is as good a way to enrich one's understanding of Beston, as walking **The Great Thoreau Hike** is to learn about Thoreau.

The Trail

➜From the parking lot, walk between the **Eastham Coast Guard Station** building and the bathhouse next door. The paved path which runs due east here formerly led to a parking lot. Today, however, it dead-ends at a small viewing area above the beach, as the parking lot was wiped out during the same harsh winter that Beston's house was destroyed.

→To access the **Coast Guard Beach**, follow the path past the bathhouse. The dunes to the left (north) of the station building are the site of an important 1990 archeological find that uncovered evidence of 3,000 to 4,000 years of human settlement.

→From the bottom of the path, strike off to the right (south) to make your way down Nauset Spit. The more substantial dunes on the right

Words to Walk By

You must walk like a camel, which is said to be the only beast which ruminates when walking. When a traveler asked Wordsworth's servant to show him her master's study, she answered, "Here is his library, but his study is out of doors."

—Walking, **1862**

are remnants of the spit's formerly greater size. Since the devastating winter storms of 1978, the dunes of Nauset Spit have only been a shadow of their former size.

→After walking about 2 miles south, estimate the former location of **The Outermost House** by lining yourself up with the roof of the pavilion at Skiff Hill across **Nauset Marsh**. As you face the marsh, Skiff Hill is the tree-covered high-point just to the left (south) of Hemenway Landing parking lot and just to the right (north) of Fort Hill. Hemenway Landing is the only parking lot clearly visible from the spit, and there are usually many skiffs moored in the marsh nearby. Fort Hill can be identified by the extensive open fields around it.

→Continue to the southernmost tip of Nauset Spit. This inlet is a popular place for striped bass fishermen and, as Thoreau pointed out, is the only regular opening in the **Great Beach** north of Chatham.

→From the inlet, retrace your steps back to the parking lot to complete this hike.●

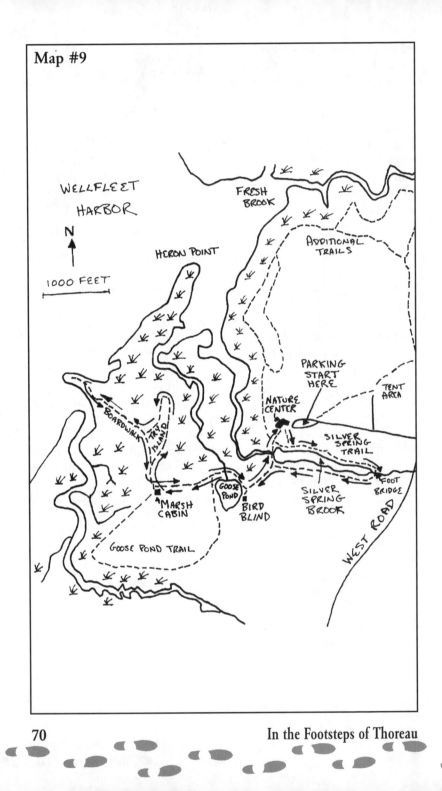

Map #9

WELLFLEET HARBOR

N
1000 FEET

FRESH BROOK

ADDITIONAL TRAILS

HERON POINT

PARKING START HERE

TENT AREA

NATURE CENTER

BOARDWALK

TRT ISLAND

SILVER SPRING TRAIL

GOOSE POND

BIRD BLIND

SILVER SPRING BROOK

FOOT BRIDGE

MARSH CABIN

GOOSE POND TRAIL

WEST ROAD

In the Footsteps of Thoreau

Wellfleet Bay Wildlife Sanctuary Trails

DISTANCE 2 miles

TIME 1 hour

RATING easy

Location

The Wellfleet Bay Wildlife Sanctuary is located on the western shore of South Wellfleet. Follow Route 6 to the Wellfleet/Eastham town line and proceed north 0.3 miles to the road on the left that is marked with a Massachusetts Audubon Society sign. Turn left onto this road and follow it 0.4 miles, across West Road, to the Sanctuary parking lot.

Description

The Wellfleet Bay Wildlife Sanctuary is owned and operated by the Massachusetts Audubon Society. It encompasses more than 700 acres of salt marsh, pine wood, fields, brooks, ponds and moor and includes 5 miles of beautiful walking trails. Described here are two of the Sanctuary trails combined into one diverse walk, the Silver Spring Trail and the Try Island Trail. The Silver Spring Trail loops around a small freshwater pond and runs through thick pine and oak woods, while the Try Island Trail runs across a unique marsh island and then stretches a full third of a mile out into the bay along a boardwalk. Although these well-kept paths thread through generally easy terrain, waterproof footwear is recommended, as the Try Island Trail can be soggy.

In the early part of this century, much of the land within today's Sanctuary was worked as a turnip and asparagus farm; but in 1928 it became the "Austin Ornithological Research Station," a family-run bird banding and research station. It was not until 1958 that the land was acquired by the Massachusetts Audubon Society. Since then, the Sanctuary has steadily developed into one of Cape Cod's most cherished institutions, as well as one of the crown jewels of the Massachusetts Audubon Society.

The Sanctuary hosts a wealth of ongoing classes and seminars on a year-round basis, on topics ranging from basic birding to canoeing. Just a sample of the activities that are offered include bird watching lessons, walks conducted by naturalists, seal watch cruises, and a summer natural history day camp for children. There is also a store at the Nature Center stocked with outdoor equipment and books. Those interested in additional walks within the Sanctuary may want to pick up a Goose Pond Trail

Guide here for $1. The guide includes a superb plant-identification scheme which matches numbered plaques along the trail. Restrooms are located in the Nature Center which is open 8:30 a.m. to 5 p.m. daily. Trails are open from 8 a.m. to 8 p.m. Entrance to the Sanctuary is free for members; but there is a $3 charge for non-members, $2 for children and seniors. Call the Sanctuary at (508) 349-2615 for further information.

Thoreau

Throughout his lifetime, Thoreau made thousands of detailed written descriptions of birds, their physical characteristics, their nests, their voices, and their habits*. But in a journal entry dated April 8, 1859, he made an ornithologically related comment that reveals more about the nature of man than the nature of birds:

> When the question of the protection of birds comes up, the legislatures regard only a low use and never a high use; the best-disposed legislators employ one, perchance, only to examine their crops and see how many grubs or cherries they contain, and never to study their dispositions, or the beauty of their plumage, or listen and report on the sweetness of their song. The legislature will preserve a bird professedly not because it is a beautiful creature, but because it is a good scavenger or the like. This, at least, is the defense set up. It is as if the question were whether some celebrated singer of the human race—some Jenny Lind** or another—did more harm or good, should be destroyed, or not, and therefore a committee should be appointed, not to listen to her singing at all, but to examine the contents of her stomach and see if she devoured anything which was injurious to the farmers and gardeners, or which they cannot spare.

Less than two years before making the above entry, Thoreau walked through the southwest corner of Wellfleet right past the present location of today's Wellfleet Bay Wildlife Sanctuary. At that time, he referred to the area as "Silver Springs" and described it simply as "an extensive bare plain tract." Like most of this part of the Cape, "Silver Springs" had been largely deforested by the 1850's. But what a difference a century and a half can make! As today's walkers will attest, the area is covered with beautiful woods and fields that support all manner of wildlife.

---

* Those interested in Thoreau's insights into the lives of birds will treasure Beacon Press' *Thoreau on Birds*, edited by Francis H. Allen with an introduction by Cape Cod nature writer John Hay. (Published in 1993, the text was originally released as *Thoreau's Bird-Lore* in 1910.)

** See the **Jenny Lind Tower** in this guide for further information on this famous 19th-century Swedish singer.

In the Footsteps of Thoreau

Given his journal entry above, there is little doubt that if Thoreau were alive today he would wholeheartedly approve of the use of this formerly "extensive bare plain tract" as a sanctuary dedicated to the protection and appreciation of the natural world. The Wellfleet Bay Wildlife Sanctuary is certainly one of the best places on Cape Cod to observe birds, "their dispositions," "the beauty of their plumage" and "the sweetness of their song."

Words to Walk By

When we walk, we naturally go to the fields and woods: what would become of us, if we walked only in a garden or a mall?

–Walking, 1862

The Trail

➡ From the front entrance of the Nature Center proceed around the right edge of the low-fenced garden to the Silver Spring Trail trailhead which is marked by a sign.

➡ Follow the trail to the left (east), along the side of Silver Spring Brook. Formerly a tidal inlet of Wellfleet Bay, the brook was separated from it in 1929 by a dike in order to form a small freshwater pond and to increase the variety of birds that are attracted to the property.

➡ After about 0.2 miles the trail turns to the right (north) and crosses the brook by way of a small bridge.

➡ On the other side of the bridge, turn right and follow the quiet pathway through a pine wood where there are views of the brook to the right.

➡ When you arrive at the t-junction at the western end of the brook, turn left and continue 0.1 miles to Goose Pond. Here, the trail crosses the earthen dike that separates the pond from the marsh. The water level and salinity of Goose Pond is regulated seasonally to attract different species of birds; and there is a bird blind set up for observation on the eastern shore of the pond, just around to the left as you face the pond from the trail.

➡ From Goose Pond, continue almost due west along the trail to the marsh cabin 0.3 miles farther. Along the way, you will pass an overlook platform and various benches that offer magnificent views of the marsh.

➡ From the marsh cabin, follow the path to the right to Try Island. Try Island is one of the last places on Cape Cod to support an oak-hickory woodland, which was formerly very common here.

➡ After making a short loop around the island, the trail winds down to the west and leads out along a boardwalk 0.3 miles into the marshes of the bay. The heavily developed land mass straight across the bay is Lieutenant

What Thoreau Saw

American Coot

There was also an almost uninterrupted line of coots rising and falling with the waves, a few rods from the shore, the whole length of the Cape. They made as constant a part of the ocean's border as the pads or pickerel-weed do of that of a pond.

Island, and the undeveloped land beyond it is Great Island. (See the **Great Island Trail**.)

➡️After traversing the boardwalk, retrace your steps back to the marsh cabin, to Goose Pond, and to Silver Spring Brook.

➡️Bear left at Silver Spring Brook and cross over the dike that separates it from the bay, then follow the short trail back to the Nature Center to complete this walk.●

I should like to know the birds of the woods better, what birds inhabit our woods? I hear their various notes ringing through them. What musicians compose our woodland choir? They must be forever strange and interesting to me.

—Henry David Thoreau, The Journal of Henry David Thoreau, 1854.

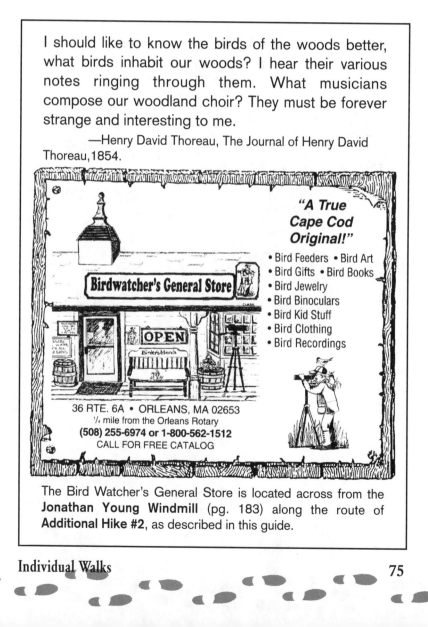

The Bird Watcher's General Store is located across from the **Jonathan Young Windmill** (pg. 183) along the route of **Additional Hike #2**, as described in this guide.

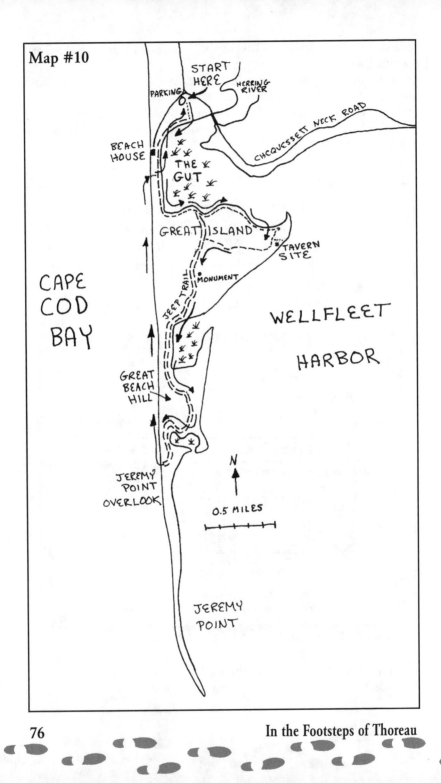

Map #10

START HERE

PARKING

HERRING RIVER

BEACH HOUSE

THE GUT

CHEQUESSETT NECK ROAD

GREAT ISLAND

TAVERN SITE

MONUMENT

CAPE COD BAY

JEEP TRAIL

WELLFLEET

HARBOR

GREAT BEACH HILL

N

JEREMY POINT OVERLOOK

0.5 MILES

JEREMY POINT

In the Footsteps of Thoreau

Great Island Trail

DISTANCE 7.7 miles

TIME 4.5 hours

RATING very difficult

Location

This trail is located on an isolated peninsula that juts into Cape Cod Bay from the western shore of Wellfleet. Follow Route 6 to the Wellfleet/Eastham town line and proceed north into Wellfleet 5.2 miles, to the traffic lights at the intersection with Main Street. Turn left onto Main Street and follow it 0.25 miles to Commercial Street. Turn left onto Commercial Street and follow it 0.75 miles to Wellfleet Harbor where the road bends hard to the right. Follow the road around to the right and stay on it for 2.5 miles, keeping the water on your left, until you arrive at the **Cape Cod National Seashore**'s Great Island parking lot, also on the left.

Description

The **Great Island Trail** is the longest self-guided hike in the **Cape Cod National Seashore** as well as the longest "Individual Walk" in this guide. While part of the path meanders through a quiet and shady pine wood, it mainly consists of challenging beach walking. The hard work is well worth the effort, however, as hikers are amply rewarded with an array of inspiring views of Cape Cod Bay, Wellfleet Harbor and small, scenic salt marshes. Although fall and spring are probably the best times to make this hike, lucky winter walkers may see harbor seals sunning themselves along the beach or swimming in the waters nearby.

While this route runs along what is presently a peninsula, the land masses visible here formerly composed a small archipelago of individual islands. Over the years these small islands became connected by barrier beaches made of sand that had eroded away from the shore to the north and was subsequently deposited between the islands by the currents of Cape Cod Bay. Geologists call such beaches "tombolos." Together they currently complete a contiguous western-facing beach stretching from Truro's Pamet Harbor south to Wellfleet's Jeremy Point, which includes Bound Brook Island, Griffin Island, Great Island, and Great Beach Hill (all located in Wellfleet).

Because of this area's unique geography, it was a prime location for Native American and Colonial whaling. In fact, one of the Pilgrims' earliest records is of Native Americans gathered around a pilot whale (also called a blackfish) along the beach near Great Island. And in Colonial times, enough fishermen used Great Island's bluffs as a lookout, and its beaches as a launching point, for small-craft whaling, that a tavern was constructed on the island to capitalize on the industry. Legend has it that this tavern, owned by one Samuel Smith, was a favored place for fishermen to eat, drink, smoke, swap stories and to consort with "sympathetic ladies." Although many dismissed this legend as mere hearsay, in 1970 archaeologists from Plimouth Plantation and the National Park Service located and excavated the foundation of a building on Great Island that was utilized from about 1690 to 1730. Some of the 24,000 artifacts found at the site include wine glass stems, clay smoking pipes, a whalebone chopping block, and a lady's fan. While this "tavern site" is today little more than a pile of rocks identified by a sign, the Cape Cod National Seashore has established display plaques along the trail which include photographs of the dig and many excavated items.

Thoreau

Thoreau explored most of Cape Cod's bay shore between Provincetown and Eastham in June of 1850, "excepting four or five miles," and was familiar with Griffin Island, Great Island and Great Beach Hill, all of which he noted on his own hand-drawn maps of the Cape. He also knew Billingsgate Island which was then located south of today's Jeremy Point in Wellfleet Harbor. He even passed close to these islands on a steamship from which he noted the shallowness of the surrounding waters. Although Billingsgate Island is today little more than a tidal flat marked on navigational charts, it was once the home of a lighthouse that served as a key Cape Cod Bay beacon for the better part of a century. The island fell victim to severe erosion at the end of the 19th century, but Billingsgate Lighthouse lasted until 1915, and bits of dry land still existed there as recently as 1942. Although some have predicted that Billingsgate Island will eventually be resurrected from the depths, or at least re-emerge through the actions of currents and tides, all that remain to speak of its past are the lighthouse foundation blocks and riprap, which are still evident at low tides.

One of the Wellfleet Oysterman's colorful Cape Cod stories, recounted by Thoreau in *Cape Cod*, offers a rich flavor of the history of these islands. He writes:

> He remembered well when gulls were taken in the gull-house, and when small birds were killed by means of a frying pan and a fire at night. His father once lost a valuable horse from this cause. A party from Wellfleet having lighted their fire for this purpose, one dark night, on Billingsgate

What Thoreau Saw

Blackfish or Pilot Whales

When I came to Great Hollow I found a fisherman and some boys on the watch, and counted about thirty blackfish, just killed, with many lance wounds, and the water was more or less bloody around. They were partly on shore and partly in the water, held by a rope round their tails till the tide should leave them. A boat had been somewhat stove by the tail of one. They were a smooth shining black, like India-rubber, and had remarkably simple and lumpish forms for animated creatures, with a blunt round snout or head, whale-like, and simple stiff-looking flippers. The largest were about fifteen feet long, but one or two were only five feet long, and still without teeth. The fisherman slashed one with his jackknife, to show me how thick the blubber was—about three inches; and as I passed my finger through the cut it was covered thick with oil. The blubber looked like pork, and this man said that when they were trying it the boys would sometimes come round with a piece of bread in one hand, and take a piece of blubber in the other to eat with it, preferring it to pork scraps.

This photograph, reproduced courtesy of Provincetown Museum, was taken by G.H. Nickerson on November 17, 1884.

 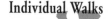

Island, twenty horses which were pastured there, and this colt among them, became frightened by it, and endeavoring in the dark to cross the passage which separated them from the neighboring beach, and which was then fordable at low tide, were all swept out to sea and drowned. I observed that many horses were still turned out to pasture all summer on the islands and beaches in Wellfleet.

The Trail

➤From the Great Island parking lot, follow the blue-stone pathway down the hill. This pathway begins near the chemical toilets that are maintained by the Park. Off to the right of this pathway, between it and the parking lot, you will find a gravestone for an "Indian Woman" who was reinterred here in 1976 by the Wampanoag Tribal Council and the Wellfleet Historical Society.

➤Follow the pathway down to the beach. To the left is a marsh area known as the "Gut." Once down by the Gut you will see the Herring River running under the Chequessett Neck Bridge to your left. The river meanders clear across Wellfleet, between Wellfleet Harbor and the kettle ponds of Wellfleet and Truro where Thoreau stayed at the Wellfleet Oysterman's house.

➤From the bottom of the blue-stone pathway, follow the beach around to the right.

➤A split-rail fence runs here between the path and the dunes. After a few hundred yards there is a gap in the fence where there is a beach-access path across the dunes. This short path is worth following for a brief look at Cape Cod Bay to the west. (Also, you will see a boxy beach house up on the hill which is worth noting, as it serves as a good marker of where to cut across the dunes from the beach at the end of the hike, on the way back to the parking lot from Jeremy Point.)

➤After taking a look at the Bay, return to the inside of the dunes by the Gut and continue south to Great Island.

➤Once at Great Island, follow the shoreline as it curves left (east), keeping the Gut to your left. You will soon come to a fork where the shoreline continues straight ahead and a jeep trail veers off to the right into the woods of Great Island. Do not take the jeep trail but instead continue along the shoreline, following the sign that points to the left to the Great Island Tavern site.

➤0.7 miles from the jeep trail you will encounter a sign marking a footpath up the hill from the shoreline into the Great Island woods.

➤Follow this footpath about 0.2 miles to the tavern site. On the way you will encounter an information plaque regarding the tavern.

➤Once at the tavern site take a brief detour along the short spur trail that

In the Footsteps of Thoreau

runs to the left of the site. This short trail leads to the top of some high bluffs that offer a spectacular view of Wellfleet Harbor. **NOTE: Do not walk on the edge of the bluffs, as they are prone to erosion and cave-ins. (See "Safe Walking.")**

→After viewing the harbor, return to the tavern site and follow the main path around

Words to Walk By

My desire for knowledge is intermittent, but my desire to bathe my head in atmospheres unknown to my feet is perennial and constant.

–Walking, 1862

to the right, where a sign points the way to Great Beach Hill and to Jeremy Point. This path meanders 0.7 miles from the tavern site to a t-junction with a jeep trail.

→ Turn left onto the jeep trail, once again following the arrows on the sign that point to Great Beach Hill and to Jeremy Point.

→About 0.2 miles along this jeep trail you will find a monument to one of Governor William Bradford's descendants who once lived here.

→From the monument follow the jeep trail until you come out to the marsh between Great Island and Great Beach Hill.

→Follow the jeep trail to the right and continue south along it, between the marsh and the dunes.

→At the southern end of the marsh, the path climbs Great Beach Hill and enters the woods here.

→After crossing Great Beach Hill, you will come out to the base of another marsh. Follow the trail as it winds and curves through the marsh for about 0.4 miles before reaching the Jeremy Point Overlook. This "overlook" is the southernmost point of the peninsula that is not submerged during high tide. **NOTE: If you choose to walk south of the Jeremy Point Overlook, along Jeremy Point itself, keep a close eye on the tide, as the water can come in rapidly.** Across Wellfleet Bay to your left (east) is Lieutenant Island, and beyond it on the mainland is the **Wellfleet Bay Wildlife Sanctuary Trails** which are described in this guide. In the winter, Jeremy Point is the most likely place along the trail to encounter harbor seals.

→From the Jeremy Point Overlook, follow the beach 2 miles north along the western side of the peninsula. Just before you get to the boxy beach house, cross the dunes back to the Gut.

→Once back at the Gut, retrace your steps along the split-rail fence to the blue-stone pathway and up the hill to the parking area to complete this walk.●

Individual Walks

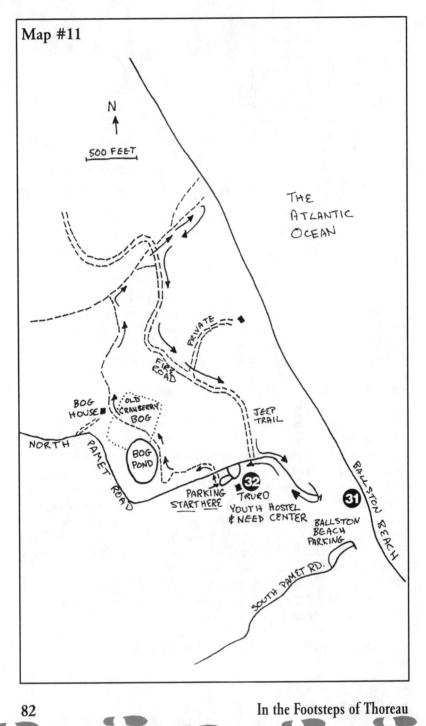

Map #11

N

500 FEET

THE
ATLANTIC
OCEAN

PRIVATE

FIRE
ROAD

BOG
HOUSE

OLD
CRANBERRY
BOG

JEEP
TRAIL

NORTH
PAMET ROAD

BOG
POND

BALLSTON BEACH

PARKING
START HERE

32

TRURO
YOUTH HOSTEL
& NEED CENTER

31

BALLSTON
BEACH
PARKING

SOUTH PAMET RD.

Pamet Cranberry & Dune Walk

No. 11

DISTANCE 1.1 miles

TIME 45 minutes

RATING easy

Location

The trailhead for this walk is located next to the **Truro Youth Hostel/NEED Center,** just across the Pamet River from the **Ballston Beach** parking lot. Follow Route 6 to the Truro/Wellfleet town line. Proceed north on Route 6 for 2.4 miles and then turn right at the well-marked "Pamet Roads" exit. Turn left at the bottom of the off-ramp and follow North Pamet Road 1.6 miles to the large red-roofed Youth Hostel/NEED Center. Parking for this walk is located to the right of the building.

Description

The Pamet River area of Truro has a rich history, with many of the houses nearby dating from Colonial times. The western end of the river was even seriously considered as a settlement site by the Pilgrims.[3] Although the Pilgrims instead chose Plymouth as their destination, the Pamet River area was nevertheless heavily settled early on, as it opens up at its western end into Cape Cod Bay to form Pamet Harbor. In addition to many businesses such as supply stores and taverns which developed around the harbor by the time Thoreau visited Truro in the 19th century, there was a tidal grist mill located along the river, as well as a windmill on a hill above the harbor, a lighthouse just inside the harbor's mouth, and a number of churches in the surrounding neighborhood. In fact, the Truro Shipwreck Monument which Thoreau wrote of in *Cape Cod* can still be found on the grounds of the Truro Congregational Church, which also overlooks the harbor and river.

Although the eastern end of the Pamet River, where this walk is located, has traditionally been less populated than the river's western end, it was the location of the once-popular Ozzie Ball Summer Resort, for which **Ballston Beach** was named. Furthermore, the beach here was the site of the Pamet Life-Saving Station, one of thirteen similar stations established along the Cape's outer shore in the 19th century. (See **Old Harbor Life-Saving Station Museum** for further information on the U.S. Life-Saving Service.) In 1933, the Pamet Life-Saving Station was replaced by a U.S. Coast Guard Station which now serves as the **Truro Youth Hostel/NEED Center** and attracts thousands of people to the area every year.

The eastern end of the river was also the location of a sizable commercial cranberry bog.[4] Established by James Howe during the 1880's, the bog changed hands many times before gradually falling into disuse. The land finally became the property of the **Cape Cod National Seashore** in 1963; and although woodlands have reclaimed much of the bog, a small patch of cranberries is still preserved by the Park in recognition of the historic landscape. The Park even maintains an old bog house nearby to complete the scene,

Words to Walk By

We should go forth on the shortest walk, perchance, in the spirit of undying adventure, never to return, prepared to send back our embalmed hearts only as relics to our desolate kingdoms. If you are ready to leave father and mother, and brother and sister, and wife and child and friends, and never see them again—if you have paid your debts, and made your will, and settled all your affairs, and are a free man—then you are ready for a walk.

–Walking, 1862

as well as a walking path between the bog house and the road. The walk described here includes this walking path, as well as a narrow footpath and a sandy fire road, the latter running through the dunes nearby.

Thoreau

Cranberries, one of the few native plants to become an important commercial crop, were discovered by early settlers to be a valuable source of Vitamin C. Unlike other sources of this vitamin, the berries could be stored for long periods of time without rotting and thus proved invaluable in the prevention of scurvy on long sea voyages. Cranberries were first grown commercially by Dennis resident Henry Hall and are today the largest export crop in Massachusetts, as well as an integral part of the Cape Cod landscape. In 1857, Thoreau made the following journal entry about a Cape Cod cranberry bog he encountered on one of his walks:

> They formed a handsome, perfectly level bed, a field, a redeemed meadow, adjoining the pond, the plants in perfectly straight rows eighteen inches apart, in coarse sand which had been carted in. What with the runners and the moss, etc., between, they made a uniform green bed, very striking and handsome.

Thoreau spent a substantial amount of time in Truro during all four of his Cape visits and did not fail to write abut the Pamet River in *Cape Cod*. In fact, he even spoke to "one who lives nearby" it and recorded information about the erosion of the beach near this walk. See **Ballston Beach** for further information.

In the Footsteps of Thoreau

The Trail

➡ From the parking lot, follow the trail across North Pamet Road and then up the embankment via the concrete stairs.

➡ Follow the trail up the small hill to the left and then down the series of steps to the bog pond.

➡ Once at the pond, follow the trail across the bog by way of the narrow boardwalk that leads to the old bog house.

➡ Proceed along the right side of the bog house onto the narrow footpath that leads to the north.

➡ Follow this footpath north from the bog house 0.25 miles to where it intersects an east/west-running footpath.

➡ Turn right (east) onto this footpath and proceed another 0.2 miles to the junction of the path with a jeep trail. This jeep trail is also part of **The Great Thoreau Hike, Part VI,** as described in this guide.

➡ Although you are going to follow this jeep trail to the right (south), take a few minutes to follow the spur trail that runs from the footpath straight across the jeep trail (east) to the bluffs above the beach.

➡ After a look at the Atlantic from the bluffs above the beach, return to the jeep trail and follow it south 0.4 miles back to North Pamet Road near the **Truro Youth Hostel/NEED Center.**

➡ Once back at North Pamet Road, you may want to walk down to the left (east) to see where the road was buried by sand when the ocean burst through the dunes here in 1978 and again in 1991.

➡ Return to the Youth Hostel/NEED Center to complete this walk.●

Map #12

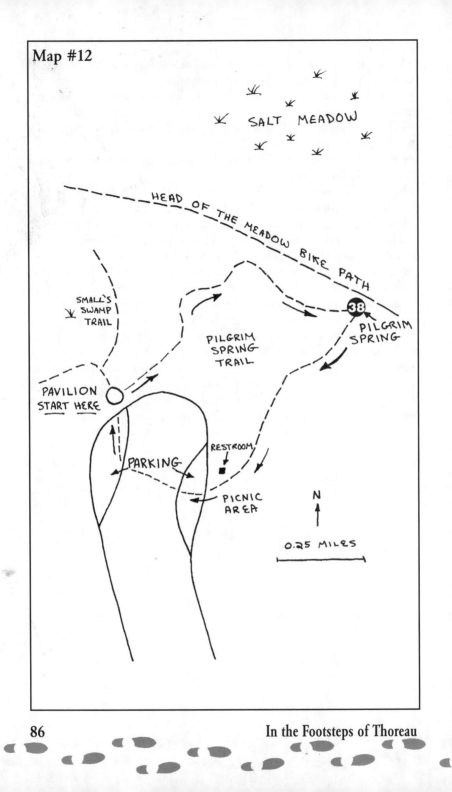

SALT MEADOW

HEAD OF THE MEADOW BIKE PATH

SMALL'S SWAMP TRAIL

PILGRIM SPRING TRAIL

38 PILGRIM SPRING

PAVILION START HERE

RESTROOM

PARKING

PICNIC AREA

N

0.25 MILES

In the Footsteps of Thoreau

Pilgrim Spring Trail

No. 12

DISTANCE 0.75 miles

TIME 30 minutes

RATING easy

Location

The **Pilgrim Spring Trail** is located within the **Cape Cod National Seashore** in North Truro. Follow Route 6 to the Truro/Wellfleet town line and then proceed north 7.4 miles to the well-marked Pilgrim Heights Area on the right. Turn right into the area and proceed 0.5 miles to the first parking lot. The trail begins at the pavilion on the left.

Description

This trail offers pleasant views of the marsh to the northwest of Pilgrim Heights and runs to **Pilgrim Spring**, the historic spring that is noteworthy as having provided the Pilgrims with their first fresh drinking water in North America.

After 65 days at sea in extremely cramped quarters, the 101 passengers on board the *Mayflower* were grateful to safely enter Provincetown Harbor on November 11, 1620. But alone in a strange land, and with dwindling reserves of food and drink, their work had just begun. Thus, one of the Pilgrims' first orders of business was to organize a group to search the area for supplies, and on November 13th a party of 15 men left the *Mayflower* to explore the region. *Mourt's Relation*, an account of the Pilgrims' experiences that is considered to have been written by William Bradford and Edward Winslow, relates the discovery of a freshwater spring by the Pilgrims, after they had pursued Native Americans near today's Pilgrim Heights:

> In the morning so soon as we could see the trace, we proceeded on our journey, and had the track until we had compassed the head of a long creek [probably Pilgrim Lake/Provincetown East Harbor], and there they took into another wood, and we after them, supposing to find some of their dwellings, but we marched through boughs and bushes, and under hills and valleys, which tore our very armor in pieces, and yet could meet with none of them, nor their houses, nor find any fresh water, which we greatly desired, and stood in need of, for we brought neither beer nor water with us, and our victuals was only biscuit and Holland cheese, and a little bottle of aquavitae [probably gin[5]], so as we were sore athirst. About ten o'clock we came into a deep valley, full of brush, wood-gaile, and long grass, through which we found little paths or tracks,

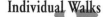

and there we saw a deer, and found springs of fresh water, of which we were heartily glad, and sat us down and drunk our first New England water with as much delight as ever we drunk in all our lives.

History buffs will note, however, that while plaques at Pilgrim Spring commemorate it as the place where William Bradford, Captain Miles Standish and their Pilgrim comrades first tasted New World water, its actual location has never been accurately established. Although Pilgrim Spring is in the general vicinity of the spring that the Pilgrims drank from more than 375 years ago, it has only recently been identified as such, and there is no conclusive evidence that it is the same.

Thoreau
Thoreau probably knew Truro better than he knew any other part of Cape Cod, as it was the town in which he spent the most time. Of course he also knew its history, having read every book on the subject that he could lay his hands on. He quotes *Mourt's Relation* in *Cape Cod*:

> They say that, just after passing the head of East Harbor Creek, the boughs and bushes "tore" their "very armor in pieces" (the same thing happened to such armor as we wore, when out of curiosity we took to the bushes); or they came to deep valleys, "full of brush, wood-gaile, and long grass," and "found springs of fresh water."

Thoreau certainly was familiar with the area that we now call Pilgrim Heights, as a number of main roads—including parts of the **Old Kings Highway**—once ran adjacent to it. In fact, it wasn't far from the Pilgrim Heights Area that Thoreau discovered artifacts left by the Native Americans who had settled here. He records the event in a journal entry:

> As I was approaching the Bay through a sandy hollow a mile east of High Head, I found two or three arrow-points and a rude axe or hammer, a flattish stone from the beach with a deep groove chipped around it.

Those interested in additional information on this area should see **Pilgrim Lake/Provincetown**'s **East Harbor, Head of the Meadow Beach, High Head Parking Area**, and **Small's Swamp Trail** in this guide.

The Trail
This trail begins at the pavilion located next to the area's first parking lot, the same place that the **Small's Swamp Trail** begins.

➜From the pavilion follow the trail to the right.

➜After about 0.2 miles you will reach a scenic overlook that offers a great view of the marsh, with the rolling dunes of the **Great Beach** beyond it.

In the Footsteps of Thoreau

The **Cape Cod National Seashore** has erected informative plaques nearby with information on the Native Americans who inhabited this area for some 4,000 years.

➡️From the overlook follow the trail down to the Head of the Meadow Bike Path, where the spring is located. (This bike path is also part of **The Great Thoreau Hike, Part VII,** as described in this guide.) This is also a great place to take a break, as there is a picnic table located near the spring. (Those interested in more information regarding the spring should turn to the **Pilgrim Spring** entry in this book.)

➡️From the bike path and spring, follow the trail up the hill to the left. After about 0.25 miles you will arrive at a picnic area where you will find seasonally operated restrooms.

➡️Follow the trail across the area's second parking lot and through a short path to return to the area's first parking lot to conclude this walk.●

Words to Walk By

I walk out into a nature such as the old prophets and poets, Menu, Moses, Homer, Chaucer, walked in. You may name it America, but it is not America; neither Americus Vespuccius, nor Columbus, nor the rest were the discoverers of it. There is a truer account of it in mythology than in any history of America, so called, that I have seen.

–Walking, 1862

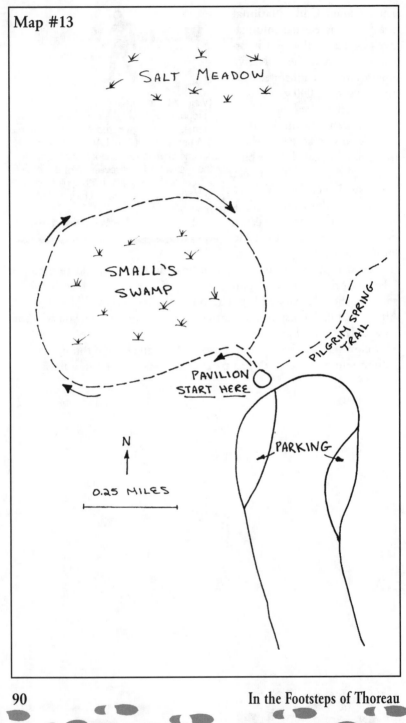

Map #13

SALT MEADOW

SMALL'S SWAMP

PILGRIM SPRING TRAIL

PAVILION
START HERE

PARKING

N

0.25 MILES

In the Footsteps of Thoreau

Small's Swamp Trail

No. 13

DISTANCE 0.75 miles

TIME 30 minutes

RATING easy

Location

The **Small's Swamp Trail** is located within the **Cape Cod National Seashore** in North Truro. Follow Route 6 to the Truro/Wellfleet town line and then proceed north 7.4 miles to the well-marked Pilgrim Heights Area on the right. Turn right into the area and proceed 0.5 miles to the first parking lot. The trail begins at the pavilion on the left.

Description

A short simple loop, this walk offers a number of great views and interesting insights into Cape Cod history.

Small's Swamp is one of many kettle holes in the area. Similar to kettle ponds, kettle holes are the products of glaciers. After the glaciers that formed Cape Cod receded some thousands of years ago, massive chunks of ice remained embedded in the Cape's soil. When these chunks finally melted, the earth around them collapsed and left huge holes in their stead. Those holes that were as deep as the ground water were flooded and formed kettle ponds (See **Little Cliff Pond Trail**); but those that did not reach as deep as the ground water simply remained kettle holes. The kettle hole that formed Small's Swamp happens to be somewhat unique in that it is deep enough to have taken on some water, but not deep enough to have formed a proper kettle pond. As a result, it has served as a fertile breeding ground for plants as well as a sheltered location for homes, including the farmhouse of Thomas Small for whom it was named.[6]

Although the aforementioned geological processes behind the formation of kettle holes had not yet been identified in Thoreau's time, the author described those he encountered in North Truro, like Small's Swamp, with amazing insight:

> Some of the valleys, however, are circular, a hundred feet deep and without any outlet, as if the Cape had sunk in those places, or its sands had run out. The few scattered houses which we passed, being placed at the bottom of these hollows for shelter and fertility, were, for the most part, concealed entirely as much as if they had been swallowed up by the earth.

Always alert and ready for discovery, Thoreau found a number of arrowheads and stone tools not far from Small's Swamp, a fact that is not surprising given the history of the area. Archaeological evidence indicates that the swamp was inhabited by Native Americans for some 4,000 years. These people appear mainly to have been migrants who grew corn, pumpkin, squash and beans, and who regularly cleared fields with forest fires. Soil samples also indicate that these inhabitants utilized environmentally intelligent agricultural methods, only working individual fields for limited numbers of seasons before moving on to others, and thus allowing the earth to recover before being completely depleted of its nutrients.

Unfortunately, this was not the method employed by many early European settlers who quickly clear-cut and then over-farmed and over-grazed the land. By the time Thomas Small set up his farmhouse in the swamp in 1860, most of the surrounding land was completely deforested. Only by selecting a wise variety of crops and harvesting salt hay from the nearby marsh were he and his son, Warren Small, able to keep their 200-acre farm going until about 1920, when it was finally abandoned.[7]

Words to Walk By

When I would recreate myself, I seek the darkest wood, the thickest and most interminable and, to the citizen, most dismal, swamp. I enter a swamp as a sacred place, a "sanctum sanctorum." There is the strength, the marrow, of Nature. The wildwood covers the virgin mould, and the same soil is good for men and for trees. A man's health requires as many acres of meadow to his prospect as his farm does loads of muck. There are the strong meats on which he feeds. A town is saved, not more by the righteous men in it than by the woods and swamps that surround it. A township where one primitive forest waves above while another primitive forest rots below—such a town is fitted to raise not only corn and potatoes, but poets and philosophers for the coming ages. In such a soil grew Homer and Confucius and the rest, and out of such a wilderness comes the Reformer eating locusts and wild honey.

–Walking, 1862

Thoreau

Thoreau wrote enthusiastically of this part of Truro and commented on its interesting landscape, particularly on the contrasts between the open plains and the kettle holes:

> This part of Truro affords singularly interesting and cheering walks for me, with regular hollows or dimples shutting out the sea as completely as if in the midst of the continent, though when you stand on the plain you commonly see the sails of vessels standing up or down the coast on

each side of you, though you may not see the water…. That solitude was sweet to me as a flower. I sat down on the boundless level and enjoyed the solitude, drank it in, the medicine for which I had pined, worth more than the bear-berry so common on the Cape.

Thoreau spent a substantial amount of his time on Cape Cod in Truro and probably knew today's Pilgrim Heights Area well. See **Pilgrim Lake/Provincetown East Harbor, Head of the Meadow Beach, Pilgrim Spring** and **High Head Parking Area** for more information regarding the history of this area.

The Trail

This loop starts at the pavilion at the corner of the area's first parking lot, the same place that the **Pilgrim Spring Trail** begins. Off to the west, Provincetown's **Pilgrim Monument** can be seen almost four miles away on clear days.

➜Take the **Small's Swamp Trail** from the pavilion and follow the log steps down to the swamp. Be sure to bear left at the fork you will encounter on the way.

➜Once down in the swamp, follow the wide sandy path around to the left. The Park has built boardwalks through the swamp over the wettest areas and posted signs that mark a variety of plants. Common species include swamp azalea, highbush blueberry, black cherry, beach heather and bearberry.

➜Remnants from Small's farm can also be spotted here and there, including grape vines, apple trees and lilac bushes.

➜As you follow the trail out of the swamp, views of the marsh, dunes, and even the distant Atlantic will open up on the left. You will also encounter plaques commemorating the Pilgrim's 1620 explorations of the area and the 1778 wreck of the British man-of-war *Somerset*, as well as the history of **Pilgrim Lake/Provincetown's East Harbor** and its estuary, East Harbor Creek, now called "Salt Meadow."

➜Follow the trail back up to the pavilion to conclude this walk. Seasonal restrooms are located by the area's second parking lot.●

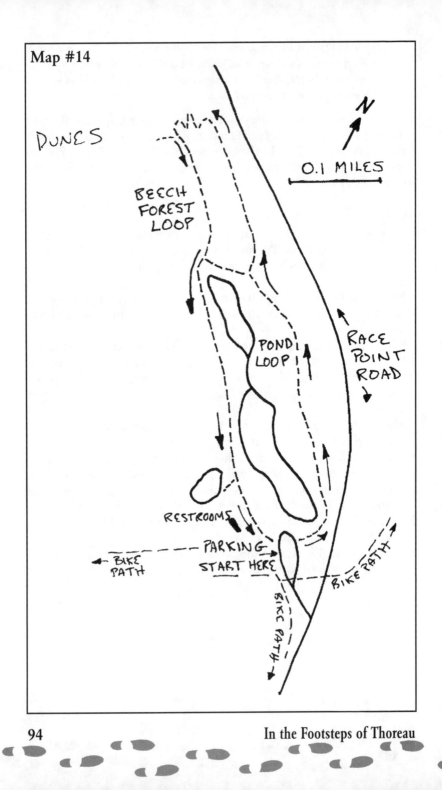

Map #14

DUNES

BEECH
FOREST
LOOP

POND
LOOP

RACE
POINT
ROAD

N

0.1 MILES

RESTROOMS

PARKING
START HERE

BIKE
PATH

BIKE PATH

BIKE PATH

In the Footsteps of Thoreau

Beech Forest Trail

No. 14

DISTANCE 1 mile
TIME 45 minutes
RATING easy

Location

The **Beech Forest Trail** is located in the town of Provincetown, within the **Cape Cod National Seashore**-managed **Province Lands**. Follow Route 6 to the Provincetown/Truro town line and proceed west 2.25 miles to the traffic lights at Race Point Road. Turn right onto Race Point Road and continue 0.5 miles north to the Beech Forest parking lot on the left.

Description

Although the **Beech Forest Trail** is located within the boundaries of the **Province Lands**, the largest dune environment on Cape Cod, it was not named for the nearby sandy *beaches*, but for the many *beech* trees within its environs. Beech Forest is, in fact, the only mature hardwood forest in the area and is often described as an oasis within the desert-like Province Lands.

Trees have not always been as scarce in the Province Lands as they are today, however. In fact, when the Pilgrims first dropped anchor in Provincetown Harbor in 1620, most of the area was covered by a substantial woodland. It was only after years of clear-cutting and over-grazing by early settlers that the Province Lands was reduced to the harsh, almost barren environment that Thoreau encountered in 1849 and that largely remains today. It should be noted, however, that Beech Forest is not a virgin wood. The land around Beech Forest Pond was also over-exploited by early settlers, and the reestablishment of the forest is the result of a 19th-century replanting program that was sponsored by the state.

The Beech Forest Trail makes a great short walk in any season, with many lovely views of lily-filled Beech Forest Pond. And there is ample opportunity to spot a variety of animal and plant species along the way. Walkers should be especially alert for birds, as Beech Forest is one of the premier birding locations on Cape Cod, particularly during the spring passerine and warbler migrations. There are also a number of interesting places along the trail where one can see the surrounding dunes that have encroached on the forest.

The **Cape Cod National Seashore** has placed picnic tables near the parking lot, and also maintains seasonal restrooms here.

Thoreau

The **Province Lands** had changed so much in the two centuries separating the Pilgrims' explorations and Thoreau's walks, that Thoreau could not resist humorously contrasting his observations with those of his country's forefathers. He writes in *Cape Cod*:

> It is remarkable that the Pilgrims (or their reporter) describe this part of the Cape, not only as well wooded, but as having a deep and excellent soil, and hardly mention the word sand. Now, what strikes the voyager is the barrenness and desolation of the land. They found "the ground or earth sand-hills, much like the downs in Holland, but much better; the crust of the earth, a spit's depth, excellent black earth." We found that the earth had lost its crust—if, indeed, it ever had any—and that there was no soil to speak of. We did not see enough black earth in Provincetown to fill a flower-pot, unless in the swamps. They found it "all wooded with oaks, pines, sassafras, juniper, birch, holly, vines, some ash, walnut; the wood for the most part open and without underwood, fit either to go or ride in." We saw scarcely anything high enough to be called a tree, except a little low wood at the east end of the town, and the few ornamental trees in its yards—only a few small specimens of some of the above kinds on the sand-hills in the rear; but it was all thick shrubbery, without any large wood above it, very unfit either to go or ride in. The greater part of the land was a perfect desert of yellow sand, rippled like waves by the wind, in which only a little Beach-grass grew here and there.

Thoreau spent two full days walking in the Province Lands in 1849, and questions in *Cape Cod* the accuracy of the Pilgrims' claim that there was once a forest there. He even theorizes that the Pilgrims exaggerated the fertility of the area in order to impress their countrymen back in England. Although there may be some truth to Thoreau's suspicions that the Pilgrims may have exaggerated somewhat, there remains no doubt that a hardwood forest once covered the Province Lands. Certainly, Beech Forest is the best place in Provincetown for one to get an unblemished sense of what the area was like prior to the 17th century.

The Trail

This trail consists of two overlapping loops, the 0.75-mile "Pond Loop" to the south and the 0.25-mile "Beech Forest Loop" to the north.

➔The trailhead to the walk is located on the right side of the parking lot, adjacent to the grassy clearing by the edge of the pond.

➔Just a few steps from the parking lot, the trail crosses a small bridge that features an exceptional view of the pond.

➔From the bridge, proceed 0.3 miles to the fork in the trail. You may

What Thoreau Saw

Beach Grass

Thus Cape Cod is anchored to the heavens, as it were, by a myriad of little cables of beach-grass, and, if they should fail, would become a total wreck, and erelong go to the bottom. Formerly, the cows were permitted to go at large, and they ate many strands of the cable by which the Cape is moored, and wellnigh set it adrift, as the bull did the boat which was moored with a grass rope; but now they are not permitted to wander.

notice that up until this point in the walk, the woods are dominated more by pine and oak than by beech trees.

➜At the fork, continue straight ahead onto the Beech Forest Loop where you will cross a short boardwalk. Here, you will notice a steadily increasing number of beech trees. These smooth, silver-barked trees create a high, thick canopy that is a joy to walk under.

➜0.2 miles along the Beech Forest Loop, the trail bends hard to the left and climbs a

Words to Walk By

If a man walk in the woods for the love of them half of each day, he is in danger of being regarded as a loafer; but if he spends his whole day as a speculator, shearing off those woods and making earth bald before her time, he is esteemed an industrious and enterprising citizen. As if a town had no interest in her forests but to cut them down!

–Life Without Principle, 1863

small knoll by way of a log-framed stairway.

➜Once you've passed this knoll you will come to a number of places where the desert-like **Province Lands** landscape is just visible off to the right. A short walk off the trail at these places yields great views across the adjacent dunes and provides a sense of just how unique Beech Forest is within the environs of today's Province Lands.

➜After winding over some small hills, the Beech Forest Loop reconnects with the Pond Loop. Bear right at this junction and follow the path another 0.25 miles back to the parking lot. On the way, you may notice more places where the woods meet the dunes off to the right.

➜As the trail returns to the parking lot, just before the public restrooms, a spur trail to the right (west) offers a pleasant look at a nearby pond. A little farther toward Race Point Road, you will encounter the Province Lands Bike Path. This bike path makes a long loop around the Province Lands and is included in **Additional Walk #2**, described in this guide.

➜After the walk, a short drive from Beech Forest will bring you to a number of interesting sites. Turn left out of the parking lot to drive to the **Province Lands Visitor Center**, 0.9 miles to the north on the right; or to Race Point Beach, 1.8 miles to the north. At **Race Point Beach** you will find the **Old Harbor Life-Saving Station Museum** and the **Race Point Ranger Station**. A right-hand turn out of the Beech Forest Parking Lot will bring you into Provincetown, less than 1 mile away, where you will find the **Pilgrim Monument & Provincetown Museum**, as well as the town waterfront and the **Provincetown Center Walk.**●

In the Footsteps of Thoreau

The landscape painter is said to use the figures of men to mark a road. He would not make use of my figure. I walk out into nature such as the old prophets and poets, Menu, Moses, Homer, Chaucer, walked in.

—Henry David Thoreau, Walking, 1862.

"High Head Path–Overcast" by Heather Bruce

The Julie Heller Gallery

2 Gosnold Street, Provincetown, MA (508) 487-2169
Across from Adams Pharmacy, Town Landing on the Beach

At the Julie Heller Gallery you'll discover fine art by more than just landscape painters. You'll find the finest Provincetown painters of every sort, from Thoreau's day to our own. Stop in for an in-depth, eclectic look at Provincetown's great fine art tradition.

Located along the **Provincetown Center Walk** in this guide.

www.capecodaccess.com/Gallery/julieheller/jhg.htm

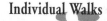

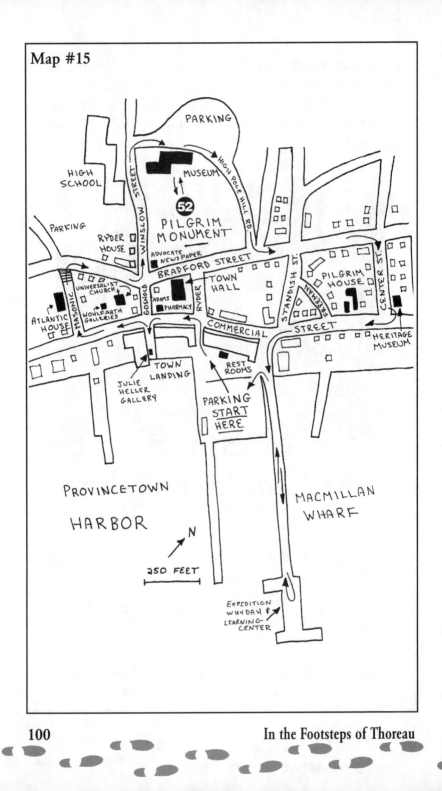

Map #15

PARKING

HIGH SCHOOL

WINSLOW STREET

MUSEUM

HIGH POLE HILL RD.

52
PILGRIM MONUMENT

PARKING

RYDER HOUSE

ADVOCATE NEWSPAPER

BRADFORD STREET

TOWN HALL

PILGRIM HOUSE

STANDISH ST.

FREEMAN ST.

CENTER ST.

MASONIC

UNIVERSALIST CHURCH

GOSNOLD

ADAMS PHARMACY

RYDER

ATLANTIC HOUSE

WOHLFARTH GALLERIES

COMMERCIAL STREET

HERITAGE MUSEUM

TOWN LANDING

JULIE HELLER GALLERY

REST ROOMS

PARKING START HERE

PROVINCETOWN

HARBOR

N

250 FEET

MACMILLAN WHARF

EXPEDITION WHYDAH & LEARNING CENTER

Provincetown Center Walk

No. 15

DISTANCE 1.3 miles
TIME 1-2 hours
RATING easy

Location

This walk begins at the town parking lot at the base of MacMillan Wharf in Provincetown. Follow Route 6 to the Provincetown/Truro town line and proceed 2.25 miles west on to the intersection with Conwell Street (to the left) and Race Point Road (to the right). Turn left and follow Conwell Street 0.4 miles to the t-junction at Bradford Street. Turn right on Bradford and drive 0.15 miles before taking the second left onto Standish Street. Follow Standish 0.1 miles across Commercial Street to the town parking lot where parking fees are charged from spring through fall. If the lot is full, the town lot at Provincetown High School on Bradford Street is a good alternative.

Description

This enjoyable walk—the only one in this guide to be set in an urban environment—is composed of a relatively short loop that runs along paved walkways but includes a number of hills. The trail begins at Provincetown's scenic waterfront and then works its way through the center of town to the **Pilgrim Monument & Provincetown Museum**. From the monument, the route winds down eastwardly to the Provincetown Heritage Museum before returning to the waterfront and ending with a stroll along MacMillan Wharf.

While this guide focuses on the historic aspects of the town, walkers are bound to encounter dozens of other delightful buildings, views, shops, galleries, restaurants and clubs. Walkers are encouraged to explore the town, as it is difficult to get lost in Provincetown, but easy to have fun.

Restrooms and public telephones are located at the parking lot at the beginning of the route.

Thoreau

Thoreau stayed in Provincetown during all four of his visits to the Cape and dedicated Chapter 10, by far the longest chapter in *Cape Cod*, to the town. Thoreau's Provincetown chapter is filled with historical information regarding early explorations of the area, as well as pages of detailed descriptions of the town and its inhabitants. At one point in the chapter, however, Thoreau sums up Provincetown rather succinctly:

> This was the most completely maritime town that we were ever in.
> It was merely a good harbor, surrounded by land dry, if not firm—an
> inhabited beach, whereon fishermen cured and sorted their fish, without
> any back country.

Today, while the fishing industry has suffered in a period of great decline, life in Provincetown continues to be dominated by the ubiquitous presence of the ocean.

The Trail

Looking inland from the town parking lot on MacMillan Wharf, Provincetown's public restrooms are visible just to the left of the Chamber of Commerce building next to the bus stop.

➡️From the bus stop proceed to the left (west), to Ryder Street.

➡️Turn right onto Ryder Street and follow it just a few steps north to Commercial Street. Approximately three miles long, Commercial Street was laid out in 1835. Thoreau observed that the road was very sandy and that "in some pictures of Provincetown the persons of the inhabitants are not drawn below the ankles, so much being supposed to be buried in the sand!" Not long before Thoreau's arrival the town had constructed a wooden sidewalk along Commercial Street, known as the "Four Planks of Provincetown." (See illustration opposite.) Prior to the construction of Commercial Street most of the waterfront houses faced the beach, which was used as the main road in town. Although many of the houses have since been turned around to face Commercial Street, a few still front the beach. (A good example is the Martin House Restaurant, 157 Commercial Street, to the west of this walk.)

➡️At the corner of Commercial and Ryder Streets is the heart of the community, the Provincetown Town Hall. During Thoreau's first two visits to Provincetown in 1849 and 1850, there was no official Town Hall, and church buildings were used instead. But in 1853, in time for Thoreau's last two visits, the town built its first Town Hall on High Pole Hill, now the location of the **Pilgrim Monument & Provincetown Museum**. Although the first Town Hall offered a spectacular view of the harbor and was itself a grand sight for incoming ships to see, the physical location was considered a bane by many citizens who complained about the chore of trudging up and down the hill every time they had Town Hall business. Thus, after the first Town Hall burned down in 1877, the present building was erected at its current location in 1885. In addition to housing government offices and Town Meetings, the building is a museum of sorts, with many paintings from the town's priceless collection displayed on its walls. It is

What Thoreau Saw

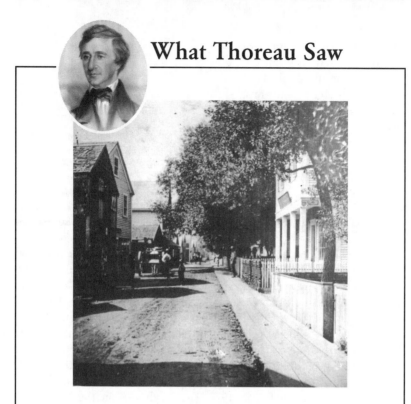

Four Planks of Provincetown

We learned that the four planks on which we were walking had been bought by the town's share of the Surplus Revenue, the disposition of which was a bone of contention between the inhabitants, till they wisely resolved thus to put it under foot. Yet some, it was said, were so provoked because they did not receive their particular share in money, that they persisted in walking in the sand a long time after the side-walk was built. This is the only instance which I happen to know in which the surplus revenue proved a blessing to any town. A surplus revenue of dollars from the treasury to stem the greater evil of a surplus revenue of sand from the ocean. They expected to make a hard road by the time these planks were worn out. Indeed, they have already done so since we were there, and have almost forgotten their sandy baptism.

Photo courtesy of Provincetown Museum.

also utilized for a variety of community activities, including school proms, public concerts and theater productions. There are public restrooms available inside during regular business hours.

→While facing Town Hall, proceed to your left (west) along Commercial Street to Adam's Pharmacy on the right; established in 1868, it is the oldest business in continuous operation in Provincetown.

Words to Walk By

I set out once more to climb the mountain of the earth, for my steps are symbolical steps, and in my walking I have not reached the top of the earth yet.

–The Journal of Henry D. Thoreau, March 21, 1853

→Across Commercial Street from Adam's Pharmacy is the Gosnold Street Town Landing. Town landings like this one are still located up and down the shore. Thoreau observed wheelbarrows full of fish "cured and sorted" at these landings before they were carted off for drying. Art lovers will enjoy a visit to the Julie Heller Gallery at 2 Gosnold Street, adjacent to the landing, which specializes in both classic and contemporary Provincetown painters. The gallery building once served as the ticket booth and green room for the Provincetown Playhouse on the Wharf, which was founded in 1940 and remained active as a theater until it was destroyed in an arson fire in 1977. The Playhouse on the Wharf was dedicated to the spirit of Eugene O'Neill and the Provincetown Players. Among the many actors who performed at the Playhouse was a young Richard Gere who acted here in 1969.

→Continuing west along Commercial Street you will soon come to Provincetown's Unitarian Universalist Meeting House on the right. Erected in 1847, the building was virtually brand new when Thoreau first encountered it. Today, however, it is the oldest house of worship in the community. Its tower was modeled after designs by Christopher Wren, and its interior features mahogany pews, a sandwich-glass chandelier and a 130-year-old English organ.[8] Tucked away next to the church is Wohlfarth Galleries, 234 Commercial Street. Wohlfarth Galleries is known for specializing in artists from the Cape Cod School of Art, the oldest art school in the town, and one of the oldest in the country. The Cape Cod School of Art was founded by Charles Brewster Hawthorne in 1899 and is still thriving. Emphasizing landscape painting in the American Impressionist style, the school is largely credited with establishing Provincetown as an "artist colony," one of the most famous in the world to this day.

→Continuing west along Commercial Street, Masonic Place is just a few hundred feet farther on the right. Turn onto Masonic Place and on the left you will encounter the oldest hotel and one of the best-known buildings in Provincetown, the Atlantic House. The Atlantic House opened in 1798 as a bar, with a hotel added in 1812. Thoreau spent a night at the Atlantic House during his 1855 visit, when the structure was known as Gifford's Hotel or Gifford's Union House. At that time the Atlantic House was also a stopping point for the stagecoach which Thoreau took to North Truro on his way to **Highland Light**. But Thoreau isn't the only world-renowned writer to have slept under this roof. Eugene O'Neill worked on four of his early sea plays while rooming at the Atlantic House; and Tennessee Williams was also a boarder there for a time. The A-House, as it is affectionately known, was owned for many years by Provincetown native Reginald Cabral (1924-1996) who was famous not only for his business acumen but for his renowned collection of works by Provincetown artists and writers, as well as his knowledge of Provincetown history.

➡️Proceeding past the Atlantic House, take the steps up to Bradford Street and continue down the hill to the right. At the bottom of the hill turn left onto Winslow Street at the building which houses *The Advocate* newspaper.

➡️Just a few steps up Winslow Street on the left is the Godfrey Ryder House, 4 Winslow Street, a private residence. Built in 1770, the house was originally located in the center of town, on the property of the present Town Hall. The house was moved to Winslow Street after the Ryder family generously donated the land for the construction of today's Town Hall. During the Civil War the house served as an underground railroad station for the smuggling of runaway slaves en route to freedom in Canada.[9]

➡️Continuing up Winslow Street 0.1 miles, bear right just past the high school onto High Pole Hill Road where the **Pilgrim Monument & Provincetown Museum** are located. Thoreau spent some time on this hill in 1849 when it was undeveloped. From his perch here he enjoyed a bird's-eye view of the town and talked with some boys who were "endeavoring in vain to fly their kite." While the view has certainly changed since the mid-19th century, the perspective offered from the monument is well worth the price of admission as well as the climb up its 167 steps and 60 ramps.

➡️From the monument and museum, continue down the hill along High Pole Hill Road, to Bradford Street and turn left (east).

➡️Follow Bradford past the convenience stores/gas stations on both sides of the road up the hill to Center Street on the right.

➡️Turn right onto Center Street and follow it 0.1 miles back to Commercial Street where you will encounter the Provincetown Heritage Museum on the left. Constructed as a Methodist Church, the Provincetown Heritage Museum was sold to automobile heir Walter

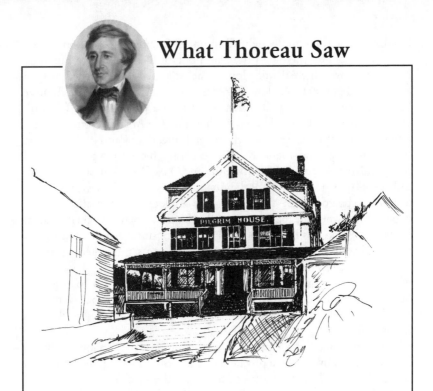

The Pilgrim House

At the Pilgrim House, though it was not crowded, they put me into a small attic chamber which had two double beds in it, and only one window, high in a corner, twenty and a half inches by twenty-five and a half, in the alcove when it was swung open, and it required a chair to look out conveniently. Fortunately, it was not a cold night and the window could be kept open, though at the risk of being visited by the cats, which appear to swarm on the roofs of Provincetown like the mosquitoes on the summits of its hills. I have spent four memorable nights there in as many different years, and have added considerable thereby to my knowledge of the natural history of the cat and the bedbug. Sleep was out of the question…

Illustration by Richard Brown.

Chrysler who turned it into a fine arts museum in 1958. In 1974 it was sold again and used as a center for the arts, until it was purchased by the town for use as a museum. Today the Heritage Museum displays "the world's largest indoor model of a grand banks fishing schooner," fire engines, a model of Harry Kemp's dune shack (see **Province Lands Dune Shacks**), wax figures and more. It is open 10 a.m. to 5:30 p.m. 7 days a week, Memorial Day through Columbus Day.

➜ From the Heritage Museum, proceed right (west) onto Commercial Street and follow it 0.1 miles to the Pilgrim House on the right. Built in 1781, the Pilgrim House was the oldest hotel in Provincetown until it recently burned down and was rebuilt as a shopping and business center. In 1857, Thoreau stayed at the Pilgrim House for "four memorable nights." (See the illustration opposite.)

➜From the Pilgrim House continue west along Commercial Street to Standish Street.

➜Turn left onto Standish Street, and MacMillan Wharf will be directly ahead and the town parking lot will be just to the right. MacMillan Wharf was named for Provincetown native and world-famous Arctic explorer, Admiral Donald Baxter MacMillan. Built in 1883, MacMillan Wharf was formerly called the Old Colony Railroad Wharf, because the tracks went right out to its end. When Thoreau visited Provincetown there were dozens of wharves stretching into the harbor, almost all since fallen victim to weather, age or the drastically reduced fishing industry. Walk MacMillan Wharf today to enjoy the town's renowned waterfront, a view of Provincetown from the water, and a closer look at **Long Point** and **Wood End** across the harbor. Along the wharf, you will notice a number of ticket booths for whale watches, harbor cruises and fishing trips. Also located at the end of the wharf is the Expedition *Whydah* & Learning Center which offers a unique look into the 1717 wreck of the pirate ship *Whydah*, which was recently discovered off the eastern coast of Wellfleet. Admission to the center is $5 for adults, $3.50 for children. Hours vary seasonally, so call ahead at (508) 487-7955.

➜ After visiting the wharf, return to the parking lot to complete this walk.●

What Thoreau Saw

Piping Plover

But if I were required to name a sound, the remembrance of which most perfectly revives the impression which the beach has made, it would be the dreary peep of the piping plover, which haunts there. Their voices, too, are heard as a fugacious part in the dirge, which is ever played along the shore for those mariners who have been lost in the deep since first it was created. But through all this dreariness we seemed to have a pure and unqualified strain of eternal melody, for always the same strain which is a dirge to one household is a morning song of rejoicing to another.

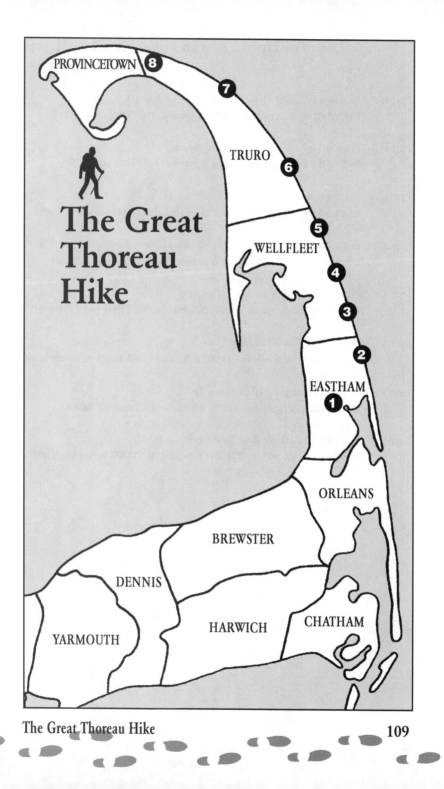

PROVINCETOWN

TRURO

WELLFLEET

EASTHAM

ORLEANS

BREWSTER

DENNIS

CHATHAM

YARMOUTH

HARWICH

The Great
Thoreau
Hike

The Great Thoreau Hike, Parts I–VIII

Part I: Salt Pond Visitor Center to Nauset Light Beach
             DISTANCE 6.2 miles TIME 4 hours RATING difficult

Part II: Nauset Light Beach to Marconi Beach
             DISTANCE 6.4 miles TIME 4 hours RATING difficult

Part III: Marconi Beach to LeCount Hollow Beach
             DISTANCE 8.1 miles TIME 5 hours RATING very difficult

Part IV: LeCount Hollow Beach to Newcomb Hollow Beach
             DISTANCE 9 miles TIME 6 hours RATING very difficult

Part V: Newcomb Hollow Beach to Ballston Beach
             DISTANCE 9.6 miles TIME 6.5 hours RATING very difficult

Part VI: Ballston Beach to Highland Beach
             DISTANCE 10.5 miles TIME 6.5 hours RATING very difficult

Part VII: Highland Beach to High Head Parking Area
             DISTANCE 5.6 miles TIME 3 hours RATING difficult

Part VIII: High Head Parking Area to Race Point Beach
             DISTANCE 15 miles TIME 11 hours RATING extremely difficult

In the Footsteps of Thoreau

Introduction to
The Great Thoreau Hike

The Great Thoreau Hike section of this guide is based on Thoreau's 1849 Cape hike that forms the narrative structure of his book, *Cape Cod*. The hike begins at the **Salt Pond Visitor Center** in Eastham where Thoreau "left the road" on his way to the Cape's Outer Beach. It then continues north all the way to **Race Point Beach** where he turned inland en route to the village of Provincetown.

Thoreau completed his 1849 walk up the Cape in three days. The first day he walked to the approximate location of what is now known as **Newcomb Hollow Beach** where he spent the night at the nearby Wellfleet Oysterman's house. On his second day he followed the shoreline to **Highland Light** in North Truro and stayed with the lighthouse keeper. And on his final day, he proceeded to Race Point Beach.

To make The Great Thoreau Hike easier to follow for today's hikers, it has been divided into eight separate but connected sections, Parts I-VIII, with each hike conveniently finishing at the same place that it starts. Each part consists of two components: an "Initial Route" that essentially runs from the south to the beginning of the next hike to the north*, and a "Return Route" that returns to the hike's starting point. The Initial Routes mainly run inland through woodlands and dunes and along roads and paths, while the Return Routes primarily follow the shoreline along the beach.

As hikers are sure to discover, the Initial Routes and Return Routes complement each other nicely. The Initial Routes feature tours of the Cape's "inner" landscape—its woodlands, ponds, marshes, rivers, dunes and man-made structures—while the Return Routes offer the incomparable experience of walking along the **Great Beach**.

Challenging

Unlike most of the fifteen routes in the **Individual Walks** section of this book, all eight parts of **The Great Thoreau Hike** are very lengthy and challenging. While this may be just what some hikers are looking for, The Great Thoreau Hike is nevertheless not for everyone. These routes include such diverse terrain as narrow footpaths, busy bike paths, sandy jeep trails, regular paved roads and ocean beaches. Furthermore, these routes are not maintained by any organization and do not include regular trail-marks.

---

* This is true for each section of The Great Thoreau Hike except Part VIII in which the Initial Route actually runs east to west and the Return Route runs west to east.

Some sections are even prone to becoming overgrown with vegetation and can change from year to year.

The Great Thoreau Hike has been developed to aid ambitious hikers in their exploration of places on Cape Cod that tend to be "off the beaten path." Hikers need to use good common sense to insure their own safety. Each hike includes potential danger from severe storms and high tides along the beach. Furthermore, all but Part I of The Great Thoreau Hike includes some walking through areas where hunting is allowed from September 1 through March 31. (See **Safe Walking**.)

The Great Thoreau Hike should only be followed by experienced hikers who are in good physical condition and have solid map-reading skills*. Studying each route before heading out and carrying a compass is strongly advised.

Customizing

Like the rest of this book, **The Great Thoreau Hike** has been designed in such a way that it can easily be customized to meet individual needs. Each of the eight parts in this section includes information about Thoreau, insights into the history of the area, and a walking route. Each part may be considered a section of the larger Great Thoreau Hike *and* a complete hike in its own right. As a result, hikers can follow The Great Thoreau Hike in a variety of ways.

For example, some hikers may attempt to complete each part of The Great Thoreau Hike as quickly as they can. Some may choose to complete one part a day for eight consecutive days, while others may choose to follow only one hike a week, month or year. Still other hikers may not wish to follow every part of The Great Thoreau Hike, but may be content to follow only one or two parts of it at any time.

Furthermore, the different parts of The Great Thoreau Hike can be combined in a variety of other ways. Because each part is connected, two or more hikes can be easily combined to create a longer hike that starts and ends at the same spot. For example, Part II of The Great Thoreau Hike runs from **Nauset Light Beach** in Eastham to **Marconi Beach** in Wellfleet; and Part III of The Great Thoreau Hike runs from Marconi Beach to **LeCount Hollow Beach**, also in Wellfleet. By combining the Initial Routes of these two parts, hikers can walk from Nauset Light Beach all the way to LeCount Hollow Beach. Then, by combining the Return Routes of these two parts, they can make their way back from LeCount Hollow

---

*Some walkers may choose to bring along topographical maps of the areas covered by The Great Thoreau Hike as supplementary resources. "Topo maps" are available at the **Salt Pond Visitor Center**, at the **Province Lands Visitor Center**, and at various sporting goods stores across the region. (See **Safe Walking**.)

Beach along the shoreline to Nauset Light Beach.

Furthermore, by arranging for transportation at a given destination, hikers can eliminate the need for starting and finishing at the same place and thereby expand their options even further. By doing this, hikers may follow just the Initial Routes, just the Return Routes or switch between Initial Routes and Return Routes. There is, of course, nothing to prevent hikers from following any route in a reverse direction either.

By customizing walks, each hiker will be able to make The Great Thoreau Hike into his or her own "Great Hike."●

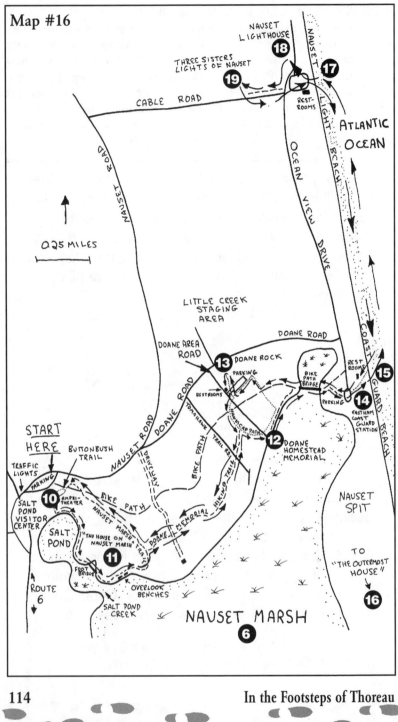

Map #16

0.25 MILES

START HERE

NAUSET MARSH

In the Footsteps of Thoreau

The Great Thoreau Hike

PART I

Salt Pond Visitor Center to Nauset Light Beach

DISTANCE 6.2 miles

TIME 4 hours

RATING difficult

Location

This walk begins and ends on the grounds of the **Cape Cod National Seashore**'s **Salt Pond Visitor Center**. From the Orleans Rotary, follow Route 6 north 3 miles to the traffic lights at the intersection with Nauset Road. Turn right, and the entrance to the parking lot is immediately on the right.

Description

Although this is one of the shorter parts of **The Great Thoreau Hike** section of this guide, it includes some of the most diverse terrain and most interesting historic sites. The trail winds its way through a shady Cape Cod wood, over well-marked walking paths, paved trails and a number of short bridges. It also includes a 2.2-mile round-trip stretch along the **Great Beach**.

Before even starting the hike, there is plenty to see at the **Salt Pond Visitor Center**, which serves as the main welcoming center to the **Cape Cod National Seashore** and offers free educational movies, museum exhibits and a variety of other programs. Directly across Nauset Road from the Visitor Center is the **Eastham School House Museum**; and across Route 6 from the Visitor Center, just up Salt Pond Road, is the **Old Eastham Town Center**. Furthermore, the hill on which the Visitor Center stands was formerly the site of **Eastham Windmill**. Also noteworthy is that the surrounding land formerly served as the location of "one of the world's most beautiful golf courses," the **Cedar Bank Golf Course**.

Along the trail walkers can also see the farmhouse where Wyman Richardson wrote *The House on Nauset Marsh*; as well as the beach where Henry Beston composed his American nature classic, *The Outermost House*. The route offers many different views of **Nauset Marsh** and runs by the **Doane Homestead Memorial**, **Doane Rock**, and the **Eastham Coast Guard Station**. It also passes by the site of the American terminus of the French Transatlantic Cable, **Nauset Lighthouse**, and the **Three Sisters Lights of Nauset**.

What Thoreau Saw

Sand-piper

Sometimes we sat on the wet beach and watched the beach birds, sand pipers, and others, trotting along close to each wave, and waiting for the sea to cast up their breakfast. The former ran with great rapidity and then stood stock still remarkably erect and hardly to be distinguished from the beach.

Thoreau

This hike serves as a fine introduction to **The Great Thoreau Hike**, as it provides a comfortable transition between the civilization of mainland Cape Cod and the wildness of the **Great Beach**.

In 1849, Thoreau experienced this same transition as he walked about 5 miles along the **Old Kings Highway** from Orleans to Eastham until "at length, before we got to Eastham Meeting House, we left the road and struck across the country for the eastern shore, at Nauset Lights." From these directions, we know that Thoreau "left the road" very close to the location of the start of this hike (today's **Salt Pond Visitor Center**) en route to **Nauset Light Beach**, which is also the terminus of this walk. He described the exhilaration he felt as he headed for the shore:

> I was glad to have got out of the towns, where I am wont to feel unspeakably mean and disgraced—to have left behind me for a season the bar-rooms of Massachusetts, where the full-grown are not weaned from savage and filthy habits—still sucking a cigar. My spirits rose in proportion to the outward dreariness. The towns need to be ventilated. The gods would be pleased to see some pure flames from their altars. They are not to be appeased with cigar-smoke.

It should be noted that Thoreau actually cut a straight path from the road, across the dreary "Plains of Nauset" (now mainly residential neighborhoods), to Nauset Light Beach. However, this hike follows a more scenic route along the shoreline of **Nauset Marsh** and up the Great Beach.

The Trail
Initial Route

The trailhead to this hike is also the trailhead to the Nauset Marsh Trail, a popular 1-mile loop maintained by the Park and encompassed within this route. (Nauset Marsh Trail guides can be picked up at the **Salt Pond Visitor Center**.)

➡️From the Visitor Center parking lot follow the paved path to Salt Pond down the hill past the amphitheater. Salt Pond was originally a glacially-formed kettle pond which has since become a tidal inlet of **Nauset Marsh**.

➡️Follow the bank of Salt Pond around to the left to Salt Pond Creek. The creek was the former site of a tidal grist mill. To power the mill, the miller waited for high tides to fill Salt Pond and then shut flood gates built across the creek to entrap the water. Once the tide began to recede in the rest of the marsh, the miller allowed just enough water to escape Salt Pond to power his mill and grind his grain.

➡️Follow the trail along Salt Pond Creek and across the short footbridge. The windowless structures on both sides of the creek are privately owned boathouses.

→Just after the bridge you will approach the mouth of Salt Pond Creek. Be sure to follow the trail here as marked, up the hill to the right. The jeep trail to the left is on private property.

→A short distance beyond this hill you will arrive at the Nauset Marsh Overlook benches, the perfect place to recall the marsh's most famous bards: Henry Beston and Wyman Richardson. Straight across the marsh from the overlook is

The chivalric and heroic spirit which once belonged to the Rider seems now to reside in, or perchance to have subsided into, the Walker—not the Knight, but Walker, Errant. He is a sort of fourth estate outside of Church and State and People.

–Walking, 1862

Nauset Spit, the low-lying barrier beach that separates Nauset Marsh from the Atlantic. This beach is the former location of the "Fo'castle," the dune shack where Beston wrote *The Outermost House*. In the opposite direction, just a few hundred yards behind the overlook benches (to the north), is the old farmhouse where Richardson wrote his memorable nature study, *The House on Nauset Marsh*.

→From the Nauset Marsh Overlook, continue along the Nauset Marsh Trail just a few hundred feet farther and turn right onto the path marked with a sign that reads "Hiking Trail to Doane Memorial, 0.9 miles."

→Follow this trail 0.9 miles across a dirt and stone driveway, and then across an unmarked paved road called Tomahawk Trail, to where you will arrive at a t-junction with a narrow paved pathway for the handicapped. One sign at this junction points to the right and reads "**Coast Guard Beach**"; and another sign points to the left and reads "**Doane Rock**" and "Little Creek". Turn right to head toward Coast Guard Beach.

→After turning right on the pathway, proceed just a couple hundred feet farther to the Doane Area Road, where the **Doane Homestead Memorial** is located straight ahead. The memorial marks the site of the home of early Eastham settler Deacon John Doane.

→From the memorial follow the hiking trail down the hill to the left. This trail is marked with another sign pointing to Coast Guard Beach, and is labelled with the figure of a hiker. **NOTE: Do not follow the handicap pathway which also continues to the left of the memorial.**

→From the memorial, the hiking path winds along the edge of the marsh and offers a number of lovely views, including a distant look at the path's ultimate destination, the **Eastham Coast Guard Station**.

→After passing over a boardwalk through a cluster of cattails, the path comes to a t-junction with a bike path.

➔Follow the bike path to the right and cross the bike path bridge.

➔Just after crossing the bridge turn right onto the white-shelled walking path that climbs the hill to the Coast Guard Beach parking lot and the Eastham Coast Guard Station.

➔The parking lot provides yet another grand marsh vista, as well as a panoramic look at the Atlantic, and is also the starting point of another walk in this book, **The Outermost Walk.**

➔From the parking lot, follow the paved path between the station and the restrooms down to Coast Guard Beach.

➔Turn left and follow Coast Guard Beach 1.1 miles north to **Nauset Light Beach.**

➔At the Nauset Light Beach parking lot you will find seasonally operated restrooms and public telephones. This beach was also the former location of the American terminus of the **French Transatlantic Cable.**

➔The **Three Sisters Lights of Nauset,** three restored wooden lighthouses that formerly composed Nauset Lighthouse Station, are located 0.25 miles west along nearby Cable Road. If time allows, the "Sisters" are well worth the walk to view them, for they serve as marked contrasts to the more modern **Nauset Lighthouse.**

Return Route

➔When you are ready to leave Nauset Light Beach, follow the stairs down from the parking lot to the beach and retrace your way south 1.1 miles back to Coast Guard Beach.

➔From the Coast Guard Beach parking lot, follow the white-shelled path back down the hill to the bike path.

➔Turn left on the bike path and cross the bike path bridge. **NOTE: After crossing the bridge, do not turn left onto the hiking trail that leads to the Doane Homestead Memorial. Instead, continue along the bike path.**

➔About 0.15 miles past the bike path bridge, the bike path is crossed by the narrow, paved handicap pathway that encircles the Doane Area. This junction is marked by three white stripes on the bike path signifying a crosswalk. Leave the bike path at this point and follow the handicap pathway to the right.

➔Proceed along the handicap pathway to the Doane Area parking lot.

➔Follow the handicap pathway along the left side of the parking lot to where it comes to a t-junction.

➔From the t-junction, turn right and follow the handicap pathway past the restrooms to **Doane Rock,** the largest above-ground glacier erratic boulder known on Cape Cod.

➔After visiting Doane Rock, return along the handicap pathway past the

The Great Thoreau Hike

What Thoreau Saw

Poverty Grass or Beach Heather

In summer, if the poverty-grass grows at the head of a Hollow looking toward the sea, in a bleak position where the wind rushes up, the northern or exposed half of the tuft is sometimes all black and dead like an oven-broom, while the opposite half is yellow with blossoms, the whole hillside thus presenting a remarkable contrast when seen from the poverty-stricken and the flourishing side. This plant, which in many places would be esteemed an ornament, is here despised by many on account of its being associated with barrenness. It might well be adopted for the Barnstable coat-of-arms, in a field sableux. I should be proud of it.

restrooms and parking lot, across the Doane Area Road, and across the bike path, to the junction with the Doane Memorial Hiking Trail. This hiking trail is marked with a sign that points to the right and reads "Hiking Trail to Visitor Center (40 minutes)."

➡Turn right onto the Doane Memorial Hiking Trail and follow it 0.9 miles back to the Nauset Marsh Trail. Along the way you will cross the paved Tomahawk Trail Road and a dirt and stone driveway.

➡Once back at the Nauset Marsh Trail, you will see a glimpse of Nauset Marsh off to the left and encounter a sign with an arrow pointing to the right to the Salt Pond Visitor Center.

➡Turn right and follow the Nauset Marsh Trail 0.7 miles back to the Visitor Center to complete this walk.●

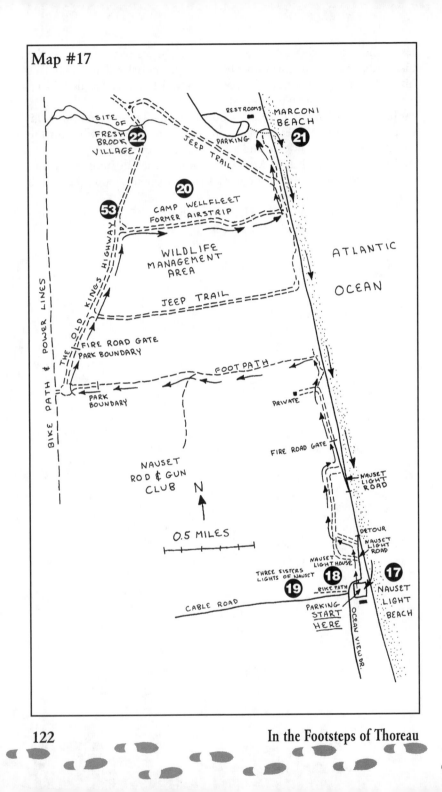

Map #17

SITE OF FRESH BROOK VILLAGE **22**

RESTROOMS
PARKING
MARCONI BEACH **21**

JEEP TRAIL

53

20 CAMP WELLFLEET FORMER AIRSTRIP

WILDLIFE MANAGEMENT AREA

ATLANTIC OCEAN

JEEP TRAIL

THE OLD KINGS HIGHWAY

FIRE ROAD GATE
PARK BOUNDARY

FOOTPATH

BIKE PATH & POWER LINES

PARK BOUNDARY

PRIVATE

FIRE ROAD GATE

NAUSET ROD & GUN CLUB

N

NAUSET LIGHT ROAD

0.5 MILES

DETOUR
NAUSET LIGHT ROAD

THREE SISTERS LIGHTS OF NAUSET

NAUSET LIGHTHOUSE **18**

17

19

BIKE PATH

PARKING START HERE

NAUSET LIGHT BEACH

CABLE ROAD

OCEAN VIEW DR.

In the Footsteps of Thoreau

The Great Thoreau Hike

PART II

Nauset Light Beach to Marconi Beach

DISTANCE 6.4 miles

TIME 4 hours

RATING difficult

Location

Begin this loop at **Nauset Light Beach** in North Eastham. Follow Route 6 to the Orleans Rotary, and then continue north on Route 6 for 3 miles to the second set of traffic lights. Turn right onto Nauset Road. After 0.7 miles Nauset Road bears off to the left and Doane Road continues straight ahead. Proceed straight ahead onto Doane Road. 1.7 miles from Route 6 you will arrive at a junction. Turn left onto Ocean View Drive and proceed 1 mile north to the beach parking lot on the right. A $7 daily fee or a $20 seasonal fee is charged for daytime summer parking at this and all **Cape Cod National Seashore** managed beaches.

Description

If you are familiar with Cape Cod but have never visited the Wellfleet Wildlife Management Area you are bound to find this hike a real treat. The Management Area is administered by the Massachusetts Division of Fisheries and Wildlife and the **Cape Cod National Seashore** and is one of the Outer Cape's best kept secrets, offering nature lovers some 1,200 acres of undeveloped woodlands to explore.

After meandering through a quiet residential neighborhood, this route threads through narrow footpaths and then opens up into a series of long, secluded jeep trails within the thick woods of the Management Area. One of these jeep trails is actually a little-known section of the **Old Kings Highway,** and another originally served as an airstrip for drone planes at the former **Camp Wellfleet** during World War II. From the jeep trails, the route next runs along the top of the breathtaking bluffs of South Wellfleet to **Marconi Beach,** and then concludes with a 2.2-mile beach walk back to **Nauset Light Beach.**

Visitors to Nauset Light Beach will encounter a number of informative plaques erected by the Cape Cod National Seashore. Topics covered by the plaques include nearby **Nauset Lighthouse** and the **French Transatlantic Cable.** Additionally, the **Three Sisters Lights of Nauset**—three restored 19th-century wooden lighthouses—are located just 0.25 miles west of the beach parking lot on Cable Road. Seasonal restrooms and public telephones are maintained at both the Nauset Light Beach and the Marconi Beach parking lots.

Thoreau

During his 1849 walk between **Nauset Light Beach** and **Marconi Beach**, Thoreau encountered a "beach wrecker" who was scavenging the storm-washed sands for valuable wood and other items. The semi-satirical description Thoreau wrote of that wrecker forms one of the most entertaining and vivid vignettes in *Cape Cod*:

> We soon met one of these wreckers—a regular Cape Cod man, with whom we parleyed, with a bleached and weather-beaten face—within whose wrinkles I distinguished no particular feature. It was like an old sail endowed with life—a hanging-cliff of weather-beaten flesh—like one of the clay boulders which occurred in that sand-bank. He had on a hat which had seen salt water, and a coat of many pieces and colors, though it was mainly the color of the beach, as if it had been sanded. His varie gated back—for his coat had many patches, even between the shoulders—was a rich study to us, when we had passed him and looked round. It might have been dishonorable for him to have so many scars behind, it is true, if he had not had many more and more serious ones in front. He looked as if he sometimes saw a dough-nut, but never descended to comfort; too grave to laugh, too tough to cry; as indifferent as a clam—like a sea-clam with hat on and legs, that was out walking the strand. He may have been one of the Pilgrims—Peregrine White*, at least—who has kept on the back side of the Cape, and let the centuries go by. He was looking for wrecks, old logs, water-logged and covered with barnacles, or bits of boards and joists, even chips which he drew out of the reach of the tide, and stacked up to dry...You may see his hooked pike-staff always lying on the bank ready for use. He is the true monarch of the beach whose "right there is none to dispute," and he is as much identified with it as a beach-bird.

While "wrecking," or beachcombing, has long since died out as a regular Cape Cod profession, it nevertheless remains a favored pastime of locals and visitors alike. Who hasn't felt their spirits jump at the prospect of discovering some unexpected treasure along the beach? Thoreau, who was noted for his ability to find things along his walks, discovered "a French Crown Piece" on the Cape's shore, as well as a piece of rope which he carried all the way back to Concord for use as a clothes line. As recently as 1996, one lucky beachcomber even found an old musket from the pirate ship *Whydah* which was wrecked in 1717 about 2 miles north of this walk.

* Peregrine White was the first Pilgrim child to be born in the New World.

In the Footsteps of Thoreau

What Thoreau Saw

Sea-Jellies

The beach was also strewn with beautiful sea-jellies, which the wreckers called sun-squall, one of the lowest forms of animal life, some white, some wine-colored, and a foot in diameter. I at first thought that they were a tender part of some marine monster, which the storm or some other foe had mangled. What right has the sea to bear in its bosom such tender things as sea-jellies and mosses, when it has such a boisterous shore, that the stoutest fabrics are wrecked against it? Strange that it should undertake to dandle such delicate children in its arms.... They say that when you endeavor to take one up, it will spill out the other side of your hand like quicksilver. Before the land rose out of the ocean, and became dry land, chaos reigned; and between high and low water mark, where she is partially disrobed and rising, a sort of chaos reigns still, which only anomalous creatures can inhabit.

The Trail
Initial Route

➡Begin this hike by bearing to the right out of the **Nauset Light Beach** parking lot and proceeding north on Nauset Light Road, past **Nauset Lighthouse** on the left. Nauset Lighthouse was moved to its present location, away from the eroding cliffs on the opposite side of the road, in the fall of 1996. The cover photo for this book, was taken just a few months before the lighthouse was moved, and provides a sense of just how close the cliff-edge had encroached on the lighthouse before the move.

➡After 0.2 miles on Nauset Light Road, you will encounter a detour where the road has been wiped out by erosion. Turn left at this detour and pro-

Words to Walk By

I know of but one or two persons with whom I can afford to walk. With most the walk degenerates into a mere vigorous use of your legs, ludicrously purposeless, while you are discussing some mighty argument, each one having his say, spoiling each other's day, worrying one another with conversation, hustling one another with our conversation. I know of no use in the walking part in this case, except that we may seem to be getting on together toward some goal; but of course we keep our original distance all the way. Jumping every wall and ditch with vigor in the vain hope of shaking our companion off. Trying to kill two birds with one stone though they sit at opposite points of the compass, to see nature and do the honors to one who does not.

–The Journal of Henry D. Thoreau, November 8, 1858

ceed 0.1 miles west along the dirt road to a t-junction.

➡Turn right at the t-junction and follow the dirt road north. It winds 0.3 miles before turning sharply to the right and reconnecting with a still-intact section of the paved Nauset Light Road.

➡Turn left onto this section of Nauset Light Road and follow it north 0.1 miles to the fire road gate.

➡Continue past the fire road gate 0.25 miles to where the jeep trail bends sharply to the left and a narrow walking path continues through the low brush straight ahead to the north.

➡Proceed straight ahead to the north on the walking path, keeping the bluffs to your right. This very narrow path winds through the brush for about 0.2 miles. **NOTE: This path skirts the edge of the bluffs above the beach in various places. Walkers are reminded not to get too close to the edge of the bluffs, as they are prone to cave-ins. (See "Safe Walking.")**

➡After 0.2 miles this narrow walking path opens up to a wider walking path that runs directly inland to the left (west). **NOTE: Do not continue north past this east/west-running path.**

➡Follow this wider walking path west for about 1 mile to the small

In the Footsteps of Thoreau

t-junction where you should bear to the right. Do not turn left at this junction, as this walking path leads to the Nauset Rod & Gun Club, from which you can frequently hear gunshots.

➡From the junction continue west another 0.5 miles to the **Cape Cod National Seashore** Park boundary which is marked by a small split-rail fence. At this point, the path widens into a jeep trail and continues in the same westerly direction.

➡Just 0.2 miles from the Park boundary you will reach a junction where the Wellfleet power lines and a bike path are ahead to the west, and another jeep trail runs off to the right, in a northeasterly direction. Turn right at this junction and avoid the power lines and bike path. This jeep trail is a part of the **Old Kings Highway**, which served for many generations as the primary stagecoach route on the Cape from Sandwich to Provincetown.

➡After about 0.2 miles along the Old Kings Highway you will come to the Park boundary again, which is marked by a fire road gate.

➡Continue straight ahead past the fire road gate along the Old Kings Highway and about 0.2 miles farther you will come to a jeep trail on the right. Do not turn right onto this jeep trail but continue along the Old Kings Highway another 0.5 miles to the next jeep trail on the right.

➡Turn right onto this jeep trail. It was originally built as an airstrip within **Camp Wellfleet**, a U.S. Army base that once included all of today's Wellfleet Wildlife Management Area and much of the land to the north.

➡As you continue west along this 0.9-mile jeep trail you will notice new-growth trees on both sides of the trail, indications of the airstrip's former width.

➡After following the jeep trail/"airstrip" to the top of the bluffs above the beach, turn left and follow the trail north, keeping the ocean on your right.

➡**NOTE: After less than 0.2 miles, this jeep trail veers off to the left (west), away from the bluffs. Do not follow the jeep trail at this point but continue straight ahead to the walking path that continues in a northerly direction parallel with the cliffs.**

➡After about 0.1 miles, this walking path rises to a small hill that offers a spectacular view of the **Marconi Beach** area, including the Marconi Beach bathhouses, parking lot and the beach itself. You may also be able to see the pavilion at the **Marconi Station Site** about two miles farther to the north.

➡Continue along the walking path until you arrive at the Marconi Beach area.

Return Route

➡Take the stairs from the bluffs down to Marconi Beach and head right (south) along the beach.

➡The stairs to the Nauset Light Beach parking lot are located 2.2 miles south of Marconi Beach.●

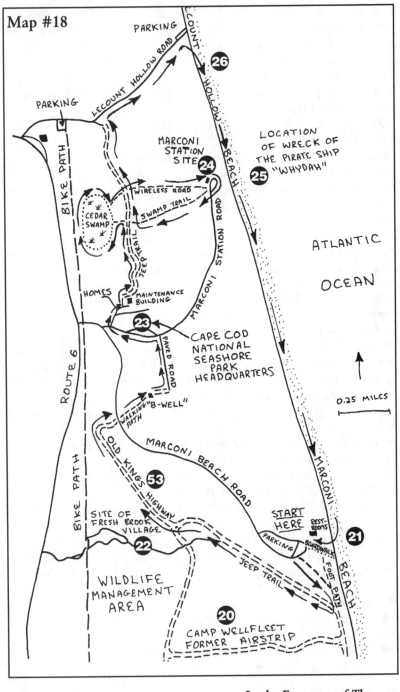

Map #18

PARKING

PARKING

LECOUNT HOLLOW ROAD

LECOUNT HOLLOW BEACH

26

MARCONI STATION SITE

24

WIRELESS ROAD

SWAMP TRAIL

CEDAR SWAMP

JEEP TRAIL

BIKE PATH

ROUTE 6

HOMES

MAINTENANCE BUILDING

23

MARCONI STATION ROAD

CAPE COD NATIONAL SEASHORE PARK HEADQUARTERS

PAVED ROAD

WALKING PATH "B-WELL"

OLD KINGS HIGHWAY

MARCONI BEACH ROAD

53

BIKE PATH

SITE OF FRESH BROOK VILLAGE

22

WILDLIFE MANAGEMENT AREA

LOCATION OF WRECK OF THE PIRATE SHIP "WHYDAH"

25

ATLANTIC OCEAN

0.25 MILES

MARCONI BEACH

START HERE

PARKING

REST-ROOMS

21

BOARDWALK

FOOT PATH

JEEP TRAIL

20

CAMP WELLFLEET FORMER AIRSTRIP

In the Footsteps of Thoreau

The Great Thoreau Hike

PART III

Marconi Beach to LeCount Hollow Beach

DISTANCE 8.1 miles

TIME 5 hours

RATING very difficult

Location

This hike begins at **Marconi Beach** in South Wellfleet. Follow Route 6 to the Wellfleet/Eastham town line and then proceed 2 miles north to the first set of traffic lights. Turn right at the lights and continue straight ahead 1.4 miles to the parking lot. A $7 daily fee or a $20 seasonal fee is charged at this and all other **Cape Cod National Seashore** managed beaches.

Description

This section of **The Great Thoreau Hike** is one of the most enjoyable and includes a dramatic variety of terrain and many intriguing historic sites, as well as some truly unforgettable views. The trail begins with a short stretch above the panoramic cliffs of **Marconi Beach** before entering the woods and running along a little-known section of the **Old Kings Highway** near the site of historic **Fresh Brook Village**. From there the trail cuts through a narrow footpath to an old paved road that was once part of **Camp Wellfleet**, a former World War II Army base. It next passes by the **Cape Cod National Seashore Park Headquarters** on its way down into the dark recesses of an Atlantic White Cedar Swamp. The trail continues up to the scenic cliff-side **Marconi Station Site**, where the world's first transatlantic radio messages were received and transmitted. Finally, after a short stretch along a public road, the trail returns to the shore at **LeCount Hollow Beach** and finishes with a 2.3-mile walk along the **Great Beach** past the location of the wreck of the ill-fated pirate ship *Whydah*.

Thoreau

In his narrative of Cape Cod, between his stop at **Marconi Beach** and his clam lunch at **LeCount Hollow Beach**, Thoreau provides a timeless description of the experience of hiking the Cape's **Great Beach**:

> I was comparatively satisfied. There I had got the Cape under me, as much as if I were riding it bare-backed. It was not as on the map, or seen from the stage-coach; but there I found it all out of doors, huge and real, Cape Cod! as it cannot be represented on a map, color it as you will; the thing itself, than which there is nothing more like it, no truer picture or

account; which you cannot go further and see. I cannot remember what I thought before that it was. They commonly celebrate those beaches only which have a hotel on them, or those which have a humane house alone. But I wished to see that sea-shore where man's works are wrecks; to put up at the true Atlantic House, where the ocean is land-lord as well as sea-lord, and comes ashore without a wharf for the landing; where the crumbling land is only invalid or at best but dry land, and that is all you can say of it.

The Trail
Initial Route
Although this trail leads to **LeCount Hollow Beach**, which is located north of **Marconi Beach**, it starts with a 0.2-mile walk *south* from Marconi Beach, along the top of the bluffs above the shore.

➡From the Marconi Beach parking lot walk to the boardwalk that leads to the beach. Instead of going onto the boardwalk, however, follow the split-rail fence to the right, along the side of the parking lot. Near the end of this fence, at the southeast corner of the parking lot, you will find a footpath that leads to the bluffs above the beach to the right.

➡Proceed south along this footpath and about 0.2 miles from the parking lot you will meet up with a sandy jeep trail. **NOTE: Be sure to make a hard right turn onto this jeep trail, and to follow it into the woods away from the bluffs to the northwest.**

➡After 0.9 miles the jeep trail intersects another jeep trail which is actually a part of the **Old Kings Highway**. This junction is very near the former location of **Fresh Brook Village**, a 19th-century fishing village which was once a regular stagecoach stop along the Old Kings Highway. Unfortunately, no signs of the village are visible from the jeep trail today.

➡Turn right onto the Old Kings Highway and walk north 0.6 miles to where the trail bends sharply to the right and meets up with the paved Marconi Beach Road.

➡Continue directly across Marconi Beach Road to a narrow walking path. Follow this path 0.2 miles to the water pump station labeled "B-Well."

➡From B-Well follow the dirt road up to the right 0.1 miles to where it meets up with a paved road. This paved road is one of the last remnants of **Camp Wellfleet**, a World War II Army base that once encompassed most of the land around this hike.

➡Turn left on this paved road and follow it 0.25 miles to the t-junction with Marconi Station Road.

➡Turn left onto Marconi Station Road and follow it to the **Cape Cod National Seashore Park Headquarters** on the right. The Park Headquarters are open weekdays 9 a.m. to 5 p.m. Public restrooms and a small book store are located inside. This is also the best place in the area to inquire about the Park.

→Continue just 0.1 miles past the Park Headquarters on Marconi Station Road and turn onto the first road on the right.

→After turning right, continue straight ahead toward the maintenance building. **NOTE: Do not turn right into the parking lot behind the Park Headquarters or left into the residential housing area.**

→As you approach the maintenance building, which is surrounded by a high fence, stay to the left and walk to the end of the parking lot to the jeep trail which begins there.

→Follow this jeep trail behind

Words to Walk By

I t is a certain faeryland where we live. You may walk out in any direction once on the earth's surface, lifting your horizon, and everywhere your path, climbing the convexity of the globe, leads you between heaven and earth, not away from the light of the sun and stars and the habitations of men. I wonder that I ever get five miles on my way, the walk is so crowded with events and phenomena.

—The Journal of Henry D. Thoreau, June 7, 1851

the maintenance building 0.3 miles to where it crosses the **Cape Cod National Seashore**'s Atlantic White Cedar Swamp Trail, a park-maintained 1.2-mile nature trail that makes a loop between the Marconi Station parking lot and the swamp. Wooden poles have been set in the ground across the fire road here to designate where the Atlantic White Cedar Swamp Trail crosses it.

→Turn left and follow the Atlantic White Cedar Swamp Trail into the swamp. After a short distance you will arrive at the boardwalk which makes a 0.4-mile loop through the swamp.

→After a few steps along the boardwalk you will arrive at a fork. Turn left at the fork and follow the boardwalk clockwise around the swamp until you arrive at the next fork. When you get to this fork bear left and follow the trail out of the swamp to where it once again intersects the jeep trail.

→At this junction, proceed straight ahead up the hill along the trail marked "Wireless Road." Wireless Road was once the main road from Marconi Radio Station (or "wireless telegraphy" station) to Wellfleet village.

→Follow Wireless Road 0.4 miles up the hill to the parking lot.

→Once at the parking lot, turn left and proceed to the **Marconi Station Site** and the nearby overlook platform. Although the majority of the station site has eroded away since it was established at the turn of the century, there are still a number of foundation blocks and other remnants present. The Park has also placed informative plaques and a miniature model of the station beneath a pavilion here. On clear days, the overlook platform boasts extraordinary views of the area, including glimpses of Cape Cod Bay to the west. Seasonally operated restrooms are also located next to the parking lot.

→When you are ready to leave the station site, head back across the parking lot to the start of the Atlantic White Cedar Swamp Trail. Do not retrace your steps back down Wireless Road, however, but take the path on the left for a change of scenery. The surrounding vegetation becomes larger and more substantial the farther you get from the cliffs. Many of the plants along this trail are marked with identification plaques placed by the Park.

→After 0.4 miles, you will arrive back at the jeep trail.

→Turn right onto the jeep trail and follow it 0.1 miles back to the intersection with Wireless Road.

→At the intersection with Wireless Road proceed straight ahead 0.3 miles to the north to LeCount Hollow Road.

→Turn right onto LeCount Hollow Road, and the LeCount Hollow Beach parking lot is just 0.4 miles farther to the east. Seasonal restrooms are located at this beach which is managed by the Town of Wellfleet.

Return Route

→From the Lecount Hollow Beach parking lot, walk down to the beach and proceed to the right (south).

→Just 0.6 miles south of Lecount Hollow is the approximate location of the wreck of the pirate ship, *Whydah*, which sank in 1717. Although much of the ship has been salvaged, pieces of it still remain buried along the shoreline, presumably strewn up and down the beach for some distance. In fact, as noted elsewhere in this guide, one lucky beachcomber found a musket from the *Whydah* along the beach here in 1996. Who knows what remains to be discovered?

→After walking 2.3 miles south from LeCount Hollow Beach, climb the stairs to the Marconi Beach parking lot to conclude this hike.●

What Thoreau Saw

Great Black Backed Gull and Herring Gull

A remarkable method of catching gulls, derived from the Indians, was practiced in Wellfleet in 1794. "The Gull House," it is said, "is built with crotchets, fixed in the ground on the beach," poles being stretched across the top, and the sides made close with stakes and sea-weed. "The poles on the top are covered with lean whale. The man being placed within, is not discovered by the fowls, and while they are contending for and eating the flesh, he draws them in, one by one, between the poles, until he has collected forty or fifty." Hence, perchance, a man is said to be gulled, when he is taken in.

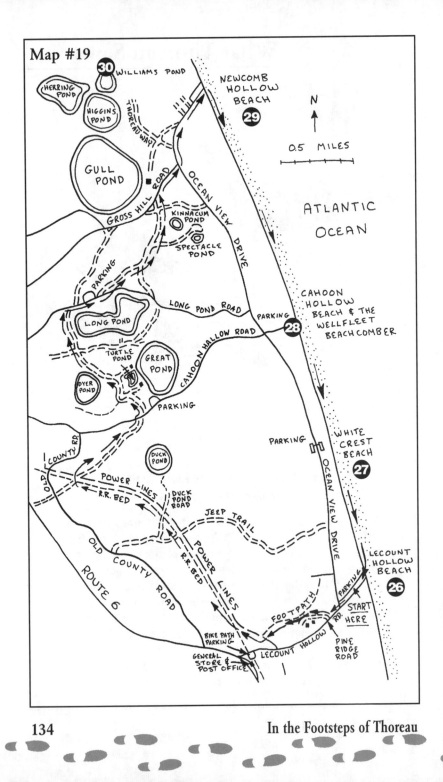

Map #19

HERRING POND

WILLIAMS POND

30

HIGGINS POND

NEWCOMB HOLLOW BEACH

29

N

0.5 MILES

THOREAU WAY

GULL POND

GROSS HILL ROAD

KINNACUM POND

SPECTACLE POND

OCEAN VIEW DRIVE

ATLANTIC OCEAN

PARKING

LONG POND ROAD

PARKING

CAHOON HOLLOW BEACH & THE WELLFLEET BEACHCOMBER

28

LONG POND

TURTLE POND

GREAT POND

DYER POND

CAHOON HOLLOW ROAD

PARKING

PARKING

WHITE CREST BEACH

27

DUCK POND

OLD COUNTY RD.

POWER LINES

R.R. BED

DUCK POND ROAD

JEEP TRAIL

OCEAN VIEW DRIVE

LECOUNT HOLLOW BEACH

26

OLD COUNTY ROAD

POWER LINES

R.R. BED

PARKING

FOOT PATH

START HERE

ROUTE 6

BIKE PATH PARKING

GENERAL STORE & POST OFFICE

LECOUNT HOLLOW

PINE RIDGE ROAD

In the Footsteps of Thoreau

The Great Thoreau Hike

PART IV

LeCount Hollow Beach to Newcomb Hollow Beach

DISTANCE 9 miles

TIME 6 hours

RATING very difficult

Location

Begin this hike at **LeCount Hollow Beach** in Wellfleet. Follow Route 6 to the Wellfleet/Eastham town line, and then proceed north 2.7 miles to LeCount Hollow Road on the right. Turn right onto LeCount Hollow Road and proceed 0.8 miles east to the LeCount Hollow Beach parking lot. Unfortunately, no parking is permitted at the lot from 9 a.m. to 5 p.m. July through Labor Day, except for Town of Wellfleet resident sticker-holders. Free summer parking is permitted, however, 0.6 miles west on LeCount Hollow Road at the Cape Cod Rail Trail Bike Path parking lot. Summer parking is also available for a fee at **White Crest Beach**, which is located 1 mile north on Ocean View Drive.

Description

This lengthy loop is one of the most challenging in this guide. Although the "Initial Route" runs through inland portions of Wellfleet, and does not include many historic sites, it nevertheless offers walkers an intimate look at the local landscape. The trail passes through thick Cape Cod woods and by a number of idyllic kettle ponds before finishing with a stint along the **Great Beach**. Aside from the beach, the terrain mainly includes quiet jeep trails, power-line access trails, and some paved roads. Along the trail is the **Wellfleet Beachcomber** at **Cahoon Hollow Beach**, where in 1849 Thoreau encountered the **Humane House** which he wrote so extensively about in *Cape Cod*.

Thoreau

On his first hike between **LeCount Hollow Beach** and **Newcomb Hollow Beach**, Thoreau discovered a **Humane House**, or "Charity House," in the dunes above today's **Cahoon Hollow Beach**. This so-called Humane House was just one of a number of such structures established along secluded sections of the coast as emergency shelters for shipwreck survivors. These huts were built and maintained by the Massachusetts Humane Society as early as 1786, long before the development of the U.S. Life-Saving Service or the U.S. Coast Guard. For the better part of a century Humane Houses were the only formally organized resources for shipwreck survivors on Cape Cod.

Still, Thoreau was unimpressed with the Humane House he encountered. Having become acquainted with the immensity and seclusion of the **Great Beach**, as well as with the regularity of shipwrecks along the Atlantic coast, he considered Humane Houses woefully inadequate. To Thoreau, these huts seemed more like empty gestures than genuine resources. He provided the following account of his walk north from today's LeCount Hollow Beach, and of his subsequent discovery at Cahoon Hollow Beach:

> At length, by mid-afternoon, after we had two or three rainbows over the sea, the showers ceased, and the heavens gradually cleared up, though the wind still blowed as hard and the breakers ran as high as before. Keeping on, we soon after came to a charity house, which we looked into to see how the shipwrecked mariner might fare. Far away in some desolate hollow by the sea-side, just within the bank, stands a lonely building on piles driven into the sand, with a slight nail put through the staple, which a freezing man can bend, with some straw, perchance, on the floor on which he may lie, or which he may burn in the fire-place to keep him alive. Perhaps this hut has never been required to shelter a shipwrecked man, and the benevolent person who promised to inspect it annually, to see that the straw and matches are here, and that the boards will keep off the wind, has grown remiss and thinks that storms and shipwrecks are over; and this very night a perishing crew may pry open its door with their numbed fingers and leave half their number dead here by morning. When I thought what must be the condition of the families which alone would ever occupy or had occupied them, what must have been the tragedy of the winter evenings spent by human beings around their hearths, these houses, though they were meant for human dwellings, did not look cheerful to me. They appeared but a stage to the grave*.

Present day Cahoon Hollow is one of the most popular places on Cape Cod during the summer and is often overrun with sunbathers, swimmers and surfers. Winter walkers, however, will have little difficulty imagining the bleak scene as described by Thoreau nearly a century and a half ago.

---

*The Humane House Thoreau encountered at Cahoon Hollow was only a fraction of the size of the hut in which Thoreau had dwelt just a couple of years earlier at Walden Pond. While Thoreau's Walden home was just "ten feet by fifteen long," offering only 150 square feet of floor space, Humane Houses were merely eight feet long on each side, providing just 64 square feet of floor space.

In the Footsteps of Thoreau

The Trail
Initial Route
➜From the parking lot at **LeCount Hollow Beach** proceed west along LeCount Hollow Road 0.1 miles past Ocean View Drive, to the first road on the right. This unmarked and unpaved road is labelled Pine Ridge Road on the map.

➜Follow Pine Ridge Road 0.2 miles to the point where it bends hard to the left, just beyond the first private home located here. As the road bends to the left, you will notice a split-rail fence on the right. At the end of the fence is the start of a narrow walking path.

➜Step from Pine Ridge Road onto this walking path and bear to the left (west). **NOTE: Be sure not to follow the walking path to the right (north).**

Words to Walk By

I do not know how to entertain one who can't take long walks. The first thing that suggests itself is to get a horse to draw them, and that brings us at once into contact with the stablers and dirty harness, and I do not get over my ride for a long time. I give up my forenoon to them and get along pretty well, the very elasticity of the air and promise of the day abetting me, but they are as heavy as dumplings by mid-afternoon. If they can't walk, why won't they take an honest nap and let me go in the afternoon. But, come two o'clock they alarm me by an evident disposition to sit. In the midst of the most glorious Indian summer afternoon, there they sit, breaking your chairs and wearing out the house, with their backs to the light, taking no note of the lapse of time.

–The Journal of Henry D. Thoreau, October 7, 1857

➜After turning to the left on the walking path, follow it straight ahead through the woods 0.3 miles to where it meets up with the Wellfleet power lines.

➜Turn right onto the jeep trail by the power lines and follow it 0.2 miles to where it bends to the right. At this location the power lines run alongside the old Wellfleet railroad bed which is located just to the left (west) of the power lines. Most walkers will want to cut from the jeep trail onto the railroad bed when they get the chance, as the railroad bed makes for easier walking.

➜Follow the power lines and railroad bed north 0.6 miles across one unmarked dirt road to where they are crossed by Duck Pond Road, which is clearly marked by a sign pointing to Duck Pond on the right. **NOTE: Duck Pond Road leads 0.2 miles to the right to Duck Pond, one of the most scenic and secluded ponds in the area. If you choose to visit Duck Pond, where there is a small but pleasant beach, plan on adding an extra half hour to this walk.**

➜From Duck Pond Road, continue north along the railroad bed and power lines 0.6 miles farther until you arrive at the next dirt road that crosses the power lines. This dirt road is easily identified by the split-rail fence near it on the right side of the power lines. Turn right (east) onto this dirt road and follow it into the woods. **NOTE: If you accidentally pass this dirt road, you will arrive at Old County Road, a regular paved road 0.2 miles farther on.**

➜Follow the dirt road 0.6 miles from the power lines to where it intersects with Cahoon Hollow Road, a regular paved road.

➜Turn right onto Cahoon Hollow Road and walk just a few feet to where you will encounter a jeep trail on the opposite side of the road.

➜Cross Cahoon Hollow Road and proceed onto the jeep trail. Follow this jeep trail 0.7 miles, past Dyer Pond on the left, to where there is a four-way junction with another jeep trail. **NOTE: There will be a number of driveways leading off this jeep trail, marked as private ways or with the name of the property owner nailed to a tree. Be sure to avoid these private driveways and to pay close attention to the map in order to stay on the main jeep trail.**

➜When you reach the four-way junction, proceed straight across it and continue 0.3 miles farther to where the jeep trail forms a t-junction with Long Pond Road, a regular paved road.

➜Turn right onto Long Pond Road and proceed 0.2 miles past the parking lot for the beach at Long Pond, and then turn left onto the unmarked jeep trail.

➜Follow the jeep trail about 0.5 miles to the first fork, at which point you should bear to the left and continue toward the north.

➜0.1 miles past the first fork in the jeep trail, you will arrive at another fork at which point you should also bear left.

➜Continue 0.3 miles from the second fork to where the jeep trail forms a t-junction with paved Gross Hill Road.

➜Turn right onto Gross Hill Road and follow it 0.3 miles to the Stop sign at the intersection with Ocean View Drive.

➜Bear left at this Stop sign and continue 0.4 miles to **Newcomb Hollow Beach.**

Return Route
➜From Newcomb Hollow Beach turn to the right and follow the beach south.

➜If conditions allow, follow the shoreline south 1.5 miles to **Cahoon Hollow Beach**, the site of the **Wellfleet Beachcomber**. As stated, Cahoon Hollow Beach is where Thoreau encountered a **Humane House**. With its proximity to the trail, the Beachcomber is an ideal place to stop for a bite to eat in the summer.

➜Continue 0.7 miles south along the shore to **White Crest Beach**. The Town of Wellfleet also maintains seasonal restrooms here.

➜Continue south from White Crest Beach 0.8 miles to LeCount Hollow Beach to complete this loop.●

In the Footsteps of Thoreau

What Thoreau Saw

Kettle Ponds of Wellfleet and Truro

Our host took pleasure in telling us the names of the ponds, most of which we could see from his windows, and making us repeat them after him, to see if we had got them right. They were Gull Pond, the largest and a very handsome one, clear and deep, and more than a mile in circumference, Newcomb's, Swett's, Slough, Horse-Leech, Round, and Herring Ponds, all connected at high water, if I do not mistake. The coast-surveyors had come to him for their names, and he told them of one which they had not detected. He said they were not so high as formerly. There was an earthquake about four years before he was born, which cracked the pans of the ponds, which were of iron, and caused them to settle.

From left to right, the ponds shown in this photograph are today called, Gull Pond, Higgins Pond, Williams Pond, Herring Pond, Slough Pond, Horseleech Pond and Round Pond. Newcomb Hollow Beach is visible in the foreground; and that's Great Island across the Cape, in the top left corner.

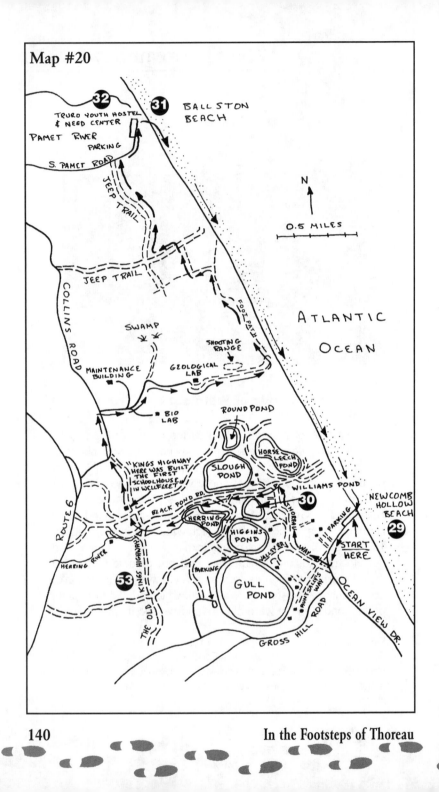

Map #20

32 TRURO YOUTH HOSTEL & NEED CENTER

31 BALLSTON BEACH

PAMET RIVER PARKING

S. PAMET ROAD

JEEP TRAIL

JEEP TRAIL

COLLINS ROAD

SWAMP

MAINTENANCE BUILDING

GEOLOGICAL LAB

SHOOTING RANGE

FOOTPATH

N

0.5 MILES

ATLANTIC OCEAN

BIO LAB

ROUND POND

"KINGS HIGHWAY HERE WAS BUILT THE FIRST SCHOOLHOUSE IN WELLFLEET"

SLOUGH POND

HORSE LEECH POND

WILLIAMS POND

NEWCOMB HOLLOW BEACH

29

30

BLACK POND RD.

HERRING POND

HIGGINS POND

THOREAU WAY

PARKING

START HERE

ROUTE 6

HERRING RIVER

THE OLD KINGS HIGHWAY

53

PARKING

VALLEY BR.

AUNT SALLY'S WAY

GULL POND

OCEAN VIEW DR.

GROSS HILL ROAD

In the Footsteps of Thoreau

The Great Thoreau Hike

PART V
Newcomb Hollow Beach to Ballston Beach

DISTANCE 9.6 miles

TIME 6.5 hours

RATING very difficult

Location

This loop begins at **Newcomb Hollow Beach** in north Wellfleet. Follow
Route 6 to the Wellfleet/Eastham town line, and then proceed north 2.6
miles to LeCount Hollow Road on the right. Follow LeCount Hollow
Road 0.7 miles east to the intersection with Ocean View Drive and the
LeCount Hollow Beach parking lot. Turn left onto Ocean View Drive and
continue 3.3 miles to the Newcomb Hollow Beach parking lot.
Unfortunately, no parking is permitted at the beach from 9 a.m. to 5 p.m.
July through Labor Day, except for Town of Wellfleet resident sticker-hold-
ers. The nearest public parking is located 1.5 miles south off Ocean View
Drive at Cahoon Hollow Beach, where parking fees are charged.

Description

As magnificent as any hike on Cape Cod, this unforgettable route consists
mainly of quiet jeep trails and little-known walking paths, with just a few
stretches along paved roads. The trail runs by half a dozen placid kettle
ponds (including **Williams Pond** where Thoreau stayed at the Wellfleet
Oysterman's house) and offers many spectacular ocean views from the
secluded, hundred-foot cliffs of South Truro. **NOTE: This hike is very
difficult and, because of its remote situation and terrain, requires particularly careful readings of both the map and the directions listed below.**

Thoreau

After spending the night at the Wellfleet Oysterman's house, Thoreau
returned to his Cape Cod walk near Newcomb Hollow on Friday,
October 12, 1949. He carried with him a copy of a small book, published in 1803, entitled *A Description of the Eastern Coast of the County of
Barnstable*, which he referred to as a "Shipwrecked Seamen's Manual."
Thoreau quoted from this book numerous times in *Cape Cod* and
commented that although half a century had elapsed since it was
printed, it still presented a "true description" of the landscape between

"Newcomb's and Brush Hollows*," the same area that is covered by this route.

Amazingly enough, and thanks in large part to the resource management of the **Cape Cod National Seashore**, this area continues to retain many of the characteristics that defined it nearly 200 years ago. As today's hikers are sure to discover, the landscape is still marked by a "very high and steep" cliff, "almost impassable" brush, and woods "in which not a house is to be discovered." Thoreau tells the story of his 1849 morning walk which began just to the north of today's **Newcomb Hollow Beach**:

> The sun rose visible at such a distance over the sea, that the cloud-bank on the horizon, which at first concealed him, was not perceptible until he had risen high behind it, and plainly broke and dispersed it, like an arrow. But as yet I looked at him rising over the sea. Already I saw some vessels on the horizon, which had rounded the Cape in the night, and were now well on their watery way to other lands. We struck the beach again in the south part of Truro in the early part of the day, while it was flood tide, and the beach was narrow and soft. We walked on the bank, which was very high here, but not so level as the day before, being more interrupted by slight hollows. The author of the *Description of the Eastern Coast* says of this part, that "the bank is very high and steep. From the edge of it west, there is a strip of sand a hundred yards in breadth. Then succeeds low brushwood, a quarter of a mile wide, and almost impassable. After which comes a thick perplexing forest, in which not a house is to be discovered. Seamen, therefore, though the distance between these two hollows (Newcomb's and Brush Hollows) is great, must not attempt to enter the wood, as in a snow-storm they must undoubtedly perish." This is still a true description of the country, except that there is not much high wood left.

The Trail
Initial Route
→From the parking lot at **Newcomb Hollow Beach** head southwest up Gross Hill Road 0.3 miles to Thoreau Way, which was named in honor of Thoreau's walks here. Thoreau Way is located at the beginning of the first bend in Gross Hill Road and is the fourth unpaved way on the right. While it is not labelled with a street sign, Thoreau Way can be identified by the nearly 25 small signs with residents' names that are posted on a tree at the corner of it and Gross Hill Road. (If you accidentally pass Thoreau Way, you will come to the intersection with Gross Hill Road and know you have gone too far.)

*While today's Brush Hollow, which is located just south of **Ballston Beach**, is little more than a footpath through the dunes, in Thoreau's time it was a primary access point to the **Great Beach**.

In the Footsteps of Thoreau

➡️After just a few hundred feet along Thoreau Way, you will arrive at a four-way junction with another dirt road, Aunt Sally's Way. Proceed straight across this junction and stay on Thoreau Way. **NOTE: Many of the dirt roads and driveways in the area look very similar, and there are no official street signs. However, most of the driveways are marked either as a "Private Way" or with a sign indicating the name of the resident. Be sure not to follow these private driveways and stay on the main roads as shown on the map.**

Words to Walk By

It requires considerable skill in crossing a country to avoid houses and cultivated parts—some what of the engineer's or gunner's skill—to pass a house, if you must go near it through high grass—pass the enemy's lives where houses are thick—as to make a hill or wood screen you—to shut every window with an apple tree for that route which most avoids the houses is not only the one in which you will be least molested, but it is by far the most agreeable.

–The Journal of Henry D. Thoreau, June 19, 1852

➡️Follow Thoreau Way 0.6 miles to the junction with Black Pond Road, an unmarked dirt road that runs east to west. This junction is marked by a small triangular green that causes travelers on Thoreau Way to bear either left (west) or right (east) onto Black Pond Road.

➡️Bear left (west) onto Black Pond Road. (Just after you turn onto Black Pond Road you will come to an intersection with a resident's driveway that is marked with a pair of white fences and the resident's name. Be sure to avoid walking between these fences and stay on Black Pond Road.)

➡️As you follow Black Pond Road west, you should be able to spot **Williams Pond** through the trees to the left (after walking 0.1 miles); Slough Pond through the trees to the right (after walking 0.2 miles); and Herring Pond through the trees to the left (after 0.4 miles).

➡️After walking west along Black Pond Road a total of 0.9 miles from Thoreau Way you will come to a four-way intersection with an unmarked dirt road that runs downhill to the left (south) and uphill to the right (north). This intersection can be identified by the "Private Homes" sign that faces away from the direction you are coming from. **NOTE: If you mistakenly pass this intersection, you will come to a private home that is surrounded by a high stockade fence, at which point you will know you have gone too far.**

➡️Turn right at the four-way intersection and follow the narrow jeep trail up the hill to the north. Although this dirt road is fairly narrow and does not currently get much use, it is actually a part of the **Old Kings Highway**,

The Great Thoreau Hike

formerly the main stagecoach route from Sandwich to Provincetown.

→After about 0.1 miles on the Old Kings Highway you will come to an intersection with another unmarked dirt road. Proceed straight ahead (to the north) at this intersection, and within a few hundred feet you will encounter a stone marker on the left that identifies the former location of the first schoolhouse in Wellfleet.

→From the schoolhouse marker continue straight ahead 0.3 miles to the intersection with Collins Road, a regular paved road.

→Bear right onto Collins Road and follow it to the north.

→After 0.3 miles on Collins Road, you will encounter a paved access road on the right marked with a sign for "Authorized Vehicles Only." Turn right onto this access road. Although it is marked for "Authorized Vehicles Only," walking is permitted here.

→Follow the access road 0.2 miles straight ahead to the fire road gate. **NOTE: Do not turn left off this access road onto the road marked "Warehouse." Likewise, do not turn right onto the road that leads to a biological laboratory.**

→Proceed straight past the fire road gate and continue east on this narrow paved road. After 0.7 miles you will arrive at an old building that once served as a geological laboratory and is currently surrounded by a high wire fence.

→Follow the dirt road around the geological lab building.

→About 0.25 miles from the geological lab building you will pass a shooting range, and 0.25 miles farther you will arrive at the bluffs above the beach.

→Once at the top of the bluffs follow the jeep trail to the left (north), more or less parallel to the cliffs.

→After a few hundred feet, the jeep trail narrows to a walking path. Follow this thin—and at some points vaguely defined—walking path 0.7 miles as it skirts the tops of the bluffs.

→After 0.7 miles, turn left (west) onto the walking path that runs directly away from the cliffs into the vegetation. **NOTE: If you mistakenly continue too far along the path to the north, and miss the turn-off to the left, you will come to a dead end.**

→After turning left (west), proceed 0.1 miles and turn onto the first walking path on the right (north).

→Follow this path 0.25 miles to where it comes to a t-junction with a jeep trail.

→Turn left onto the jeep trail and follow it west 0.3 miles to the four-way intersection with another jeep trail, which runs north to south.

→Turn right (north) at this four-way jeep trail junction and follow this jeep trail as it winds through the woods 1 mile to paved South Pamet Road.

→Turn right onto South Pamet Road and follow it 0.6 miles to the Ballston Beach parking lot where the Town of Truro maintains chemical toilets. The marsh area to the left (north) of the parking lot is the eastern end of the

Pamet River. The handsome red-roofed building on the other side of it is the **Truro Youth Hostel/NEED Center.**

Return Route
➡To complete this hike, follow the path from the Ballston Beach parking lot out to the beach, and proceed to the right (south) 2.8 miles back to Newcomb Hollow Beach.●

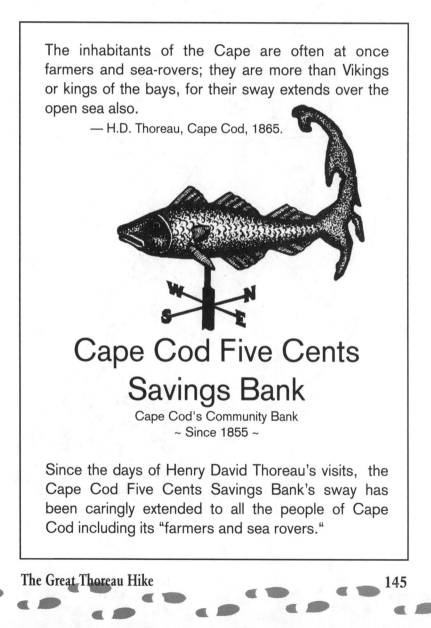

The inhabitants of the Cape are often at once farmers and sea-rovers; they are more than Vikings or kings of the bays, for their sway extends over the open sea also.
— H.D. Thoreau, Cape Cod, 1865.

Cape Cod Five Cents Savings Bank
Cape Cod's Community Bank
~ Since 1855 ~

Since the days of Henry David Thoreau's visits, the Cape Cod Five Cents Savings Bank's sway has been caringly extended to all the people of Cape Cod including its "farmers and sea rovers."

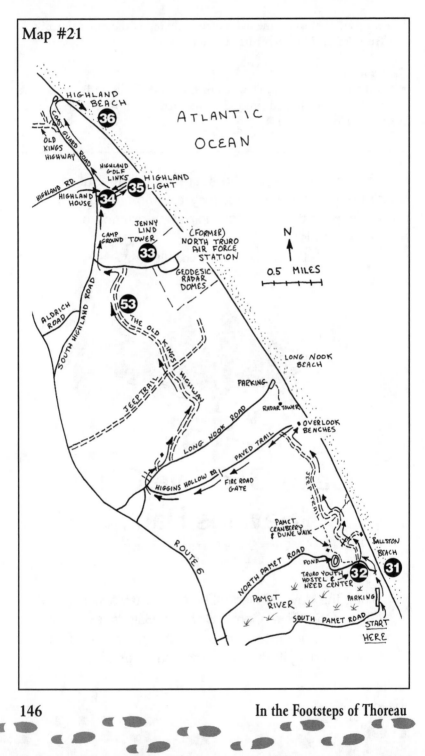

Map #21

HIGHLAND BEACH
36
COAST GUARD ROAD
OLD KINGS HIGHWAY
HIGHLAND RD.
HIGHLAND HOUSE
34
HIGHLAND GOLF LINKS
35 HIGHLAND LIGHT
CAMP GROUND
JENNY LIND TOWER
33
(FORMER) NORTH TRURO AIR FORCE STATION
GEODESIC RADAR DOMES

ATLANTIC OCEAN

N
0.5 MILES

ALDRICH ROAD
SOUTH HIGHLAND ROAD
53
THE OLD KINGS HIGHWAY
JEEP TRAIL
LONG NOOK BEACH
PARKING
RADAR TOWER
OVERLOOK BENCHES
LONG NOOK ROAD
PAVED TRAIL
HIGGINS HOLLOW RD.
FIRE ROAD GATE
JEEP TRAIL
PAMET CRANBERRY & DUNE WALK
POND
BALLSTON BEACH
32 **31**
TRURO YOUTH HOSTEL & NEED CENTER
PARKING
ROUTE 6
NORTH PAMET ROAD
PAMET RIVER
SOUTH PAMET ROAD
START HERE

In the Footsteps of Thoreau

The Great Thoreau Hike

PART VI

Ballston Beach to Highland Beach

DISTANCE 10.5 miles

TIME 6.5 hours

RATING very difficult

Location

Begin this route at **Ballston Beach** in Truro. Follow Route 6 to the Truro/Wellfleet town line, proceed north 2.4 miles and turn right onto the well-marked "Pamet Roads" exit. At the end of the off-ramp turn right at the t-junction. 0.1 miles farther, you will arrive at another t-junction. Turn left onto South Pamet Road and follow it 1.7 miles to the parking lot at Ballston Beach. Unfortunately, no parking is permitted at the beach from 9 a.m. to 5 p.m. July through Labor Day, except for Town of Truro resident sticker-holders. Limited parking is permitted year-round, however, at the small parking area at the trailhead to the **Pamet Cranberry & Dune Walk**, located next to the **Truro Youth Hostel/NEED Center** on North Pamet Road.

Description

This lengthy but lovely loop follows miles of little-known jeep trails and runs across the historic Highlands of North Truro. It finishes with a walk of more than 4 miles along one of the most secluded stretches of beach on all of Cape Cod. The hike runs past a former U.S. Coast Guard Station (now the **Truro Youth Hostel/NEED Center**) which is located along a part of the **Pamet Cranberry & Dune Walk**, as described in this guide, and then through some of the prettiest dunes anywhere. After ascending to a spectacular overlook viewing area, the trail cuts through a quiet Cape Cod neighborhood; it then makes its way through a thick pitch-pine and scrub-oak wood via a long section of the **Old Kings Highway** to Truro's Highlands. At the Highlands, walkers will encounter the oldest lighthouse on Cape Cod, **Highland Light**; the **Highland House**, home of the Truro Historical Society Museum; the oldest golf course on Cape Cod, **Highland Golf Links**; and the romantic **Jenny Lind Tower**.

Thoreau

Whatever else Thoreau thought of the **Great Beach**, he was keenly aware of its capacity for destruction. On his way to the Cape in 1849, he viewed numerous corpses of would-be Irish immigrants collected from the wreck of the *Saint John* in Cohasset (about 35 miles north of Cape Cod) of which he offers the following account:

> I saw many marble feet and matted heads as the cloths were raised, and one livid, swollen and mangled body of a drowned girl—who probably had intended to go out to service to some American family—to which some rags still adhered, with a string, half concealed by the flesh, about its swollen neck; the coiled up wreck of a human hulk, gashed by the rocks or fishes, so that the bone and muscle were exposed, but quite bloodless—merely red and white—with wide-open and staring eyes, yet lusterless, dead-lights; or, like the cabin windows of a stranded vessel, filled with sand. Sometimes there were two or more children, or a parent and child in the same box...

Surprisingly enough, the carnage of the *Saint John* may have also reached as far as the Cape's coast, in the vicinity of today's **Ballston Beach** and **Highland Beach** where this walk is located. Sometime after his 1849 Cape beach walk, Thoreau met a man from Truro who discovered the bodies of two shipwreck victims, probably of the *Saint John*, washed up at the clay-filled cliffs below Truro's Highlands that are locally known as the "Clay Pounds." The event inspired the following passage in *Cape Cod*:

> The annals of this voracious beach! who could write them unless it were a shipwrecked sailor? How many who have seen it have seen it only in the midst of danger and distress, the last strip of earth which their mortal eyes beheld. Think of the amount of suffering which a single strand has witnessed. The ancients would have represented it as a sea monster with open jaws, more terrible than Scylla and Charybdis. An inhabitant of Truro told me that about a fortnight after the St. John was wrecked at Cohasset he found two bodies on the shore at the Clay Pounds. They were those of a man, and a corpulent woman. The man had thick boots on, though his head was off, but "it was alongside." It took the finder some weeks to get over the sight. Perhaps they were man and wife, and whom God had joined the ocean currents had not put asunder. Yet by what slight accidents at first may they have been associated in their drifting. Some of the bodies of those passengers were picked up far out at sea, boxed up and sunk; some brought ashore and buried. There are more consequences to a shipwreck than the underwriters notice. The Gulf Stream may return some to their native shores, or drop them in some out-of-the-way cave of Ocean, where time and the elements will write new riddles with their bones.—But to return to land again.

The Trail
Initial Route
➡️From the end of the parking lot at **Ballston Beach**, cross the marshy

In the Footsteps of Thoreau

Bank Swallow

In this bank, above the clay, I counted in the summer, two hundred holes of the Bank Swallow within a space of six rods long, and there were at least one thousand old birds within three times that distance, twittering over the surf. I had never associated them in my thoughts with the beach before. One little boy who had been a-bird's-nesting had got eighty swallows' eggs for his share! Tell it not to the Humane Society.

eastern end of the Pamet River to North Pamet Road. North Pamet Road formerly connected with South Pamet Road and the Ballston Beach parking lot and ran between the eastern edge of the river and the dunes. However, a 1978 and a 1991 storm sent the ocean surging through the dunes and across the road, burying it beneath tons of sand.

Words to Walk By

I think that I cannot preserve my health and spirits unless I spend four hours a day at least—and it is commonly more than that—sauntering through the woods and over the hills and fields, absolutely free from all worldly engagements.

–Walking, 1862

→Once you arrive at North Pamet Road, continue up the hill toward the red-roofed **Truro Youth Hostel/NEED CENTER**.

→Just before reaching the Youth Hostel/NEED Center, turn off North Pamet Road onto the unmarked jeep trail on the right.

→0.2 miles along this jeep trail, a driveway forks off to a large house on the right, and a fire road gate marks the entrance to the rest of the jeep trail straight ahead.

→Continue past the fire road gate and follow the jeep trail as it winds north through the dunes.

→About 0.2 miles past the fire road gate, there will be a small junction where walking paths cross the jeep trail. These walking paths are part of the **Pamet Cranberry & Dune Walk** described in this guide. Follow the path to the right for a view of the beach, but then return to the jeep trail to continue with this hike.

→About 1 mile past the above-mentioned junction, the jeep trail forms a t-junction with a narrow paved trail that runs east and west.

→Turn right onto this paved trail for a brief detour to a scenic overlook where you will find a picnic table and some benches.

→From the overlook, walk back down the hill along the narrow paved trail and follow it west 0.6 miles to the fire road gate located at the end of Higgins Hollow Road.

→Continue west on Higgins Hollow Road 0.6 miles farther to the intersection with Longnook Road, which is marked by a small triangular island in the road.

→Turn right onto Longnook Road and proceed 0.25 miles east. After passing two driveways on the left, you will come to an unmarked jeep trail on the left. This jeep trail is the start of a section of the **Old Kings Highway**, once the main thoroughfare on Cape Cod and well-known to Thoreau.

➡️Proceed north along the Old Kings Highway. **NOTE: This section of the Old Kings Highway intersects a number of other jeep trails and walking paths. Be sure to continue straight ahead (north) at all of these junctions, and stay on the Old Kings Highway.**

➡️After 1.7 miles, the Old Kings Highway comes to a t-junction with a paved road. Turn left and walk 0.3 miles to the junction with South Highland Road.

➡️Turn right onto South Highland Road and walk 0.5 miles to Highland Light Road on the right.

➡️Turn right onto Highland Light Road to view the **Highland House**, the **Highland Golf Links**, and **Highland Light**. Thoreau stayed at Highland Light, as well as at an earlier version of the Highland House Hotel located here. While standing in front of Highland Light, look to the right to see the top of the gothic-style **Jenny Lind Tower** above the low-growth trees. Beyond the Jenny Lind Tower are a pair of geodesic radar domes at the North Truro Air Force Station.

➡️Walk back down Highland Light Road to South Highland Road and proceed to the right (north).

➡️0.1 miles along South Highland Road you will arrive at a junction, with Coast Guard Road straight ahead and Highland Road to the left.

➡️Continue straight ahead at this junction onto Coast Guard Road and proceed 0.8 miles to **Highland Beach**. Coast Guard Road was named in recognition of the Highland Life-Saving Station which was formerly located at the beach here. (See **Old Harbor Life-Saving Station Museum** for more information on the Life-Saving Service.) The Town of Truro stations chemical toilets at the beach in the summer.

Return Route

➡️From the Highland Beach parking lot, walk to the beach and proceed 4.3 miles to the right (south) back to Ballston Beach to complete this walk.

➡️As you proceed south notice the rich deposits of clay in the cliffs below the Highlands.

➡️2.7 miles south of Highland Beach you will come to a small hollow, Long Nook Beach. The Town of Truro also manages this beach and maintains seasonal restrooms here.

➡️**NOTE: the pathway to the parking lot at Ballston Beach, unlike the pathway to the Long Nook Beach parking lot and other small paths off the beach, is easy to recognize by the many houses surrounding it.●**

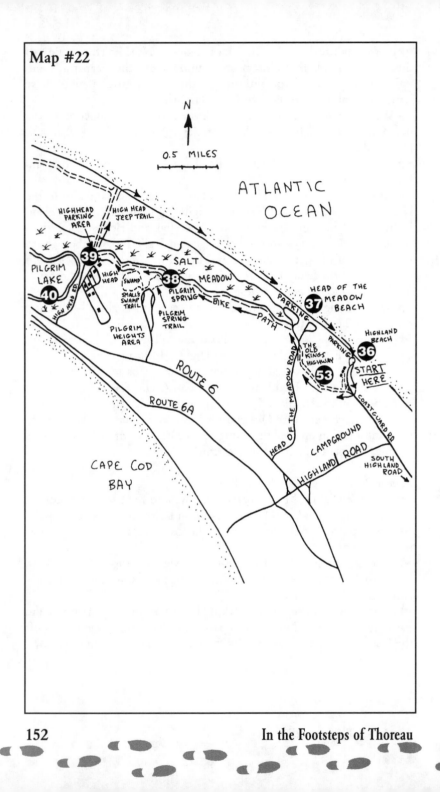

Map #22

N

0.5 MILES

ATLANTIC OCEAN

HIGHHEAD PARKING AREA

HIGH HEAD JEEP TRAIL

39

HIGH HEAD

PILGRIM LAKE

40

HIGH HEAD RD.

SALT

MEADOW

SWAMP

SMALLS SWAMP TRAIL

PILGRIM SPRING

38

PILGRIM HEIGHTS AREA

PILGRIM SPRING TRAIL

BIKE PATH

PARKING

37

HEAD OF THE MEADOW BEACH

HIGHLAND BEACH

36

PARKING

THE OLD KINGS HIGHWAY

53

START HERE

HEAD OF THE MEADOW ROAD

COAST GUARD RD.

ROUTE 6

ROUTE 6A

CAMPGROUND

HIGHLAND ROAD

SOUTH HIGHLAND ROAD

CAPE COD BAY

In the Footsteps of Thoreau

The Great Thoreau Hike

—————— PART VII ——————

Highland Beach to High Head Parking Area

DISTANCE 5.6 miles

TIME 3 hours

RATING difficult

Location

Begin this route at **Highland Beach** in Truro. Follow Route 6 to the Truro/Wellfleet town line, proceed north 5.8 miles and turn right at the well-marked Highland Road exit. At the bottom of the off-ramp, turn right and proceed 0.7 miles east to the t-junction. Turn left and follow Coast Guard Road 0.8 miles northeast to the Highland Beach parking lot. Unfortunately, no parking is permitted at the beach from 9 a.m. to 5 p.m. July through Labor Day, except for Town of Truro resident sticker-holders. The nearest non-restricted public parking lots to Highland Beach are at **Highland Light** to the south, and at the **Cape Cod National Seashore** parking lot at **Head of the Meadow Beach** to the north.

Description

One of the shortest sections of **The Great Thoreau Hike**, this walk is also one of the most delightful and features many historical sites and scenic views. The inland portion of the trail runs almost exclusively along a section of the **Old Kings Highway**, which was once the main road on Cape Cod but currently consists of a quiet jeep trail and a scenic bike path. The route passes by **Head of the Meadow Beach**, **Pilgrim Spring**, the **Pilgrim Spring Trail** and the **Small's Swamp Trail**. It then makes its way out to the **Great Beach** and concludes with the 2.4-mile stretch between High Head and **Highland Beach**.

NOTE: Some walkers may choose to include the Pilgrim Spring Trail and/or the Small's Swamp Trail with this hike. See the descriptions of these trails in this guide for further information.

Thoreau

After spending the night at **Highland Light** in 1849, Thoreau returned to the Cape's outer shore at **Highland Beach** near the starting point of this hike. Although he had already dedicated the better part of two full days to hiking the beach, he was anything but weary of it and offered the following memorable description of his morning:

> The light-house lamps were still burning, though now with a silvery

lustre, when I rose to see the sun come out of the Ocean; for he still rose eastward of us; but I was convinced that he must have come out of a dry bed beyond that stream, though he seemed to come out of the water.... Again we took to the beach for another day (October 13), walking along the shore of the resounding sea, determined to get it into us. We wished to associate with the Ocean until it lost the pond-like look which it wears to a countryman. We still thought that we could see the other side. Its surface was still more sparkling than the day before, and we beheld "the countless smilings of the ocean waves"; though some of them wore pretty broad grins, for still the wind blew and the billows broke in foam along the beach.

Throughout *Cape Cod*, Thoreau examines the **Great Beach** from a multitude of perspectives. He writes of the power of the ocean, the feel of the sand underfoot, the sounds of the shore, the history and natural history of the Cape, and the characters of the people and creatures that inhabit it. And, as demonstrated by the passage above, Thoreau took plenty of time to contemplate the dazzling visual beauty of the place. He also writes in *Cape Cod*:

To-day it was the Purple Sea, an epithet which I should not before have accepted. There were distinct patches of the color of purple grape with the bloom rubbed off. But first and last the sea is of all colors. Well writes Gilpin concerning "the brilliant hues which are continually playing on the surface of a quiet ocean," and this was not too turbulent at a distance from the shore. "Beautiful," says he, "no doubt in a high degree are those glimmering tints which often invest the tops of mountains; but they are mere coruscations compared with these marine colors, which are continually varying and shifting into each other in all the vivid splendor of the rainbow, through the space often of several leagues." Commonly, in calm weather, for half a mile from the shore, where the bottom tinges it, the sea is green, or greenish, as are some ponds; then blue for many miles, often with purple tinges, bounded in the distance by a light almost silvery stripe, beyond which there is generally a dark-blue rim, like a mountain ridge in the horizon, as if, like that, it owed its color to the intervening atmosphere. On another day it will be marked with long streaks, alternately smooth and rippled, light colored and dark, even like our inland meadows in a freshet, and showing which way the wind sets. Thus we sat on the foaming shore, looking on the wine colored ocean.

The Trail
Initial Route
→From the **Highland Beach** parking lot proceed inland up Coast Guard Road 0.25 miles and turn onto the unmarked jeep trail on the right. This jeep trail is a section of the **Old Kings Highway**.

→Just after the start of this jeep trail, you will encounter a fork in the trail where you should bear to the left, as the trail to the right is a private driveway.

→From the fork, follow the Old Kings Highway 0.6 miles to the northwest to where it meets Head of the Meadow Road.

→Once at Head of the Meadow Road, walk to the right (east) and you will quickly arrive at a fork where the **Cape Cod National Seashore** parking lot for **Head of the Meadow Beach** is located on the left; and the Town of Truro parking lot for the beach is located on the right. Bear to the left, toward the Park-managed lot.

→Just before the entrance to this parking lot, turn left onto the Head of the Meadow Bike Path.

Words to Walk By

What is it that makes it so hard sometimes to determine whither we will walk? I believe that there is a subtle magnetism in Nature, which, if we unconsciously yield to it, will direct us aright. It is not indifferent to us which way we walk. There is a right way; but we are very liable from heedlessness and stupidity to take the wrong one. We would fain take that walk, never yet taken by us through this actual world, which is perfectly symbolical of the path which we love to travel in the interior and ideal world; and sometimes, no doubt, we find it difficult to choose our direction, because it does not yet exist distinctly in our idea.

–Walking, 1862

→Follow this bike path 1.2 miles to **Pilgrim Spring** on the left. Pilgrim Spring is a small active spring, honored as the location of the first source of fresh water discovered by the Pilgrims upon arriving in North America in 1620. A picnic table adjacent to the spring makes a nice place for a break. **NOTE: Pilgrim Spring also marks the intersection of The Great Thoreau Hike with the Pilgrim Spring Trail, described in this guide. The Pilgrim Spring Trail in turn connects to the Small's Swamp Trail, also described in this guide. Combined, they make for a great 1.5-mile walk.**

→From Pilgrim Spring continue along the Head of the Meadow Bike Path an additional 0.8 miles to the **High Head Parking Area**. The Park maintains chemical toilets here, but there are no other services available.

Return Route

→From the High Head Parking Area proceed to the northeast along the High Head jeep trail 0.3 miles to the **Great Beach**. This jeep trail is also one of the main access roads to the beach for four-wheel-drive vehicles.

→Once on the beach turn right and continue 1.8 miles back to Head of the Meadow Beach. There are restrooms operated seasonally at the Park-managed parking lot, and chemical toilets operated seasonally at the town parking lot.

→From Head of the Meadow Beach, complete this hike by continuing just 0.6 miles farther southeast along the shoreline to Highland Beach.●

The Great Thoreau Hike

The Great Thoreau Hike

PART VIII

High Head Parking Area to Race Point Beach

DISTANCE 15 miles
TIME 11 hours
RATING extremely difficult

Location

This hike begins at the **High Head Parking Area** in North Truro. Follow Route 6 to the Truro/Wellfleet town line and proceed north 8.3 miles to High Head Road on the right, just before **Pilgrim Lake**. Turn right onto High Head Road and proceed 0.4 miles to the fork. Bear left onto the unpaved road and continue 0.3 miles to the parking lot.

Description

NOTE: This hike requires a high level of physical fitness and should not be attempted by inexperienced walkers, as it runs through isolated areas that are particularly exposed to the elements. Care must be taken to bring ample supplies and to begin this hike early enough in the day so that there is enough daylight remaining to complete it. The jeep trails through the dunes are also subject to change and can be difficult to follow, especially during and after bad weather.

This longest section of **The Great Thoreau Hike** is also the most arduous. The route runs almost exclusively through thick, soft sand that makes the going slow, both on the jeep trails through the dunes and along the almost 8 miles of beach. This having been said, the hike is not without its rewards. In fact, it is one of the most gratifying hikes in this guide.

Reconstructing the path Thoreau followed a century and a half ago, this hike crosses the largest dune area in the region, the **Province Lands**, providing an intimate look at one of the most unique coastal environments in New England. Formerly covered by a substantial forest, the area was clear-cut and overgrazed by early settlers—acts which lead to the loss of its once fertile topsoil. Today, the sand in the Province Lands that does not blow about freely is held in place by many species of vegetation. As emphasized by Thoreau, this beach grass, poverty grass, seaside goldenrod, rose hips, bayberry, cranberry and beach plum make for a truly inspiring landscape, especially where they intermingle with swampy patches of scrub oak and pitch pine. And there is always the ubiquitous presence of the ocean, with sea birds, sea breezes and ocean views at every turn.

Along the route, hikers will also encounter many different rustic huts, the renowned **Province Lands Dune Shacks**. Plus, there is **Mount Ararat** (a prominent dune that was well known to Thoreau), as well as the **Old Harbor Life-Saving Station Museum** and the remains of the **Peaked Hill Bars Life-Saving Station**. Furthermore, **Race Point Lighthouse**, **Pilgrim Lake** and the **Pilgrim Monument** are all visible from the trail. Of course, the most impressive aspect of this hike is the sheer quantity and quality of time walkers get to spend along the **Great Beach**, an experience that is not easily forgotten.

Depending on the season, a variety of useful services may be available at **Race Point Beach**, including public telephones and restrooms. The **Race Point Ranger Station** is also located at the beach and serves as the administrative center for the **Cape Cod National Seashore** which manages the area.

Thoreau

Thoreau first came to the Cape in October, the month that he later declared "is the best time to visit this shore." Today, many would still agree with Thoreau and for a number of reasons, not the least of which being the often underrated beauty of the Cape's autumn landscape. Thoreau's eloquent description of the **Province Lands**, as viewed from **Mount Ararat** in October of 1849, captures the enticing aspects of the area that have attracted so many people to it over the centuries:

> Not withstanding the universal barrenness, and the contiguity of the desert, I never saw an autumnal landscape so beautifully painted as this was. It was like the richest rug imaginable spread over an uneven surface; no damask nor velvet, nor Tyrian dye or stuffs, nor the work of any loom, could ever match it. There was the incredibly bright red of the Huckleberry, and the reddish brown of the Bayberry mingled with the bright and living green of small Pitch Pines, and also the duller green of the Bayberry, Boxberry, and Plum, the yellowish green of the Shrub Oaks, and the various golden and yellow and fawn colored tints of the Birch and Maple and Aspen—each making its own figure, and, in the midst, the few yellow sand-slides on the sides of the hills looked like the white floor seen through rents in the rug. Coming from the country as I did, and many autumnal woods as I had seen, this was perhaps the most novel and remarkable sight that I saw on the Cape. Probably the brightness of the tints was enhanced by contrast with the sand which surrounded this tract. This was part of the furniture of Cape Cod. We had for days walked up the long and bleak piazza which runs along her Atlantic side, then over the sanded floor of her halls, and now we were being introduced into her boudoir.

The Trail
Initial Route
→From the far end of the **High Head Parking Area**, proceed 0.4 miles

Map #23A

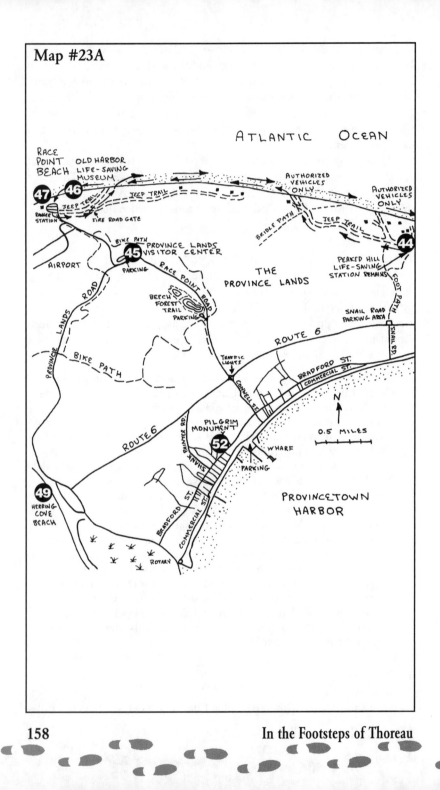

ATLANTIC OCEAN

RACE
POINT
BEACH

OLD HARBOR
LIFE-SAVING
MUSEUM

AUTHORIZED
VEHICLES
ONLY

AUTHORIZED
VEHICLES
ONLY

47 **46**

JEEP TRAIL

JEEP TRAIL

BRIDLE PATH

JEEP TRAIL

RANGER
STATION

FIRE ROAD GATE

44

BIKE PATH

PROVINCE LANDS
VISITOR CENTER

PEAKED HILL
LIFE-SAVING
STATION REMAINS

45

FOOT PATH

AIRPORT

PARKING

RACE POINT ROAD

THE
PROVINCE LANDS

SNAIL ROAD
PARKING AREA

PROVINCE LANDS ROAD

BEECH
FOREST
TRAIL

PARKING

SNAIL RD.

BIKE PATH

ROUTE 6

TRAFFIC
LIGHTS

BRADFORD ST.
COMMERCIAL ST.

CONNELL ST.

N

ROUTE 6

PILGRIM
MONUMENT

0.5 MILES

SHANK PAINTER RD.

52

WHARF

BRADFORD ST.

PARKING

49

HERRING
COVE
BEACH

COMMERCIAL ST.

PROVINCETOWN
HARBOR

ROTARY

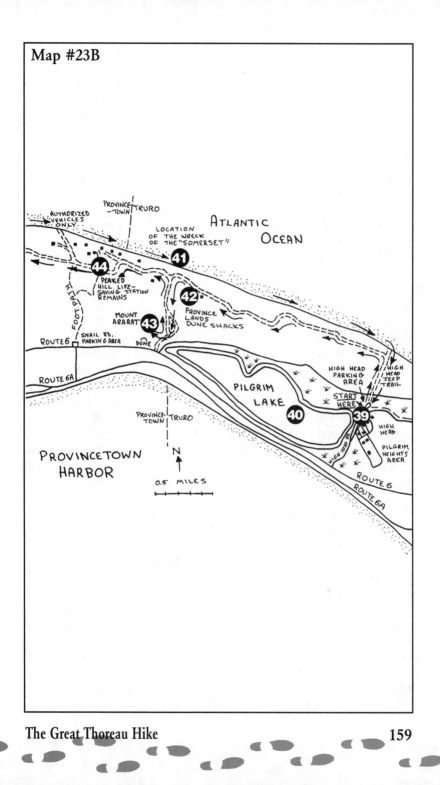

Map #23B

AUTHORIZED VEHICLES ONLY

PROVINCE-TOWN|TRURO

ATLANTIC OCEAN

LOCATION OF THE WRECK OF THE "SOMERSET"

44

41

PEAKED HILL LIFE-SAVING STATION REMAINS

42

PROVINCE LANDS DUNE SHACKS

FOOTPATH

MOUNT ARARAT

43

ROUTE 6

SNAIL RD. PARKING AREA

DUNE

PILGRIM LAKE

HIGH HEAD PARKING AREA

HIGH HEAD JEEP TRAIL

ROUTE 6A

START HERE

40

39

HIGH HEAD

PILGRIM HEIGHTS AREA

HIGH HEAD RD.

PROVINCETOWN HARBOR

PROVINCE-TOWN|TRURO

N

0.5 MILES

ROUTE 6

ROUTE 6A

north along the High Head jeep trail. This jeep trail is one of the main access roads to the **Great Beach** for four-wheel-drive vehicles.

➜Just as the High Head jeep trail rises to within site of the beach, turn left (west) onto the jeep trail that runs parallel with the shore here. This trail may be marked "Authorized Vehicles Only," but like similar trails in the **Province Lands**, it is open to the general public for walking.

➜Follow this jeep trail west, as it continues to run more or less parallel with the shore for about 1 mile. It then cuts inland and winds its way through the dunes for another mile to where it forms a t-junction with another jeep trail. Just before you arrive at this t-junction, you will pass two **Province Lands Dune Shacks**, both on the left side of the trail. NOTE: All of the dune shacks in the Province Lands are private property. Please respect owners' rights.

➜Once you arrive at the t-junction turn to the left and follow this jeep trail 0.6 miles south to **Mount Ararat**. (It was certainly not far from this junction that Thoreau, in his own words, "crossed over to the bay side, not half a mile distant, in order to spend the noon on the nearest shrubby sand-hill in Provincetown, called Mount Ararat.") NOTE: Be sure to bear right at the fork in the trail on the way to Mount Ararat.

➜As you follow the jeep trail to Mount Ararat you will approach the highway, Route 6. Just before Route 6, you will notice two large dunes on the right. The largest of the pair, and the farthest from Route 6, is Mount Ararat.

➜Climb Mount Ararat if you choose. Thoreau climbed it at least twice, once in 1849, and again in 1857. NOTE: Be careful not to tread on or damage the vegetation on Mount Ararat, or elsewhere in the Province Lands. These plants are essential to the stability of the dunes and are easily crushed underfoot. Provincetown Harbor, Pilgrim Lake, Cape Cod Bay and the Atlantic Ocean are all visible from the top of Mount Ararat. On clear days you should also be able to see **Long Point Lighthouse**, **Wood End Lighthouse** and **Race Point Lighthouse**.

➜From Mount Ararat, retrace your steps along the jeep trail, back to the above-mentioned junction that you just came from, 0.6 miles to the north.

➜Once back at this junction, turn to the left and proceed 0.5 miles to the west, past some more dune shacks.

➜After 0.5 miles, the main jeep trail curves to the left (south), and a small trail continues straight ahead (west). NOTE: Be sure to follow the main jeep trail here, as it curves to the left. The smaller trail that continues straight ahead is for the use of dune shack residents only.

➜Follow the main jeep trail 0.1 miles south, and then continue along it as it curves back to the right (west).

➜0.2 miles farther, you will arrive at the large stone-block foundation of the former **Peaked Hill Bars Life-Saving Station**.

→From the remains of the station, continue straight ahead to the west. **NOTE: Be sure not to turn left or right onto either of the two north/south-running paths that cross the main jeep trail near the station.**

→From the remains of the Peaked Hill Bars Life-Saving Station, follow the jeep trail west 1.1 miles to where it crosses a bridle path.

Words to Walk By

To preserve wild animals implies generally the creation of a forest for them to dwell in or resort to. So it is with man.

–Walking, 1862

→0.1 miles beyond the bridle path you will arrive at a small fork in the trail. Bear to the right at this fork, as the path to the left comes to a dead end at the next dune shack.

→0.1 miles past the fork, the trail runs out to the Great Beach.

→Once out on the beach follow the shoreline 2.1 miles to the left (west) to the **Race Point Beach** parking lot. Race Point Beach is also the location of the **Race Point Ranger Station** and the **Old Harbor Life-Saving Station Museum**. Also of note is the Race Point Lighthouse which is visible on clear days 1.8 miles across the dunes to the west of the parking lot.

Return Route

→From the bathhouse platform at Race Point Beach head down the hill toward the gatehouse at the parking lot entrance, where there is a four-wheel-drive jeep trail on the left.

→Follow the four-wheel-drive jeep trail 0.4 miles northeast directly back out to the beach. Do not turn onto the fire road on the right.

→Once on the beach turn right (east) and begin the beautiful 5.2-mile beach walk back to the High Head jeep trail. Before reaching the High Head jeep trail, you will pass two other jeep trails that run from the beach into the dunes, both of which are marked with "Authorized Vehicles Only" signs. Be sure not to take these trails, but stay on the beach until you reach the High Head jeep trail. (From the High Head jeep trail, you should be able to see on clear days the houses on the hill above the High Head Parking Area.)

→Follow the High Head jeep trail 0.5 miles south, back to the High Head Parking Area to complete this hike.●

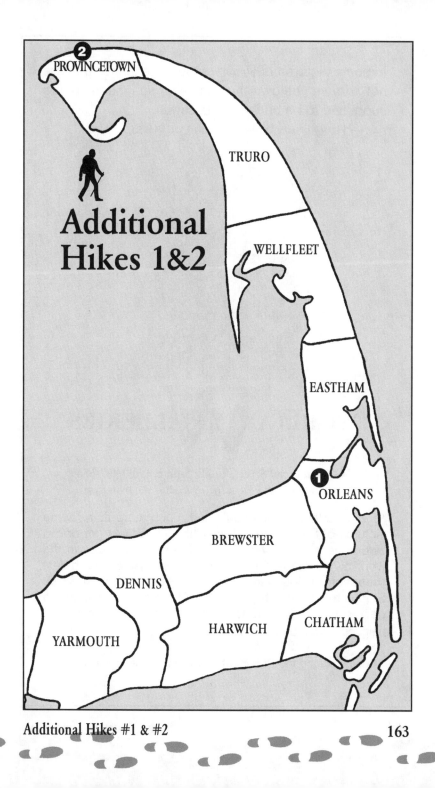

Additional Hikes #1 & #2

In some pictures of Provincetown the inhabitants are not drawn below the ankles, so much being supposed to be buried in the sand.

— Henry David Thoreau, Cape Cod, 1865.

WOHLFARTH GALLERIES

234 Commercial Street, Union Square (508) 487-6569
(Drawing of Henry Hensche by Cedric Baldwin Egeli)

At Wohlfarth Galleries you'll find much more than "some pictures of Provincetown" with "the inhabitants not drawn below the ankles." Wohlfarth Galleries specializes in the work of the Cape Cod School of Art, America's oldest school of art, founded in historic Provincetown in 1899. Stop in to examine this thriving tradition for yourself and to view some of the world's best traditional impressionist painting and fine drawing.

Located along the **Provincetown Center Walk** in this guide.

Introduction to
Additional Hikes #1 & #2

Like **The Great Thoreau Hike, Parts I-VIII** in this guide, **Additional Hikes #1 & #2** are based on Thoreau's 1849 hikes on Cape Cod that form the narrative structure of his book, *Cape Cod*. Because these walks are of such different natures from the rest of The Great Thoreau Hike, however, they have been paired off and presented separately in this section.

Additional Hike #1 covers the portion of Thoreau's 1849 travels that occurred after he left Higgins Tavern in Orleans but before he "left the road," "got out of the towns" and "left behind...for a season the bar rooms of Massachusetts," as he put it. While Thoreau recorded what he saw along this part of his hike (see **Jonathan Young Windmill**, **Eastham Windmill** and **Jeremiah's Gutter**), these descriptions form an entirely different experience in *Cape Cod* from his walks along the **Great Beach**. In fact, Thoreau's narration of his route which is covered in Additional Hike #1 can almost be said to serve as a preamble in *Cape Cod* to the wildness of the "Backside" of the Cape.

Similarly, Additional Hike #2 covers those areas that Thoreau explored after he left the Great Beach: his hike across the **Province Lands** to Provincetown, and his further explorations of the Province Lands the following day. Thoreau only gives a passing mention of his route to Provincetown from today's **Race Point Beach**, however; and his subsequent day's walk appears in his text as more of an epilogue to his hike than an integral part of his Cape adventure. To put it simply, Additional Hikes #1 & #2 cover the transitionary aspects of Thoreau's 1849 Cape Cod walks: his experiences between the relatively comfortable hotels he enjoyed in Orleans and Provincetown and the awesome danger and beauty of the Great Beach.

Thus, while most of The Great Thoreau Hike runs along quiet walking paths, jeep trails and the beach, these Additional Hikes #1 & #2 follow paved roads and bike paths. They are included here more for those who are interested in following Thoreau's 1849 route as accurately as possible, than for those who are looking for quiet, out-of-the-way nature walks. In fact, both of these routes can be followed just as easily by bicycle as on foot.

Still, while these routes have been paved over, they nevertheless offer excellent opportunities for learning more about Thoreau and the Cape Cod he memorialized. Both hikes include an extraordinary number of interesting and historic sites and closely follow the same routes taken by Thoreau. Both offer pleasant excursions into scenic Cape areas. Both run by other walks described in this guide. And both run through modern developed areas that stand in notable contrast to those undeveloped parts of the Cape that are usually associated with Thoreau.●

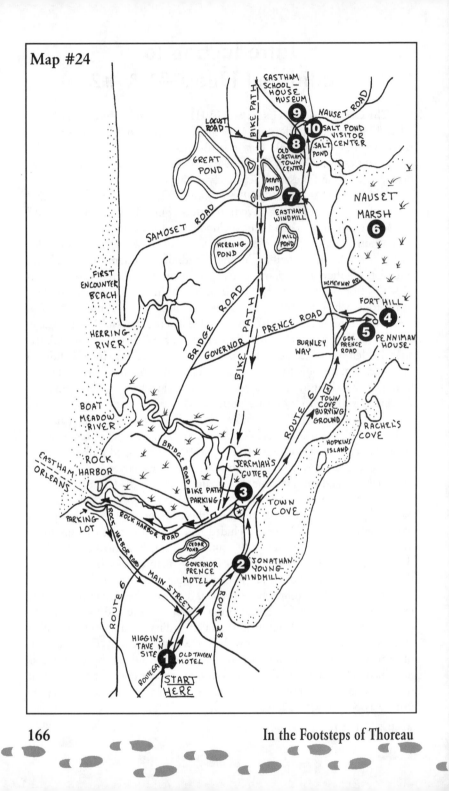

Map #24

In the Footsteps of Thoreau

Additional Hike #1

Higgins Tavern Site to Salt Pond Visitor Center

DISTANCE 10 miles
TIME 5 hours
RATING very difficult

Location

This walk begins in the center of the Town of Orleans at the historic marker designating the site of Higgins Tavern, where Thoreau slept in 1849. From mid-Cape locations follow Route 6 east to Exit 12. Turn right at the bottom of the off-ramp and follow Route 6A east 0.6 miles through one set of traffic lights, to where you will find the historical marker for the **Higgins Tavern Site** on the left side of the road. The marker is located along the sidewalk directly in front of a Citgo Station, across the street from the Old Tavern Motel. Public parking for this walk is available along Main Street, Orleans, which intersects Route 6A 0.3 miles to the east of the marker.

Description

The Great Thoreau Hike, as described in this guide, begins at the **Salt Pond Visitor Center** in Eastham, very near the site where Thoreau "left the road and struck across the country for the eastern shore." However, Thoreau actually began his famous 1849 Cape Cod walk at Higgins Tavern in Orleans, almost 5 miles south of the Salt Pond Visitor Center. This **Additional Hike #1** retraces those additional 5 miles more for the benefit of walkers who want to follow Thoreau's precise 1849 path as closely as possible, than for those who simply desire a pleasant ramble. The Initial Route retraces Thoreau's walk along the roads in Orleans and Eastham, while the Return Route follows a scenic bike path and less-travelled roads back to Orleans. In addition to the **Higgins Tavern Site** and the Salt Pond Visitor Center, there are numerous historic sites along the way, including the **Jonathan Young Windmill**, **Jeremiah's Gutter**, the Town Cove Burying Ground, the **Penniman House**, the **Fort Hill Area**, **Nauset Marsh**, the **Eastham Windmill**, the **Old Eastham Town Center**, the **Eastham Schoolhouse Museum**, and Rock Harbor.

Thoreau

After riding the stagecoach from Sandwich the previous day, Henry David Thoreau awoke on Thursday, October 11, 1849 at the Higgins Tavern in

Orleans. It was here that he began his walk to Provincetown that would later form the narrative of *Cape Cod*. Thoreau describes the initial part of that walk in the following passage:

> For the first four or five miles we followed the road, which here turns to the north on the elbow—the narrowest part of the Cape—that we might clear an inlet from the ocean [Town Cove], a part of Nauset Harbor in Orleans, on our right. We found the travelling good enough for walkers on the sides of the road, though it was "heavy" for horses in the middle. We walked with our umbrellas behind us, since it blowed hard as well as rained, with driving mists, as the day before, and the wind helped us over the sand at a rapid rate.

In Thoreau's time, the roads included in this walk were simple, narrow dirt paths, a far cry from today's great strips of pavement. Also, there was only a fraction of the number of homes and businesses along these roads than now exist. (Thoreau commented that "the houses were few and far between.") Furthermore, the landscape was virtually treeless, having been clear-cut in previous generations, and with many more water views than are available along the present route.

Although a number of historic landmarks line the road today, including two windmills seen by Thoreau, this hike serves as much as a contrast to what Thoreau saw as a reminder of it. Here, hikers will discover that the sandy Cape Cod cart tracks walked by Thoreau have been replaced by the hectic highways of the 20th century.

The Trail
Initial Route
Begin this hike at the **Higgins Tavern Site** that is identified by a marker in front of the Citgo Station on Route 6A in Orleans.

➡While facing the historical marker at the Higgins Tavern Site, proceed to the right (east) along Route 6A toward Main Street in Orleans.

➡After 0.3 miles you will arrive at the traffic lights at the intersection of Route 6A and Main Street.

➡Continue straight through the traffic lights another 0.3 miles, and you will arrive at a hill that offers a view of Town Cove straight ahead. To the left of this hill stands the Governor Prence Motel, located on the former site of the **Jonathan Young Windmill** where Thoreau probably stopped to speak to the miller.

➡From the Governor Prence Motel continue straight ahead 0.2 miles, past the junction with Route 28 on the right, to the present site of the Jonathan Young Windmill on the banks of Town Cove.

➡From the windmill continue through the next set of lights 0.3 miles to the Orleans Rotary.

→Walk to the right around the Orleans Rotary (with the traffic), and take the first road you come to, Route 6 north. You will likely notice marsh plants inside the center of the rotary; and they can also be found growing in many places on the left side of the road, opposite Town Cove. These plants are the sole remnants marking the former location of **Jeremiah's Gutter**, a small tidal creek known to Thoreau that once connected today's Boat Meadow River with Town Cove, and thus Cape Cod Bay with the Atlantic Ocean.

→From the Orleans Rotary, follow Route 6 north 1 mile to Town Cove Burying Ground on the right. This cemetery was the location of Eastham's first meeting house in the early 17th century and is also the burial place of three original Mayflower passengers.

→From Town Cove Burying Ground, continue 0.1 miles north on Route 6 to Governor Prence Road on the right, which is marked with a sign to the **Fort Hill Area**. Long before today's four-lane highway was built, this section of Governor Prence Road was part of the **Old Kings Highway**, the main thoroughfare in the area that was followed by Thoreau.

→Follow Governor Prence Road 0.25 miles to the t-junction and turn right onto Fort Hill Road. As you walk up the hill you will encounter a famous whaling captain's home, the **Penniman House**, on the right.

→Proceed past the Penniman House to the overlook parking lot at historic Fort Hill, where you will encounter a spectacular view of **Nauset Marsh**. This parking lot is also the starting place of the **Fort Hill & Red Maple Swamp Trail**, as described in this guide.

→From the overlook parking lot at Fort Hill, retrace your steps back down Fort Hill Road, past the Penniman House, to the junction with Governor Prence Road.

→From Fort Hill Road, continue straight ahead (west) on Governor Prence Road to the blinking traffic light at the intersection with Route 6, where the Eastham Chamber of Commerce Information Booth is located on the corner.

→Turn right on Route 6 and proceed north 0.8 miles to the **Eastham Windmill** on the left, on the corner of Samoset Road.

→From the Eastham Windmill, continue north 0.5 miles on Route 6 to the **Salt Pond Visitor Center** on the right. The Visitor Center is run by the **Cape Cod National Seashore** and offers a variety of useful services. The Visitor Center is also the starting point of the **Buttonbush Trail** and **The Great Thoreau Hike, Part I,** as described in this guide. The **Eastham School House Museum** is located directly across Nauset Road from the Visitor Center.

Return Route

→From the Salt Pond Visitor Center, return to the traffic lights at the corner of Nauset Road and Route 6, and follow the crosswalk across Route 6 to Salt Pond Road.

➡Continue on Salt Pond Road 0.15 miles to Locust Road. The small triangle in the road here is the **Old Eastham Town Center**.

➡Turn right onto Locust Road and follow it 0.3 miles to where it crosses the Cape Cod Rail Trail Bike Path. As its name suggests, this bike path lies along a former railroad line.

➡Turn left onto the bike path

Words to Walk By

Two or three hours' walking will carry me to as strange a country as I expect ever to see. A single farmhouse which I had not seen before is sometimes as good as the dominions of the King of Dahomey.

–Walking, 1862

and follow it 2.6 miles south. The first road you will cross on the bike path is Samoset Road, the second is Bridge Road, and the third is Governor Prence Road. After 2.6 miles, the bike path terminates in Orleans at Rock Harbor Road.

➡From the end of the bike path, turn right onto Rock Harbor Road and proceed 1 mile to the parking lot at Rock Harbor. Rock Harbor is the main harbor on Cape Cod Bay for the towns of Orleans and Eastham. It is also a great place to charter fishing boats and is one of the premiere places to view sunsets on Cape Cod.

➡As you exit the harbor parking lot turn right and follow Rock Harbor Road in a southeasterly direction toward the center of Orleans.

➡Continue along Rock Harbor Road (which soon becomes Main Street) 1.1 miles to the traffic lights at the junction of Route 6A.

➡Turn right onto Route 6A, and follow it 0.3 miles back to the Higgins Tavern Site to complete this walk.●

In the Footsteps of Thoreau

What Thoreau Saw

Blackbirds & Crows

In 1667 the town [of Eastham] voted that every housekeeper should kill twelve blackbirds, or three crows, which did great damage to the corn; and this vote was repeated for many years. In 1695, an additional order was passed, namely, that "every unmarried man in the township shall kill six blackbirds, or three crows, while he remains single; as a penalty for not doing it, shall not be married until he obey this order." The blackbirds, however, still molest corn. I saw them at it the next summer, and there were many scare-crows, if not scare-blackbirds, in the fields, which I often mistook for men. From which I concluded, that either many men were not married, or many blackbirds were.

Map #25

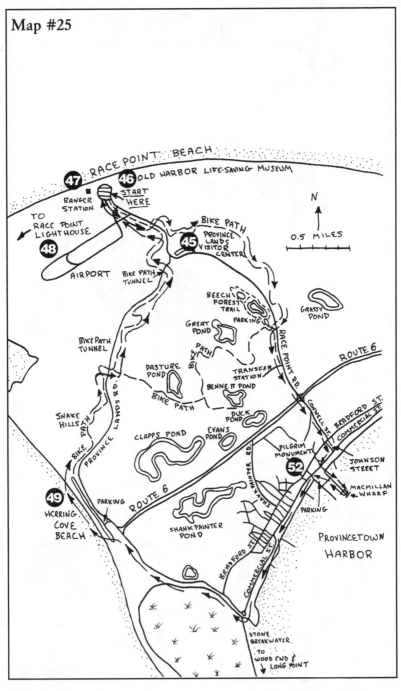

RACE POINT BEACH

47

46 OLD HARBOR LIFE-SAVING MUSEUM

START HERE

RANGER STATION

TO RACE POINT LIGHTHOUSE

48

AIRPORT

BIKE PATH TUNNEL

BIKE PATH

45 PROVINCE LANDS VISITOR CENTER

N

0.5 MILES

BEECH FOREST TRAIL

GRASSY POND

GREAT POND

PARKING

BIKE PATH

BIKE PATH TUNNEL

PASTURE POND

BIKE PATH

TRANSFER STATION

RACE POINT RD.

ROUTE 6

SNAKE HILLS

BIKE PATH

PROVINCE LANDS RD.

BENNETT POND

BIKE PATH

DUCK POND

EVANS POND

CLAPPS POND

CONNELL ST.

BRADFORD ST.

COMMERCIAL ST.

PILGRIM MONUMENT

JOHNSON STREET

52

MACMILLAN WHARF

49 HERRING COVE BEACH

PARKING

ROUTE 6

SHANK PAINTER POND

SHANK PAINTER RD.

PARKING

PROVINCETOWN HARBOR

BRADFORD ST.

COMMERCIAL ST.

STONE BREAKWATER

TO WOOD END & LONG POINT

In the Footsteps of Thoreau

Additional Hike #2

Race Point Beach to Provincetown Center

DISTANCE 9 miles
TIME 4.5 hours
RATING difficult

Location

Begin this walk at **Race Point Beach** on the north shore of Provincetown. Follow Route 6 to the Provincetown/Truro town line and proceed west 2.25 miles to the traffic lights. Turn right onto Race Point Road and follow it 2.3 miles past the **Province Lands Visitor Center** to the parking lot at Race Point Beach. A $7 daily fee or a $20 seasonal fee is charged for daytime summer parking at this and all **Cape Cod National Seashore** managed beaches.

Description

As noted elsewhere in this book, **The Great Thoreau Hike** officially ends at **Race Point Beach**. However, Thoreau actually did not finish his 1849 walk at Race Point Beach but continued on to the village of Provincetown. Furthermore, he spent an additional day hiking through the fantastic environment of the **Province Lands** before taking a steamship out of Provincetown and back to Boston at the end of his 1849 visit. This **Additional Hike #2** has been included here especially for those people who want to retrace Thoreau's route as accurately as possible, including his walk from the **Great Beach** to Provincetown village and his subsequent day's walk around the Province Lands.

The route follows the Province Lands Bike Path and runs along a number of scenic paved roads. It does not include any unpaved roads or footpaths. As such, it is perhaps most enjoyable during off-season months when bicycle and motor vehicle traffic is considerably lighter. Those people who are after a more traditional nature walk, with less paved roads and bike paths, may prefer to choose one of the other walks listed in this guide.

Still, bike paths and roads duly considered, this route can make for a truly fabulous hike, allowing walkers the opportunity to experience many of the most scenic aspects of Provincetown in a single jaunt. Wind-sculpted pine trees, tracts of wild cranberries and stretches of government-planted beach grass all greet walkers in the Province Lands to the north, while the unique streets and delightful harbor of Provincetown provide a perfect contrast to the south.

Interesting sites along the route include the **Race Point Ranger Station**, the **Old Harbor Life-Saving Station Museum** the **Province Lands Visitor Center**, **Herring Cove Beach**, Commercial Street and MacMillan Wharf. Furthermore, the hike connects with two much shorter walks included in this guide which walkers may want add to this route: the 1-mile **Beech Forest Trail** offers an enjoyable stroll through the only hardwood forest in the area; and the 1.3-mile **Provincetown Center Walk** passes by numerous historical sites, many of which were known to Thoreau.

Thoreau

By midday on Saturday, October 13, 1849, Thoreau had walked from **Highland Light** in North Truro to a "shrubby sand hill," **Mount Ararat**, near the Provincetown/Truro town line. He describes the rest of his route that day:

> As we did not wish to enter Provincetown before night, though it was cold and windy, we returned across the Deserts to the Atlantic side, and walked along the beach again nearly to Race Point, being still greedy of the sea influence. All the while it was not so calm as the reader may suppose, but it was blow, blow, blow—roar, roar, roar—tramp, tramp, tramp—without interruption. The shore now tended nearly east to west. Before sunset, having already seen the mackerel fleet returning into the Bay, we left the sea-shore on the north of Provincetown, and made our way across the Desert to the eastern extremity of the town.

Other than Race Point Road, the most reliable existing route from **Race Point Beach** to Provincetown is along the pleasant Province Lands Bike Path. This well-designed trail also winds and threads its way through the swamps and hills to the west of Race Point Road and out to **Herring Cove Beach**, a route that coincides nicely with the path Thoreau took on his second day of walking in Provincetown. He writes of his walk that day:

> The next morning, though it was still more cold and blustering than the day before, we took to the Deserts again, for we spent our days wholly out of doors, in the sun when there was any, and in the wind which never failed. After threading the shrubby hill country at the southwest end of the town, west of the Shank-Painter Swamp*, whose expressive name gave it importance in our eyes, we crossed the sands to the shore south of Race Point and three miles distant [Herring Cove Beach], and thence roamed round eastward through the desert to where we had left the sea the evening before [near Race Point Beach].

*A "shank-painter" is a chain or a rope that secures the shank of an anchor to the rail of a ship.

What Thoreau Saw

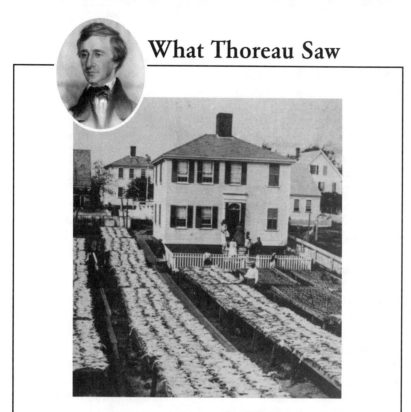

Provincetown Fish-flakes

A great many of the houses were surrounded by fish-flakes close up to the sills on all sides, with only a narrow passage two or three feet wide, to the front door; so that instead of looking out into a flower or grass plot, you looked on to so many square rods of cod turned wrong side outwards. These parterres were said to be least like a flower-garden in a good drying day in midsummer. There were flakes of every age and pattern, and some so rusty and overgrown with lichens that they looked as if they might have served the founders of the fishery here. Some had broken down under the weight of successive harvests. The principal employment of the inhabitants at this time seemed to be to trundle out their fish and spread them in the morning, and bring them in at night.

Photo courtesy of Provincetown Museum.

The Trail

Initial Route

➡️From the parking lot at **Race Point Beach** proceed south along the bike path past the Provincetown Municipal Airport.

➡️0.4 miles from the beach parking lot, there is a well-marked junction on the bike path. At this junction, turn left and follow the bike path across Race Point Road.

Words to Walk By

M̶y spirits infallibly rise in proportion to the outward dreariness. Give me the ocean, the desert, or the wilderness!

–Walking, 1862

NOTE: Be sure to follow the arrows on the sign pointing to the "Visitor Center 0.4 miles" and the "Beech Forest 1.8 miles."

➡️After crossing Race Point Road, follow the bike path 0.4 miles to the **Province Lands Visitor Center**. Operated by the **Cape Cod National Seashore**, the Visitor Center is equipped with public restrooms and telephones.

➡️From the Province Lands Visitor Center, continue south along the bike path 1.5 miles to the parking lot at Beech Forest. The **Beech Forest Trail** starts at this parking lot. (If you choose to follow the Beech Forest Trail, plan on adding 45 minutes to this walk.)

➡️After the bike path crosses the entrance to the Beech Forest parking lot, it comes to a t-junction. Turn left at this t-junction and continue south.

NOTE: Be sure to follow the arrow on the sign at the junction that points to "Route 6 & Provincetown."

➡️Continue south along the bike path 0.2 miles from Beech Forest to where it terminates near the entrance to the Provincetown Waste Transfer Station.

➡️From the entrance to the transfer station, continue south along Race Point Road 0.25 miles to the traffic lights at Route 6.

➡️Cross Route 6 and continue 0.4 miles south along Conwell Street to the t-junction with Bradford Street.

➡️Turn right onto Bradford Street and walk west a short distance to the next road on the left, Johnson Street.

➡️Turn left onto Johnson Street and follow it south 0.1 miles to the intersection with Commercial Street. Of the many roads that run north/south between Bradford Street and Commercial Street, Johnson Street boasts one of the prettiest views of Provincetown Harbor.

➡️From Johnson Street, turn right onto Commercial Street and follow it 0.1 miles to Standish Street, where a short walk to the left leads to Provincetown's waterfront. The long pier to the left is MacMillan Wharf, where you will find most of the town's fishing, sightseeing and whale-watch boats. Public restrooms are located adjacent to the bus stop at the north end of the town parking lot. (The town parking lot is also the starting point of the **Provincetown Center Walk,** described in this book. Just a few of the sites along are the walk are the **Pilgrim Monument & Provincetown Museum,** the Provincetown Heritage Museum, and the Expedition *Whydah* Sea Lab and Learning Center. If you choose to follow the Provincetown Center Walk, plan on adding 1.3 miles and 1-2 hours to this hike.)

Return Route

➔ From MacMillan Wharf, return to Commercial Street and follow it to the left (west). For most of its length Commercial Street is very straight and easy to follow; but after the first 0.5 miles toward the west end of town, it bends to the left, immediately after the Provincetown Coast Guard Station. When Commercial Street was originally laid out, this piece of property was owned by a particularly stubborn businessman who owned and operated a saltworks here. This man refused to negotiate with the town to allow them to run Commercial Street through his property. Thus, while its original designers had wanted Commercial Street to run straight along the shore, the bend here could not be avoided.[1]

➔ After following Commercial Street around the Provincetown Coast Guard Station, follow it 0.6 miles farther to the Provincetown Rotary, adjacent to the Provincetown Inn and the Provincetown breakwater. The stone breakwater here forms the western boundary of Provincetown Harbor and runs some 1.1 miles south, all the way to **Wood End.** Many people walk along the breakwater to visit the **Wood End Lighthouse,** and even continue from Wood End to **Long Point** and **Long Point Lighthouse;** however, high tides and bad weather can make the walk dangerous, so check a tide chart and weather report before venturing out.

➔ From the Provincetown Rotary, follow the road around to the right (north). After 0.25 miles you will come to the intersection of Province Lands Road and Bradford Street (Route 6A), at which point you should continue straight ahead to the north on Province Lands Road.

➔ 0.7 miles north of Bradford Street (Route 6A) you will come to the **Herring Cove Beach** parking lot. Walk across the parking lot to the beach and then follow the shore north to the other end of this very long parking lot on the left, where you will again meet up with the Province Lands Bike Path.

➔ Follow the Province Lands Bike Path 1.1 miles through the beautiful Snake Hills dune area, to the bike path tunnel that runs under Province Lands Road.

➔ Once you have passed through the tunnel, you will come to a fork in the bike path, at which point you should follow the signs that point to the left (north) to Race Point Beach.

➔ From this junction, follow the bike path 1.5 miles back to the Race Point Beach parking lot to complete this hike. Along the way, you will pass beneath Province Lands Road via another tunnel, and you will also pass the Provincetown Airport.●

Additional Hikes #1 & #2   177

What Thoreau Saw

Eastham Windmill

Being on elevated ground, and high in themselves, they [windmills] serve as landmarks—for there are no tall trees, or other objects commonly which can be seen at a distance in the horizon; though the outline of the land itself is so firm and distinct, that an insignificant cone, or even a precipice of sand is visible at a great distance from over the seas. Sailors making the land, commonly steer either by the wind-mills or the meetinghouses. In the country, we are obliged to steer by the meeting-houses alone. Yet, the meeting-house is a kind of windmill, which runs one day in seven, turned by the winds of heaven—where another sort of grist is ground, of which, if it be not all bran or musty, if it be not plaster, we trust to make bread of life.

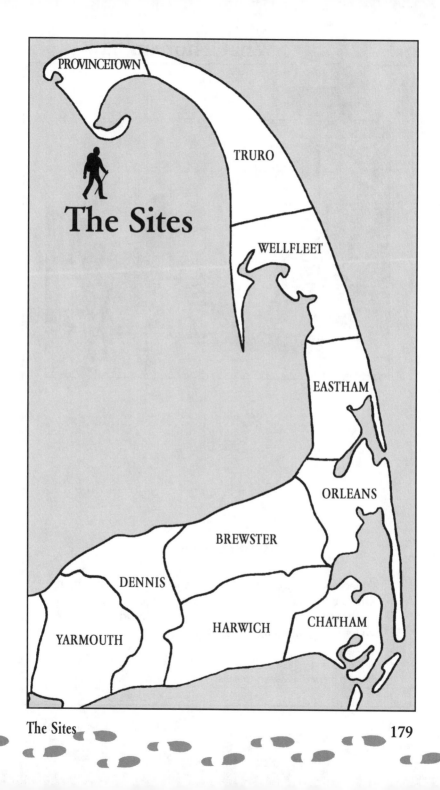

The Sites

What Thoreau Saw

Higgins Tavern

At length, we stopped for the night at Higgins's tavern, in Orleans, feeling very much as if we were on a sand-bar in the ocean, and not knowing whether we should see land or water ahead when the midst cleared away.

As indicated by the sign, this 19th-century photograph was taken in front of Higgins Tavern in Orleans. Photo courtesy of Jim Owens.

Introduction to the Sites

This section includes fifty-five historically interesting sites, the majority of which Thoreau visited and/or wrote about himself. Sites include such diverse objects as beaches, windmills, museums, lighthouses and sand dunes. They include relatively modern sites like the **Salt Pond Visitor Center**, which was constructed in 1965 by the **Cape Cod National Seashore**, and contrastingly older sites like **Doane Rock**, which was brought to its present location by the glaciers that originally formed Cape Cod during the last Ice Age. Furthermore, there are sites as diverse as **Pilgrim Spring** in North Truro, which consists of little more than a trickle of water coming out of the side of a hill; and the **Great Beach**, which stretches along some 40 miles of coastline across six different towns from Provincetown to Chatham.

Each individual site entry has been designed to stand independently from the rest of this book and includes the site's location, its relationship to Thoreau (if any), and a description of its history. By designing this section in this manner, it is hoped that the information about these sites will be easily accessible—not only to hikers, but to Cape Cod history buffs and readers of Thoreau in general.

Directions by car are provided primarily so that hikers can easily arrange to be picked up or dropped off at any site they choose. They have also been included for those who do not wish to hike to the sites, but who simply want to drive to them. Readers are encouraged to design their own driving tours of Thoreau's Cape Cod by picking out those sites that interest them and following the directions to their locations.●

#1
Higgins Tavern Site
(Map #24)

Location

The historic marker designating the **Higgins Tavern Site** stands in front of a Citgo Station on Route 6A in the center of Orleans, across from the Old Tavern Motel. From mid-Cape areas, follow Route 6 east to Exit 12. Turn right at the bottom of the off-ramp onto Route 6A and proceed east 0.6 miles, through one set of traffic lights, to where the marker is located on the left side of the road.

Thoreau

Thoreau writes in *Cape Cod*:

> At length, we stopped for the night at Higgins's tavern, in Orleans, feeling very much as if we were on a sand-bar in the ocean, and not knowing whether we should see land or water ahead when the mist cleared away.

After spending the night there, Thoreau spoke with various people at Higgins Tavern before setting out with his walking partner, poet William Ellery Channing, Jr., on their legendary walk to Provincetown:

> The next morning, Thursday, October 11th, it rained as hard as ever; but we were determined to proceed on foot, nevertheless. We first made some inquiries with regard to the practicability of walking up the shore on the Atlantic side to Provincetown, whether we should meet with any creeks or marshes to trouble us. Higgins said that there was no obstruction, and that it was not much further than by the road, but he thought that we should find it very "heavy" walking in the sand: it was bad enough in the road, a horse would sink in up to the fetlocks there. But there was one man at the tavern who had walked it, and he said that we could go very well, though it was sometimes inconvenient and even dangerous walking under the bank, when there was a great tide, with an easterly wind, which caused the sand to cave.

A century and a half after Thoreau's walk, cave-ins along the **Great Beach** can still sometimes be a danger. (See **Safe Walking.**)

The Site

Dating from 1829, **Higgins Tavern** was used as a stagecoach stop and postal relay station with coaches arriving three times per week from Sandwich and Yarmouth. Simeon Higgins was the owner and proprietor of the tavern in Thoreau's day and drove the stage between Yarmouth and Orleans. In fact, Higgins may have driven the stage that Thoreau took. By 1858, Higgins added a second building to his property which he ran as a store. At some point the tavern went out of business, and parts of the structure were moved to different sites in town and served various needs until the last identifiable portion of the building were finally burned down.●

#2
Jonathan Young Windmill
(Map #24)

Location

The **Jonathan Young Windmill** stands on the banks of Town Cove, not far from the Orleans/Eastham town line. From the Orleans Rotary proceed 0.3 miles south on Route 28, through the first set of traffic lights, to where the windmill is located on the left side of the road, along the banks of Town Cove.

Thoreau

Thoreau's route from Higgins Tavern along the **Old Kings Highway** in Orleans brought him directly past the **Jonathan Young Windmill**. The windmill was not at her present location at that time, however, but was perched on the nearby hill where the Governor Prence Motor Inn currently stands, on Route 6A across from the Orleans Christmas Tree Shop. Thoreau observed:

> The windmills on the hills—large weather-stained octagonal structures— and the salt-works scattered all along the shore with their long rows of vats resting on piles driven into the marsh, their low, turtle-like roofs, and their slighter wind-mills—were novel and interesting objects to an inlander.

This passage may well have been inspired by the Jonathan Young Windmill, as the hill she was on would have afforded a fine view of the many saltworks that were then located below her along the shores of Town Cove. Thoreau probably spoke with either the miller of the Jonathan Young Windmill or the miller of **Eastham Windmill**, for he writes in his narrative—after leaving Higgins Tavern and before passing by the **Old Eastham Town Center**—that he spoke with "a miller who was sharpening his stones."

The Site

Windmills probably struck Thoreau as "novel" because they were far more popular on Cape Cod than in Thoreau's home town of Concord or elsewhere in New England. In fact, only a few parts of Long Island and Rhode Island had nearly as many. Windmills were particularly common on Cape Cod because of the breezy climate and because of the lack of rivers and streams needed to generate power for water-driven mills. Although they were significantly harder to build and operate than water mills—and more dangerous and less reliable to run—windmills were still a far more practical alternative to carting all of a town's grain to another town for grinding.

The **Jonathan Young Windmill** was built in the early 1700's in South Orleans and was moved in 1839 to the hill now occupied by the Governor Prence Motor Inn. In 1897, she was moved again to Hyannis Port where she remained for almost a century until 1983 when she was donated to the Orleans Historical Society. After two years of refurbishing, she was finally reestablished in Orleans at what is now Town Cove Park. The mill has special historic significance because of the assortment of early machinery still intact within her structure.●

#3
Jeremiah's Gutter

(Map #24)

Location

Jeremiah's Gutter was the name of a small creek that formerly connected Town Cove and Boat Meadow River in Eastham. It was located in the general area of the Eastham/Orleans town line near the Orleans Rotary. The best remaining evidence of Jeremiah's Gutter is the cattail grass and other marsh plants that can be seen growing in the wetlands to the west of Route 6, across from Town Cove, and even in the center of the rotary itself.

Thoreau

Thoreau mentions passing **Jeremiah's Gutter** in *Cape Cod*:

> We crossed a brook, not more than fourteen rods* long, between Orleans and Eastham, called Jeremiah's Gutter. The Atlantic is said sometimes to meet the Bay here, and isolate the northern part of the Cape. The streams of the Cape are necessarily formed on a minute scale, since there is no room for them to run, without tumbling immediately into the sea, and beside, we found it difficult to run ourselves in the sand, when there was no want of room. Hence the least channel where water runs or may run, is important, and is dignified with a name.

* One rod equals 5.5 yards.

In a journal entry regarding his 1857 Cape Cod visit he adds:

Jeremiah's Gutter is what is called Boat Meadow River on the map. I saw the town bounds there. There too was somebody's Folly, who dug a canal, which the sand filled up again.

Although Thoreau initially describes Jeremiah's Gutter as an independent waterway, and later states it was another name for Boat Meadow River, it was actually an extension of Boat Meadow River that only filled up during high tides and was thus given a different name.

The Site

The historic former junction of the Atlantic with Cape Cod Bay at **Jeremiah's Gutter** is significant, not only because it was an early precursor to the Cape Cod Canal, but because its presence meant that the lands of today's Eastham, Wellfleet, Truro and Provincetown were technically once a tidal island.

This area is also the approximate meeting place of the two glacial lobes which formed today's Cape Cod during the last Ice Age—the Cape Cod Bay Lobe and the South Channel Lobe. Thus, many residents of the towns north of the Orleans Rotary claim that their communities are unique from the rest of the Cape, and there is some geological precedent for this view.

Although its presence is a little-known fact today, the historic record of boat travel through Jeremiah's Gutter is long indeed. Bartholomew Gosnold, who gave Cape Cod its name in 1602, actually referred to the lower Cape as an island. And in 1717, Captain Cyprian Southack made his way from Cape Cod Bay to the Atlantic via Jeremiah's Gutter, en route to claiming the remains of the wrecked pirate ship *Whydah*.

Jeremiah's Gutter was filled in during a great storm in 1770 but was reopened in 1804 when the Eastham-Orleans Canal Company dug what could be called the first "Cape Cod Canal" at this location. The company charged vessels ten cents per ton for passage through the canal, but only managed to stay afloat financially itself until 1817, when both it and Jeremiah's Gutter vanished from the record books.●

#4
Fort Hill Area
(Map #6, #8 & #24)

Location

The **Fort Hill Area** is situated along the banks of **Nauset Marsh** in Eastham and is administered by the **Cape Cod National Seashore**. From the Orleans Rotary proceed 1.3 miles north on Route 6 and turn right onto Governor Prence Road. Continue 0.25 miles to the small intersection with Fort Hill Road. Turn right, and proceed 0.2 miles (past the **Penniman House**) to the Fort Hill overlook parking lot. Additional parking is located across from the Penniman House.

Thoreau

In his chapter "The Plains of Nauset," Thoreau writes of one of Fort Hill's earliest colonial owners, the Reverend Samuel Treat (1648-1717), who was famous for his fire-and-brimstone sermons:

> "The effects of [Treat's] preaching," it is said, "was that his hearers were several times, in the course of his ministry, awakened and alarmed;" and on one occasion a comparatively innocent young man was frightened nearly out of his wits, and Mr. Treat had to exert himself to make hell seem somewhat cooler to him.

One of Treat's original property markers, a stone with a "T" engraved on it, sat along the **Fort Hill Trail** until recent years when it was removed by **Cape Cod National Seashore** personnel to avoid vandalism.

The Site

The **Fort Hill Area** is believed to have been farmed by Native Americans for thousands of years previous to European settlement. Thus, **Cape Cod National Seashore** authorities keep the Fort Hill pastures clear in recognition of the area's long agricultural heritage.

Fort Hill itself, on which the area's overlook parking lot is located, probably received its name from a 1653 order from Plymouth that stated, "Betwixt this present day and the first Tuesday in October next; The townsmen of every town within this government shall make and fully finish a place or places for defense of theire towne. . . a brest worke with flankers." The order came in response to a short-lived Dutch/English colonial conflict, and it is presumed that plans were subsequently made in Eastham to build a fort at this location. Although there is no record of such a fort having been built here, the location nevertheless became known as Fort Hill.

When the first settlers moved to Eastham from Plymouth in 1644, the area was deeded to its leader, Governor Prence, who (records indicate) may have built a home near the present location of the Eastham Chamber of Commerce Information Booth, on the corner of Route 6 and Governor Prence Road. After Governor Prence, the area was acquired by Reverend Treat. When Treat died, his widow sold it to the Knowles family who possessed it for more than two centuries. The large privately-owned house located between the **Penniman House** and the overlook parking lot was built by a member of that family, as was the house directly across the road from the Penniman House. Prior to the conception of the Cape Cod National Seashore in 1961, the entire area had been subdivided and slated for development. If not for the formation of the Park, it would almost certainly be a private neighborhood today.

Following the **Fort Hill & Red Maple Swamp Trail**, as described in this guide, is a great way to see the Fort Hill Area. The route features many spectacular views of **Nauset Marsh** as well as a tour through the swamp. The trail also passes by one of the most famous captain's homes on Cape Cod, the Penniman House, and leads to Skiff Hill where there is a boulder on which Nauset Indians once sharpened tools and weapons.●

#5
Penniman House
(Map #6 & #24)

Location
The **Penniman House** is located near **Nauset Marsh** in the **Fort Hill Area** of Eastham within the boundaries of the **Cape Cod National Seashore**. From the Orleans Rotary proceed north 1.3 miles on Route 6 and turn right onto Governor Prence Road. Continue 0.25 miles to the small intersection. Turn right, and proceed 0.1 miles to the parking area on the left. The Penniman House is located directly across the road from this parking area.

Thoreau
In 1849, Thoreau walked near the site of today's **Penniman House** property, as the road he followed ran adjacent to it. Thoreau did not see the present Penniman House, however, as it was not built until 1868.

At the time of Thoreau's visit, Edward Penniman (the future builder of the Penniman House) was an 18-year-old local fisherman. His future bride (Betsey Augusta Knowles) was his twelve-year-old "girl-next-door," as both their parents had homes in the area presently known as Fort Hill.

Serving as a cook on a Grand Banks fishing schooner beginning at the age of just 11 (and subsequently surviving the wreck of that ship!), Edward Penniman made numerous whaling voyages around the world in his lifetime. All told, he spent a full 22 years at sea, nine of them in the company of his wife. Although Thoreau probably did not meet the Pennimans, he certainly wrote of bold, seagoing Cape Codders like them when he observed:

> A great proportion of the inhabitants of the Cape are always thus abroad about there teaming on some ocean highway or other, and the history of their ordinary trips would cast the Argonautic expedition into the shade. I have just heard of a Cape Cod captain who was expected home in the beginning of the winter from the West Indies, but was long since given up for lost, till his relations at length have heard with joy, that, after getting within forty miles of Cape Cod light, he was driven back by nine successive gales to Key West, between florida and Cuba, and was once again shaping his course for home. Thus he spent his winter. In ancient times the adventures of these two or three men and boys would have been made the basis of a myth, but now such tales are crowded into a line of short-hand signs, like an algebraic formula in the shipping news.

The Site
Thoreau also writes of Cape Codders like the Pennimans:

> They seemed, like mariners ashore to have sat right down to enjoy the firmness of the land.... Everything told of the sea, even when we did not see its waste or hear its roar. For birds there were gulls, and for carts in the fields, boats turned bottom upward against the houses, and some times the rib of a whale was woven into the fence by the road side.

"The rib of a whale" Thoreau mentions pales in comparison with the massive whale jawbones fitted into the Penniman fence to form a grand arched gateway. Although the house sits close to **Nauset Marsh** and is a full 2 miles from the bay, the deforested state of the Cape in the late 1860's provided its upper windows with views of both shores. Originally lit by kerosene lamps, it was equipped with stained-glass windows, a marble sink, fine woodworking, and an excellent heating system. What's more, the **Penniman House** boasted the first flush toilet in Eastham.

The **Cape Cod National Seashore** offers tours of the house periodically. Stop by or call the **Salt Pond Visitor Center** at (508) 255-3421 or **Park Headquarters** at (508) 349-3785 for further information.●

#6
Nauset Marsh
(Map #6, #8 & #16)

Location

Nauset Marsh, also known as Nauset Harbor, is a large tidal inlet of the Atlantic Ocean and is located within the eastern boundaries of Eastham and Orleans.

The Site

Nauset Marsh is an excellent example of the saltwater marsh ecosystem. Strongly affected by the continuous motion of the tides, it is a fertile breeding ground for multitudinous forms of life.

As such, many local people depend on the marsh for their livelihoods, including lobstermen and fishermen who use it as a port, shellfishermen who harvest its clams and other mollusks, tour guides and even some sports fishing guides. It is also a favored birding location, with an eclectic variety of species stopping at the marsh during their seasonal migrations.

Previous to European settlement, Nauset Marsh was the site of a large Nauset Indian settlement and was the location of early encounters between Europeans and Native Americans. Samuel de Champlain (1567-1635) was the first European explorer to make a detailed map of the marsh. He served as the cartographer for the French explorer Sieur de Monts and first dropped anchor in Nauset Harbor on July 20, 1605:

> We found a very dangerous harbor in consequence of the shoals and banks, where we saw breakers in all directions. It was almost low tide when we entered, and there were only four feet of water in the northern passage; at high tide, there are two fathoms. After we had entered, we found the place very spacious, being perhaps three or four leagues in circuit, entirely surrounded by little houses around each one of which there was as much land as the occupant needed for his support.... It would be a very fine place, if the harbor were good.

A seldom-told part of the history of Nauset Marsh is that it is the site of one of the earliest clashes between Native Americans and Europeans. In the passage below Champlain gives his people's side of the story, including the death of a French carpenter named Malouin:

> On the 23rd of July, four or five seamen having gone on shore with some kettles to get fresh water, which was to be found in one of the sand-banks a short distance from our barque, some of the savages, coveting them, watched the time when our men went to the spring, and then seized one

 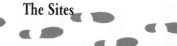

out of the hands of a sailor, who was the first to dip, and who had no weapons. One of his companions, starting to run after him, soon returned, as he could not catch him, since he ran much faster than himself. The other savages, of whom there were a large number, seeing our sailors running to our barque, and at the same time shouting to us to fire at them, took to flight. At the time there were some of them in our barque who threw themselves into the sea, only one of whom we were able to seize. Those on the land who had taken to flight, seeing them swimming, returned straight to the sailor from whom they had taken away the kettle, hurled several arrows at him from behind, and brought him down. Seeing this, they ran at once to him, and despatched him with their knives. Meanwhile, haste was made to go on shore, and muskets were fired from our barque: mine, bursting in my hands, came near to killing me. The savages, hearing the discharge of fire-arms, took to flight, and with redoubled speed when they saw that we had landed, for they were afraid when they saw us running after them. There was no likelihood of our catching them, for they are as swift as horses. We brought in the murdered man, and he was buried some hours later.

Since Champlain's time, the marsh has remained an important historical location. Nauset Spit, the barrier beach that separates the marsh from the Atlantic on the east, was the former site of nature writer Henry Beston's house, where he wrote *The Outermost House*. The marsh is also the centerpiece of Wyman Richardson's book, *The House on Nauset Marsh*. Deacon John Doane and Captain Edward Penniman, two of Eastham's most famous historical figures, also made their homes along the marsh's banks (see **Doane Homestead Memorial** and the **Penniman House**). Furthermore, the **Cape Cod National Seashore** built its southernmost welcoming center, the **Salt Pond Visitor Center**, on the shore of one of the marsh's inlets, Salt Pond.

Nauset Marsh boat tours are available through a number of organizations, including the Cape Cod Museum of Natural History which can be reached at (508) 896-3867, and Seashore Park Tours which can be reached at (508) 385-3244.●

#7
Eastham Windmill

(Map #24)

Location
The **Eastham Windmill** is located 2.5 miles north of the Orleans Rotary on the left side of Route 6, directly across from the Eastham Town Hall on the corner of Samoset Road.

Thoreau

The **Eastham Windmill** was privately owned and operated when Thoreau visited the area and observed:

> The most foreign and picturesque structures on the Cape to an inlander, not excepting the salt-works, are the windmills—gray looking octagonal towers with long timbers slanting to the ground in the rear, and there resting on a cartwheel, by which their fans are turned round to face the wind. The neighbors, who assemble to turn the mill to the wind, are likely to know which way it blows, without a weathercock. They looked loose and slightly locomotive, like huge wounded birds, trailing a wing or leg...

Thoreau followed the **Old Kings Highway** directly past Eastham Windmill, and probably spoke with its miller or the miller of the **Jonathan Young Windmill** in Orleans.

The Site

Eastham Windmill is the oldest windmill on Cape Cod, as well as the oldest building in Eastham. Built in Plymouth in 1680, she was ferried to Truro in 1770 and then relocated to Eastham in 1793, close to the present site of the **Salt Pond Visitor Center**. In 1808 she was moved to her current location in Windmill Park. Shut down around the turn of the century for lack of business, the mill was purchased by the Village Improvement Society for Preservation in 1920 and then sold to the town in 1928.

Although Thoreau speaks of "long timbers slanting down to the ground in the rear" of the windmills he saw, Eastham Windmill does not currently have such a "tailpole." Jim Owens, Eastham's current miller who operates the mill for the town, explains that in the 1850's (at about the time of Thoreau's visits) mechanical alterations were made to Eastham Windmill that probably included the removal of her tailpole. At that time, the mill's large main shaft was replaced; and it is Owens' theory that due to the scarcity and high price of lumber on Cape Cod, the former miller decided to remove the tailpole and use it instead for a new shaft. According to Owens, from then on, without the use of a tailpole to push and turn the cap, the miller probably rigged a harness to the cap and had a horse move it.

Visitors may also notice the stone watering trough in the center of Windmill Park with the inscription, "Blessed Are the Merciful." This trough once sat beneath the town water pump located in the **Old Eastham Town Center**.

Eastham Windmill is open daily from July 1 through Labor Day. Hours are Monday through Saturday 10 a.m. to 4 p.m. and Sunday 1 p.m. to 4 p.m. Call the Eastham Town Hall at (508) 240-5900 for further information.●

#8
Old Eastham Town Center
(Map #24)

Location

From the Orleans Rotary follow Route 6 north 3 miles to the traffic lights at the intersection of Route 6 and Nauset Road (to the right) and Salt Pond Road (to the left). Turn left onto Salt Pond Road and proceed 0.1 miles to the tiny triangular green that represents the **Old Eastham's Town Center**.

Thoreau

Thoreau passed the **Old Eastham Town Center** just before he "got to Eastham meeting-house" and "left the road and struck across the country for the eastern shore, at Nauset Lights."

The Site

The triangular green surrounded by a split-rail fence at the intersection of Salt Pond Road and Locust Road was once the location of Eastham's communal water pump, and is generally considered to be the location of the **Old Eastham Town Center**. Many of the houses around the green date from long before Thoreau's visits, and make it easy to imagine what that part of Eastham was once like. The stone trough that once sat beneath the pump is now located at Windmill Park in front of the **Eastham Windmill**.

At the intersection of Salt Pond Road and Route 6 stands a private residence that once served as Eastham's first Town Hall. This plain-looking building was constructed in 1851 and played an important part in town affairs until 1912, when the present Eastham Town Hall was built. Although Thoreau probably saw Eastham's first Town Hall on his last two visits to Cape Cod in 1855 and 1857, it had not yet been built at the time of his initial 1849 Cape Cod walk. That "meeting-house," referred to by Thoreau in *Cape Cod*, was actually a Congregational Church located just up the road to the north, at the Congregational and Soldiers Cemetery on the corner of Route 6 and Kingsbury Beach Road.●

#9
Eastham Schoolhouse Museum
(Map #24)

Location
The **Eastham Schoolhouse Museum** is located across Nauset Road from the **Salt Pond Visitor Center**. From the Orleans Rotary, follow Route 6 north 3 miles. Turn right onto Nauset Road, and the Schoolhouse Museum is the first building on the left.

The Site
The **Eastham Schoolhouse Museum** houses the town's Historical Society collection of mementos from various periods of Eastham's past. Exhibits include artifacts from the Nauset Indians and the town's original Pilgrim settlers, as well as farming and maritime implements and relics from the Schoolhouse itself.

Built in 1869, the Schoolhouse was abandoned in 1936. It stood unused for many years until the Eastham Historical Society purchased it in 1963 and converted it into a museum. The museum is open 1 p.m. to 4 p.m. during July and August only.

The 13-foot whale jawbone on display in the yard is from a finback whale estimated to have been 65-feet-long.●

#10
Salt Pond Visitor Center
(Map #7, #16 & #24)

Location
The **Salt Pond Visitor Center** is located in Eastham, on the corner of Route 6 and Nauset Road. From the Orleans Rotary follow Route 6 north 3 miles to the traffic lights at the intersection with Nauset Road, which is marked by a sign to the **Cape Cod National Seashore**. Turn right, and the entrance to the Visitor Center parking lot is immediately on the right.

The Site
The **Salt Pond Visitor Center** is the first **Cape Cod National Seashore** facility to be encountered by most visitors to the Park. Upon entering the Center one is immediately greeted with a familiar Cape Cod quote from Thoreau:

There I found it all out of doors, huge and real, Cape Cod! as it can not be represented on a map, color it as you will.

Emphasizing Thoreau's observation, a three-dimensional map of Cape Cod is juxtaposed with the Center's breathtaking view of Salt Pond, Salt Pond Creek and **Nauset Marsh**.

Opened to the public in 1965, the Center is one of the Cape Cod National Seashore's finest resources. It boasts an excellent museum, a small movie theater, a book and gift store, and an amphitheater. You will also find public telephones and restrooms here, along with a thorough schedule of Park Ranger-lead activities and a number of free maps and informational booklets.

The Center museum presents an eclectic collection of Cape Cod items, from natural history exhibits to historic photographs, from early agricultural and maritime tools to detailed pieces of scrimshaw. The movie theater at the Center presents a free ongoing rotation of short educational films, most about 15 minutes in length. In fact, they even have one film featuring Thoreau's *Cape Cod*. And of course, the Center is where you will find one of the most useful resources of all, Park Rangers. The Salt Pond Visitor Center is also the starting point of two walks in this guide: the **Buttonbush Trail** and **The Great Thoreau Hike, Part 1**.

Current Center hours are 9 a.m. to 4:30 p.m. seven days a week, except in July and August when it is open from 9 a.m. to 6 p.m.; and during the period from New Year's Day to President's Day when it is open only on weekends. Call the Center at (508) 255-3421 or the **Park Headquarters** at (508) 349-3785 for further information.●

#11
"The House On Nauset Marsh"
& Cedar Banks Golf Course
(Map #16)

Location

The old farmhouse that Wyman Richardson (1890-1948) writes about in his inspirational book, *The House on Nauset Marsh*, is located just to the west of the "Nauset Marsh Overlook" along the route of **The Great Thoreau Hike, Part I**, as described in this book. From the benches at the overlook, face directly away from the marsh and look up over the hill to where the 200-year-old farmhouse, a private residence, sits a few hundred yards back. Cedar Banks was the name of the 18-hole golf course that was once located on the land around Salt Pond in Eastham. It stretched along the banks of **Nauset Marsh**, between Nauset Road and Route 6.

The Site

Similar to Henry Beston's *The Outermost House*, Wyman Richardson's *The House on Nauset Marsh* builds on many of the themes established in Thoreau's *Cape Cod*. These include keen observations of the natural world and an admiration for the creatures which inhabit the area, as well as an awareness of the wildness of the ocean.

The House on Nauset Marsh originally appeared as a series of essays in the *Atlantic* magazine and was first published in book form in 1947. In the passage below, it is easy to imagine Richardson speaking to someone hiking past his house on the way to the **Great Beach**:

> From the Farm House we can look over the hill and across the Nauset Marsh to the dunes, and beyond them, where they are low or have become hollowed out, to the sea. Sometimes its color is bright blue, sometimes green, sometimes gray. Not infrequently a fog bank, lying offshore like a huge rolled-up carpet, will suddenly begin to unroll itself and to blot out sea and dunes alike. However, really to get the feel of the sea, to know its whims and caprices, its gentleness and its fury, you have to be right there, in it or by it.[1]

Today it is no small wonder to walk along the scenic trails near "The House on Nauset Marsh" and imagine that just 50 years ago there was a nearly treeless series of fairways there. Cedar Banks was built in 1928 by Quincy Adams Shaw, a wealthy Eastham summer resident, and was later hailed by *The Boston Transcript* newspaper as "one of the world's most beautiful golf courses." One of the more interesting aspects of the course was that a skiff attached to a rope and pulley was used by players to cross Salt Pond Creek, to get from the 11th-hole tee to the 11th-hole green.

The Richardsons, owners of "The House on Nauset Marsh" originally gave Shaw permission to use some of their land as part of Cedar Banks Golf Course; and their house was, for a time, within its boundaries. In the late 1930's, however, the Richardsons built a second house on their property, necessitating Cedar Banks to be scaled down from 18 holes to just nine. Today one can still spot the remnants of greens and fairways here and there among the cedar trees that abound at the site. The course remained in use from April to October each year until about 1950.●

#12
Doane Homestead Memorial
(Map #12)

Location

The **Doane Homestead Memorial** is located within the **Cape Cod National Seashore** on the banks of **Nauset Marsh** in Eastham. From the Orleans Rotary follow Route 6 north 3 miles to the second set of traffic lights. Turn right onto Nauset Road, which is marked with a sign for the Park. After 0.7 miles Nauset Road bears off to the left and Doane Road continues straight ahead. Proceed straight ahead onto Doane Road, and 1.1 miles from Route 6 you will come to the **Doane Rock** Picnic Area on the right. From the picnic area, the memorial is just a few hundred feet to the south, down the Doane Area Road that runs from the end of the parking lot.

Thoreau

Thoreau writes of the early church leaders of Eastham in *Cape Cod*, including Deacon John Doane whose property markers he apparently saw on his walk between today's **Salt Pond Visitor Center** and **Nauset Light Beach**:

> One of the first settlers of Eastham was Deacon John Doane, who died in 1707, aged one hundred and ten. Tradition says that he was rocked in a cradle several of his last years. That, certainly, was not an Achillean life. His mother must have let him slip when she dipped him into the liquor which was to make him invulnerable, and he went in, heels and all. Some of the stone bounds to his farm, which he set up, are standing to-day, with his initials cut into them.

The Site

The Doane Homestead site is marked by a pair of inscribed stones, both placed by Doane family descendants. However, it should be noted that there is some doubt about the accuracy of the claim on the markers that Doane arrived in Eastham as early as 1644; and there is also some controversy as to whether he lived to the age of 110, or to 96. What is indisputable, however, is that Doane played an important role in early American colonial life. He became a Deacon at the age of 44, was an assistant to the governor in Plymouth, served as a town Selectman until he was almost 84 and was a very successful business person throughout his life.

As for his personality, it appears that Doane could be rather tenacious. In 1636, for instance, he successfully sued a widow—one Ellen Billington—for slander and forced her to pay him five pounds, serve time in the stocks, and to be whipped! Doane had at least four children, and his many descendants include Gustavus C. Doane who played a key role in the formation of the country's first National Park, Yellowstone, in 1872.[2]●

#13
Doane Rock

(Map #16)

Location

Doane Rock is located within the **Cape Cod National Seashore** off Doane Road in Eastham. From the Orleans Rotary follow Route 6 north 3 miles to the second set of traffic lights. Turn right onto Nauset Road. After 0.7 miles Nauset Road bears off to the left and Doane Road continues straight ahead. Proceed straight ahead onto Doane Road, and 1.1 miles from Route 6 is the Doane Rock Picnic Area on the right.

Thoreau

Thoreau's observations of Cape Cod are so thorough that it sometimes seems as though he did not leave a single stone unturned. This, of course, includes **Doane Rock**, the largest above-ground boulder on the Cape. The following passage indicates that Thoreau, while he did not visit this rock, did not miss hearing about it.

> Stones are very rare on the Cape. I saw a very few small stones used for pavements and for bank walls, in one or two places in my walk, but they are so scarce, that, as I was informed, vessels have been forbidden to take them from the beach for ballast, and therefore, their crews used to land at night and steal them. I did not hear of a rod of regular stone wall below Orleans. Yet I saw one man underpinning a new house in Eastham with some "rocks," as he called them, which he said a neighbor had collected with great pains in the course of years, and finally made over to him. This I thought was a gift worthy of being recorded—equal to a transfer of California "rocks," almost. Another man who was assisting him, and who seemed to be a close observer of nature, hinted to me the locality of a rock in that neighborhood which was "forty-two paces in circumference and fifteen feet high," for he saw that I was a stranger, and, probably would not carry it off.

Doane Rock is, in fact, 18 feet high and 54 feet long.

The Site

As explained by informative plaques near **Doane Rock**, the crystallized volcanic material that composes it is very different from the bedrock underlying Cape Cod and is evidence that it was brought to its present site by glaciers.

The Wisconsin stage of the last Ice Age brought down from the north glacial ice sheets as much as two miles thick in places. Through the movement of these glaciers, great quantities of earth, known as "glacial till" were transferred from northern lands to present-day Cape Cod. Among the "till" were glacier erratics like Doane Rock. These boulders are commonly found on Cape Cod, especially along the margins of bodies of water where they are exposed by the elements.

Doane Rock is named after Deacon John Doane and his descendants who have inhabited the area since the 17th century. (See **Doane Homestead Memorial**.) The rock is also known as "Enoch's Rock," because of Enoch Doane who, it is said, played on it frequently as a child.●

#14
Eastham Coast Guard Station
(Map #8 & #16)

Location
The **Eastham Coast Guard Station**, now an environmental education center, is located just above **Coast Guard Beach** on the eastern shore of Eastham. From the Orleans Rotary, follow Route 6 north 3 miles to the second set of traffic lights. Turn right onto Nauset Road. After 0.7 miles Nauset Road bears off to the left and Doane Road continues straight ahead. Proceed straight ahead onto Doane Road, and 1.7 miles from Route 6 you will arrive at a junction. Turn right and continue 0.2 miles to the Coast Guard Beach parking lot. A $7 daily fee or a $20 seasonal fee is charged for daytime summer parking at this and all other **Cape Cod National Seashore** managed beaches. However, the small parking lot here is often filled in summer, at which times visitors are required to park at the Little Creek Staging Area and to use the beach shuttle that runs between the lot and the station. The staging area is located 0.6 miles back up Doane Road on the right.

The Site
The **Eastham Coast Guard Station** is one of the best-known Cape Cod landmarks. It is visible from most of the shore of **Nauset Marsh**, and it boasts expansive views of the marsh and **Coast Guard Beach**. Built by the Coast Guard in 1937, it was decommissioned in 1958 but is nevertheless still referred to by many as "Eastham Coast Guard Station." For a short time after it was decommissioned, the station served as the administrative

headquarters of the **Cape Cod National Seashore**. But after the current Park Headquarters was established in South Wellfleet, the building became part of the National Environmental Educational Development (NEED) Program.

Although Eastham Coast Guard Station is relatively new, historically speaking, the tradition of maritime safety resources at this site is extensive. By 1802, the Massachusetts Humane Society had established a **Humane House** at the beach.[3] The Society built such Humane Houses at various places along the Cape's eastern shore as emergency shelters for shipwreck survivors. (See **Cahoon Hollow Beach**.) The site was then upgraded in the 1850's when surf-boats, line-throwing guns and other lifesaving equipment were placed at Coast Guard Beach.[4] These "life-boat stations" remained unmanned, but the equipment was kept ready for the use of local volunteers.

The next change at Coast Guard Beach occurred in 1872, when Congress authorized the construction of nine U.S. Life-Saving Stations along the Cape's shore. (See **Old Harbor Life-Saving Station Museum** for more information about the Life-Saving Service.) The lifesavers at the Eastham Station received particular praise from Henry Beston in his classic 1928 book, *The Outermost House.*

The Eastham Life-Saving Station remained in use until 1937 when it was endangered by erosion. By that time the U.S. Life-Saving Service had been replaced by the U.S. Coast Guard, and the present Coast Guard Station was constructed.

Thus, for two centuries this site has witnessed the evolution of marine lifesaving outposts from simple Humane Houses, followed by unmanned lifeboat stations, to the U.S. Life-Saving Service and finally to the modern U.S. Coast Guard. In fact, the 1958 decommissioning of Eastham Coast Guard Station, and the subsequent ending of the site's use as a marine safety resource, can be said to represent recent movements within the Coast Guard toward centralization.

The small building to the north of Eastham Coast Guard Station was formerly the station's boathouse. Today it houses public restrooms and showers, with summer staff quarters on its second floor.●

#15
Coast Guard Beach
(Map #8 & #16)

Location

Coast Guard Beach is located on the eastern shore of Eastham, 1.1 miles south of **Nauset Light Beach** and about 2 miles north of the mouth of Nauset Harbor. From the Orleans Rotary, follow Route 6 north 3 miles to the second set of traffic lights. Turn right onto Nauset Road. After 0.7 miles Nauset Road bears off to the left and Doane Road continues straight ahead. Proceed straight ahead onto Doane Road, and 1.7 miles from Route 6 you will arrive at a junction. Turn right and continue 0.2 miles to the beach parking lot. A $7 daily fee or a $20 seasonal fee is charged for daytime summer parking at this and all **Cape Cod National Seashore** managed beaches. However, the small parking lot here is often filled in summer, at which times visitors are often required to park at the Little Creek Staging Area and to use the beach shuttle that runs between it and the station. The staging area is located 0.6 miles back up Doane Road on the right.

Thoreau

Coast Guard Beach is best known for good surfing conditions, fishing, sunbathing, and for the **Eastham Coast Guard Station,** which is located on the hill just above it. However, the beach is also the site of an important archeological find which recently provided valuable information regarding the long history of the area's occupation by Native Americans. Despite the fact that during his lifetime many of his fellow citizens were actively involved in campaigns against Native Americans, Thoreau always had a keen interest in and sympathy for them. In *Cape Cod*, he recognizes their exploitation with his famous anecdote, "Not Any":

> When the committee from Plymouth had purchased the territory of Eastham of the Indians, "it was demanded who laid claim to Billingsgate?" which was understood to be all that part of the Cape north of what they had purchased. "The answer was, there was not any who owned it. 'Then,' said the committee, 'that land is ours.' The Indians answered, that it was." This was a remarkable assertion and admission. The Pilgrims appear to have regarded themselves as Not Any's representatives. Perhaps this was the first instance of that quiet way of "speaking for" a place not yet occupied, or at least not improved as much as it may be, which their descendants have practiced, and are still practicing so extensively. Not Any seems to have been the sole proprietor of all America before the Yankees. But history says, that when the Pilgrims had held the lands of Billingsgate many years, at length

"appeared an Indian, who styled himself Lieutenant Anthony," who laid claim to them and of him they bought them. Who knows but a Lieutenant Anthony may be knocking at the door of the White House some day? At any rate, I know that if you hold a thing unjustly, there will surely be the devil to pay at last.

The Site

After a 1990 storm eroded parts of **Coast Guard Beach**, an amateur archeologist who was walking the beach noticed unusual shapes in the dunes which turned out to yield one of the most interesting archeological sites on Cape Cod. Although only preliminary reports from the dig have been completed, **Cape Cod National Seashore** archaeologists estimate that artifacts from the dig date from at least 3,000 to 4,000 years ago. Items collected included stone chips used in tool making, the remains of clay containers, a hearth consisting of a pit into which heated rocks were placed for cooking, and seven post molds indicating the walls of a dwelling. Perhaps most interesting was the discovery of many layers of artifacts from different years, suggesting that the location had been in use seasonally, off and on, for thousands of years, just as it is used seasonally today by many Cape Cod tourists. It is expected that carbon dating, pollen analysis and other scientific tools will yield more complete results from the find in the near future, and that subsequent data will help archaeologists decipher other finds in the region.

Another result of beach erosion was the 1978 destruction of a large beach parking lot. A photograph of that lot can be seen on an informative plaque between the **Eastham Coast Guard Station** and the beach. The Cape Cod National Seashore maintains restrooms on a seasonal basis and public telephones year-round at the beach, which is also the starting point for **The Outermost Walk**, also listed in this guide.●

#16
"The Outermost House"

(Map #7)

Location

Henry Beston's "Fo'castle," the 20' x 16' dune shack that was the centerpiece of his celebrated nature classic, *The Outermost House*, is gone. Washed away by a February blizzard in 1978, it lives on only in the pages of Beston's text and in the memories of those who knew it. Prior to the storm, the house was located a little less than two miles south of the **Eastham Coast Guard Station** on Nauset Spit, the barrier beach that separates **Nauset Marsh** from the Atlantic Ocean. The house was situated almost due east, or roughly straight across the marsh from Skiff Hill, part of the **Fort Hill Area** which is described in this guide. Today the former site of the house can be accessed by following **The Outermost Walk**, as described in this guide.

Thoreau

Like Henry David Thoreau, Henry Beston wrote about the Cape with inspiration, eloquence and insight. In fact, Beston's *The Outermost House* expands on many of the themes that Thoreau established in *Cape Cod*—wildness, death and disaster on the **Great Beach**, the need for a respectful relationship with the natural world, and an admiration for the creatures and people who live on Cape Cod. Beston also follows in the tradition of Thoreau's *Walden* by portraying his personal experiences in a small, simple house, alone with nature. (See the **Outermost Walk** for further information on this topic.)

The Site

Perhaps more than ever before in this century Nauset Spit remains the place that Beston described as being "in the midst of an abundance of natural life which manifests itself every hour of the day." In the last twenty years, erosion has cleared the beach of all permanent manmade structures, including Beston's house, making it—once again—a truly isolated place.

The significance of the site of the "Fo'castle" can only be appreciated by reading *The Outermost House*. A relatively short text, it is nevertheless epic in scope and mood and is composed with an elevated and poetic language rarely encountered. If there is a single book that a Cape Cod walker ought to read, other than Thoreau's *Cape Cod*, it is unquestionably *The Outermost House*. Samples of Beston's wisdom include:

> At the foot of this cliff a great ocean beach runs north and south unbroken, mile lengthening into mile. Solitary and elemental, unsullied and remote, visited and possessed by the outer sea, these sands might be the end or the beginning of a world.

> The world to-day is sick to its thin blood for lack of elemental things, for fire before the hands, for water welling from the earth, for air, for the dear earth itself underfoot. In my world of beach and dune these elemental presences lived and had their being, and under their arch there moved an incomparable pageant of nature and the year.

> To be able to see and study undisturbed the processes of nature—I like better the old Biblical phrase "mighty works"—is an opportunity for which any man might well feel reverent gratitude, and here at last, in this silence and isolation of winter, a whole

region was mine whose innermost natural life might shape itself to its ancient courses without the hindrance and interferences of man.●

#17
Nauset Light Beach & the French Transatlantic Cable
(Map #16 & #17)

Location

Nauset Light Beach, the former site of the American terminus of the **French Transatlantic Cable**, is located on the eastern shore of North Eastham, 1.1 miles north of **Coast Guard Beach** and 2.2 miles south of **Marconi Beach**. From the Orleans Rotary, follow Route 6 north 3 miles and turn right onto Nauset Road at the **Salt Pond Visitor Center**. After 0.7 miles Nauset Road bears off to the left and Doane Road continues straight ahead. Proceed straight ahead onto Doane Road, and 1.7 miles from Route 6 you will arrive at a junction. Turn left onto Ocean View Drive and continue 1 mile to the parking lot at Nauset Beach, on the right. A $7 daily fee or a $20 seasonal fee is charged for daytime summer parking at this and all **Cape Cod National Seashore** managed beaches.

Thoreau

Thoreau first encountered the **Great Beach** here, an experience which he made certain record of in *Cape Cod*:

> Crossing over a belt of sand on which nothing grew, though the roar of the sea sounded scarcely louder than before, and we were prepared to go half a mile further, we suddenly stood on the edge of the bluff overlooking the Atlantic. Far below us was the beach, from half a dozen to a dozen rods in width, with a long line of breakers rushing to the strand. The sea was exceedingly dark and stormy, the sky completely overcast, the clouds still dropping rain, and the wind seemed to blow not so much as the exciting cause, as from sympathy with the already agitated ocean. The waves broke on the bars at some distance from the shore and curving green or yellow as if over so many unseen dams, ten or twelve feet high, like a thousand waterfalls, then rolled in foam to the sand. There was nothing but that savage ocean between us and Europe.

The **French Transatlantic Cable**, an undersea telegraph cable that had its American communications station terminus at **Nauset Light Beach**, did not come into use until 30 years after Thoreau's initial visit here. Still, if Thoreau had encountered the cable at the beach, he may not have been impressed. Thoreau was frequently critical of the technological advances, and in *Walden* even rebuffs the idea of transatlantic communication:

> Our inventions are wont to be pretty toys, which distract our attentions from serious things. They are but improved means to an unimproved end.... We are in great haste to construct a magnetic telegraph from Maine to Texas; but Maine and Texas, it may be, have nothing important to communicate.... We are eager to tunnel under the Atlantic and bring the old world some weeks nearer to the new; but perchance the first news that will leak through into the broad, flapping American ear will be that the Princess Adelaide has the whooping cough![5]

No doubt Thoreau would have dismissed the Cable as a mere distraction from the Great Beach he had come to learn about.

The Site

The **Cape Cod National Seashore** maintains restrooms on a seasonal basis and public telephones year-round at **Nauset Light Beach**. The historical significance of the beach is impressive: in addition to **Nauset Lighthouse**, the **Three Sisters Lights of Nauset** are located just 0.25 miles west of the parking lot on Cable Road. Furthermore, Nauset Light Beach was the former terminus of the **French Transatlantic Cable**, which put the United States and France into virtually instantaneous communication.

The cable was laid in 1879 and ran 2,242 nautical miles from Brest, France, to St. Pierre, an island just south of Newfoundland. The cable then stretched another 827 nautical miles from St. Pierre to Eastham. After its completion, the Eastham station remained in use until 1890 when a new station was built along Town Cove in Orleans at the request of workers who found the isolation of Nauset Light Beach intolerable.

The Orleans station building is now a museum celebrating the history of the cable. It is located on the corner of Cove Road and Route 28 and is open from 2 p.m. to 4 p.m. Tuesdays through Saturdays in July and August. Contact the museum at (508) 240-1735.●

In the Footsteps of Thoreau

#18
Nauset Lighthouse

(Map #16 & #17)

Location

Nauset Lighthouse is located on the eastern shore of North Eastham, above **Nauset Light Beach**. From the Orleans Rotary, follow Route 6 north 3 miles to the second set of traffic lights and turn right onto Nauset Road, which is marked with a sign for the **Cape Cod National Seashore**. After 0.7 miles Nauset Road bears off to the left and Doane Road continues straight ahead. Proceed straight ahead onto Doane Road. 1.7 miles from Route 6 you will arrive at a t-junction. Turn left onto Ocean View Drive and proceed 1 mile north to the Nauset Light Beach parking lot on the right, from where the lighthouse will be in sight just across the road. A $7 daily fee or a $20 seasonal fee is charged for daytime summer parking at the parking lot.

Thoreau

When Thoreau visited the Nauset Lighthouse Station in 1849, it consisted of three lighthouses constructed of brick. Thoreau did not write much about Nauset's lighthouses, however—except to comment that he considered it "shiftlessness" to have three lighthouses where one could have done just as well. (See the **Three Sisters Lights of Nauset**.) Still, Thoreau's lack of commentary was not completely out of character; for while he always took due note of the works of man, it was the works of nature that interested him most. No sooner had Thoreau seen the lighthouses than he left them to walk along the **Great Beach**, which he encountered for the first time here:

> Having got down the bank, and as close to the water as we could, where the sand was the hardest, leaving the Nauset Lights behind us, we began to walk leisurely up the beach, in a north-west direction, toward Provincetown, which was about twenty-five miles distant, still sailing under our umbrellas with a strong aft wind, admiring in silence, as we walked, the great force of the ocean stream.... The white breakers were rushing to the shore; the foam ran up the sand, and then ran back as far as we could see (and we imagined how much further along the Atlantic coast, before and behind us), as regularly, to compare great things with small, as the master of a choir beats time with his white wand; and ever and anon a higher wave caused us hastily to deviate from our path, and we looked back on our tracks filled with water and foam. The breakers looked like droves of a

thousand wild horses of Neptune rushing to the shore, with their white manes streaming far behind; and when at length, the sun shone for a moment their manes were rainbow-tinted.

The Site

When lighthouse stations were initially established on the eastern shore of Cape Cod, Truro was equipped with one lighthouse, Chatham with two lighthouses, and Eastham with three—so that mariners could easily differentiate between them. Today, lighthouses are differentiated visually by the colors and blinking patterns of their lights.

The first Nauset Lighthouse Station was established in 1838 and used until 1892, when it was replaced by the wooden lighthouses that are currently on display 0.25 miles to the west of the **Nauset Light Beach** parking lot, on Cable Road. (See the **Three Sisters Lights of Nauset**.) These second generation lighthouses were used until 1911, when they were threatened by the eroding cliff. At that time the outer two towers were removed and decommissioned, and the center tower was moved back from the cliff edge and used on its own.

Finally, in 1923, the present **Nauset Lighthouse** was established in Eastham. Nauset Lighthouse was anything but new at that time, however, and had previously served as the northernmost of the pair in Chatham for almost 50 years, since 1877.

The next major change at Nauset came in the 1940's when the upper two-fifths of Nauset Lighthouse were painted bright red, as a day mark—a paint job that many credit as having helped make Nauset Lighthouse a Cape Cod icon. In the years that followed, the image of Nauset Lighthouse has decorated virtually every product imaginable, including official Massachusetts license plates, potato chip bags, book covers (including this one!), t-shirts, mugs and more. Thus, in the 1990's when Nauset Lighthouse was endangered by erosion, there was no shortage of public support to save it. Thanks to the efforts of the Nauset Lighthouse Preservation Society, the **Cape Cod National Seashore**, many local and national officials, plus innumerable citizens on Cape Cod and from across the country, Nauset Lighthouse was successfully moved to its present location in the autumn of 1996*.

For further information regarding lighthouse tours and other information, call the Salt Pond Visitor Center at (508) 255-3421, or the Park Headquarters at (508) 349-3785.●

* By the time it was relocated, Nauset Lighthouse was just 40 feet from the cliff edge. The cover photo of this book was taken in the summer of 1996, just a few months before it was moved, and gives a good idea of just how dire the situation had become.

In the Footsteps of Thoreau

#19
Three Sisters Lights of Nauset
(Map #16 & #17)

Location

The **Three Sisters Lights of Nauset** are located 0.25 miles inland of **Nauset Light Beach** on Cable Road in North Eastham. From the Orleans Rotary, follow Route 6 north 3 miles to the second set of traffic lights and turn right onto Nauset Road, which is marked with a sign for the **Cape Cod National Seashore**. After 0.7 miles Nauset Road bears off to the left and Doane Road continues straight ahead. Proceed straight ahead onto Doane Road. 1.7 miles from Route 6 you will arrive at a junction. Turn left onto Ocean View Drive and proceed 1 mile north to the stop sign where the Nauset Light Beach parking lot is located on the right. The Three Sisters Lights are 0.25 miles to the left on Cable Road.

Thoreau

Thoreau's only comment about the **Three Sisters Lights of Nauset** that he encountered in 1849 was succinct but to the point:

> We left the road and struck across the country for the eastern shore, at Nauset Lights—three lights close together, two or three miles distant from us. They were so many that they might be distinguished from others; but this seemed a shiftless and costly way of accomplishing that object.

As usual, Thoreau was right. Having three lights at Nauset was an unnecessarily expensive way of distinguishing them from other lighthouse stations, and one could have done just as well. Nevertheless, more than half a century was to pass before the U.S. Lighthouse Service was able to reach the same conclusion that Thoreau had and reduce the trio at Nauset to a solo.[6]

The first Three Sisters, observed by Thoreau, were made of brick and mortar and had been constructed in 1838. Although the technology to construct lighthouse lenses that could be distinguished from one another was available in Europe at that time, it had not yet been used in the United States. Thus, mariners were warned off the Cape's eastern shore by lighthouse stations with various numbers of lights. Truro continued with its single lighthouse (**Highland Lighthouse**, built in 1797); Chatham went on with its pair ("The Chatham Twins," built in 1808); and the Three Sisters were built in Eastham.

The original Sisters stood 15-feet high and received their nickname from mariners who claimed that from the ocean they looked like women with white dresses and black hats peering out over the cliff. Unfortunately, after having saved many a seaman's life, the Sisters became victims of the sea themselves in 1892. These original towers had been built very shoddily (perhaps another reason why Thoreau was unimpressed by them); and when the eroding cliff edge endangered them, the government simply removed their lenses and lens housings and abandoned them to their fate*.

The Site

The second set of **Three Sisters Lights of Nauset**, currently on Cable Road, were built in 1892. At that time the technology to differentiate lighthouse lights from one another was readily available, yet the government remained mired in its old ways and insisted on building three new lighthouses.

Twenty-two-feet tall, the new Sisters were placed on post foundations so that, 19 years later (60 years after Thoreau's comment!), when the cliff edge had again crept within a few feet of their bases, they were easily moved out of harm's way. Later that year, the middle tower was moved back from the cliff and used as a solo beacon, with its light set to blink three times every 10 seconds to distinguish it from other lights (and in remembrance of the three which formerly stood there).

The outer pair of Three Sisters were decommissioned and auctioned off. Purchased by Helen M. Cummings for the price of $3.50, they were incorporated into the architecture of her dance studio on Cable Road.

The remaining wooden tower, known as the Beacon, served as the lone Nauset Light until 1923, when it was replaced with one of the pair of lighthouses that had been used at Chatham. (See **Nauset Lighthouse**.) At that time, the Beacon was auctioned off to one Albert Hall for the rock-bottom price of just one dollar and used as a summer cottage, and later as a beach-side hamburger stand.

In 1963, the U.S. government bought back the outside pair for restoration; and in 1975 the Beacon was also reacquired. By 1989 the trio had been refurbished and were placed in their original positions, 150 feet apart with the Beacon once again in the middle. Visitors will notice that the outside pair remain "topless," however, having had their lens housings misplaced sometime after their initial auction. Ranger-guided tours of the Three Sisters are offered periodically by the park. Stop by or call the **Cape Cod National Seashore Headquarters** at (508) 349-3785, or the **Salt Pond Visitors Center** at (508) 255-3421 for further information.●

*Interestingly enough, the circular foundations from these original Three Sisters are still sometimes exposed on the beach below the cliff by low winter tides.

#20
Camp Wellfleet
(Map #17 & 18)

Location

Camp Wellfleet is the name of a former World War II Army base that was located in South Wellfleet. The base covered the area from about the Wellfleet/Eastham town line to the south, to LeCount Hollow Road to the north, with Route 6 on the west and the Atlantic on the east.

The Site

Surprisingly little remains of **Camp Wellfleet**, considering that it was formerly home to thousands of troops who were stationed there during World War II. The U.S. Army took control of the land just prior to the war and retained title to it until the 1961 formation of the **Cape Cod National Seashore**, when it was transferred to the Department of the Interior.

Camp Wellfleet served mainly as an anti-aircraft training base. One of the few remaining signs of its original use is a jeep trail in the woods that once served as a dirt airstrip for remote-controlled planes. These small, petroleum-powered drones trailed targets out over the ocean for use in shooting practice by gunners who were stationed on the beach. Although the former airstrip is only used today as an access trail, it is still flanked by small, new-growth trees that reveal its once greater width.

Other structures that date from Camp Wellfleet include a tall water tower to the east of the **Park Headquarters**, a water pumphouse to the south of the headquarters labelled "B-Well," and an old paved road that runs between Marconi Station Road and the pumphouse.[7]●

#21
Marconi Beach
(Map #17 & #18)

Location

Marconi Beach is located on the eastern shore of South Wellfleet, 2.2 miles north of **Nauset Light Beach** and 2.3 miles south of **LeCount Hollow Beach**. Follow Route 6 to the Wellfleet/Eastham town line and then proceed north 2 miles to the first set of traffic lights. Turn right at the lights and follow this road 1.4 miles to the beach parking lot. A $7 daily fee or a $20 seasonal fee is charged for daytime summer parking at this and all **Cape Cod National Seashore** managed beaches.

Thoreau

Although the landscape above **Marconi Beach** (which was once known as "Snows Hollow"[8]) is no longer deforested as it was in Thoreau's time, it is still as secluded and as beautiful as the author described it:

> The wrecker directed us to a slight depression, called Snow's Hollow, by which we ascended the bank—for elsewhere, if not difficult, it was inconvenient to climb it on account of the sliding sand which filled our shoes. This sand bank—the backbone of the Cape—rose directly from the beach to the height of a hundred feet or more above the ocean. It was with singular emotions that we first stood upon it and discovered what a place we had chosen to walk on. On our right, beneath us, was the beach of smooth and gently-sloping sand, a dozen rods in width—next the endless series of white breakers; further still, the light green water over the bar, which runs the whole length of the forearm of the Cape; and beyond this stretched the unwearied and illimitable ocean.... It was like the escarped rampart of a stupendous fortress, whose glacis was the beach, and whose champagne the ocean. From its surface we overlooked the greater part of the Cape. In short, we were traversing a desert, with the view of an autumnal landscape of extraordinary brilliancy, a sort of Promised Land, on the one hand, and the ocean on the other.... A thousand men could not have seriously interrupted it, but would have been lost in the vastness of the scenery as their footsteps in the sand.

The Site

Marconi Beach was named in honor of Guglielmo Marconi (1874-1937), the Nobel Prize-winning inventor of the radio. It was just north of the beach at the **Marconi Station Site** that the first transatlantic radio messages between the President of the United States and the King of England were broadcast and received in 1903.

Although there is no distinct "hollow" at Marconi Beach today, and a set of stairs have been constructed to facilitate access to the beach from the cliff top, the 1849 coastal survey map of the area indicates that in Thoreau's day there was a significant depression, or hollow, here. Prior to having been called Snow's Hollow, this narrow valley was actually referred to as Fresh Brook Hollow because of nearby Fresh Brook which flowed almost all the way across the Cape from the bay-side.[9]

The **Cape Cod National Seashore** maintains restrooms on a seasonal basis and telephones year-round at the beach parking lot.●

#22
Fresh Brook Village
(Map #17 & 18)

Location

Fresh Brook Village is the name of a small settlement that was once located along the junction of the **Old Kings Highway** and Fresh Brook in Wellfleet, approximately 1 mile west of today's **Marconi Beach**. Today, the former location of the village is only accessible by foot. (See **The Great Thoreau Hike, Part III** for directions to the area.)

The Site

Founded in 1730, **Fresh Brook Village** included about a dozen families, a store and a tavern. Fresh Brook was a regular stopping point for stagecoaches in the mid-19th century, and Thoreau—who included Fresh Brook on one of his hand-drawn maps of Cape Cod—was probably familiar with it.

Unfortunately for the residents of Fresh Brook, by 1872 the railroad had extended its tracks down the Cape and across Fresh Brook, thereby limiting the tidal flow to the village and restricting boat access to it from Cape Cod Bay. This change lead to the eventual abandonment of the village; and in 1905 Fresh Brook's last resident, Asa Cole, died. Not long thereafter the surrounding land was purchased by a Boston sportsman who used the site as a fishing camp. Finally, just prior to World War II, the Army took possession of much of the land in the area and used it as a base, **Camp Wellfleet**.[10]

Today, all that remains of Fresh Brook Village are a few scattered cellar depressions in the woods.●

#23
Cape Cod National Seashore Park Headquarters
(Map #18)

Location

The **Cape Cod National Seashore Park Headquarters** is located on Marconi Site Road in Wellfleet, about 0.9 miles west of the **Marconi Station Site**. Follow Route 6 to the Wellfleet/Eastham town line and proceed north 2 miles to the first set of traffic lights. Turn right and continue 0.1 miles west to Marconi Site Road on the left. Turn onto Marconi Site Road, and the Park Headquarters is 0.2 miles farther on the left.

The Site

The Park Headquarters is the administrative center of the **Cape Cod National Seashore**. Although the Headquarters does not have extensive visitor facilities like those at the **Salt Pond Visitor Center** and the **Province Lands Visitor Center**, it does have public restrooms, a small book store, and a useful information counter.

The Headquarters is usually the best place to direct general questions regarding the Park, especially in winter when the visitor centers have limited hours. The Headquarters is open year-round from 8 a.m. to 4:30 p.m., Monday through Friday. The telephone number is (508) 349-3785.●

#24
Marconi Station Site
(Map #18)

Location

The remains of the **Marconi Station Site** are located on the cliffs above the eastern shore of Wellfleet, approximately 1.7 miles north of **Marconi Beach** and 0.7 miles south of **LeCount Hollow Beach. NOTE: There is no direct access to the Marconi Station Site on the cliffs from the beach below it.** Follow Route 6 to the Wellfleet/Eastham town line and proceed north 2 miles to the first set of traffic lights. Turn right and continue 0.2 miles west to Marconi Site Road on the left. Turn onto Marconi Site Road and follow it 1.1 miles, past the **Cape Cod National Seashore Park Headquarters**, to the station site.

The Site

The Marconi Wireless Station in Wellfleet was the site of the first transmission and reception of radio messages across the Atlantic. Guglielmo Marconi (1874-1937), known as "The Wizard of Wireless," was only 28-years-old when he performed this feat that earned him a Nobel Prize and permanently altered human communications. By 1903, he had constructed three long-distance radio transmission sites: one in Wellfleet, one in Poldhu, England, and one in Glace Bay, Canada. Through the development of his own "grounding techniques," Marconi had by then already received international fame for transmitting the first long-distance radio transmissions, which included a Morse code "s", from England to Newfoundland.

On January 18th, 1903, Marconi marked the dawn of a new era by sending detailed messages between the President of the United States and the King of England. Interestingly, when the President's message had been sent from Wellfleet, Marconi had only expected it to reach Glace Bay, where he had hoped it would be relayed to England. But history was made when the message travelled clear across the Atlantic and was answered directly by the King's message. Both communications consisted of a few lines of formally worded salutations.[11]

One of the most entertaining tales about the Marconi Station is that of Charlie Paine, a native Cape Codder who was hired by Marconi to be a messenger between the station and Wellfleet Village*. When the world's first transatlantic radio messages had finally been sent and received, Paine had the important task of delivering the news to Wellfleet Village where it could be spread to the waiting world via traditional telegraph equipment. Paine's version of his historic role reveals a quality of independent-mindedness reminiscent of Thoreau's Wellfleet Oysterman. Paine was quoted:

> Diamond and I had been waiting around for about six days. I never knew when Mr. Marconi was going to need me to rush to the telegraph office down here at the depot with the message he was praying for. When the great moment came, Mr. Marconi came dashing out of the station very excited carrying two messages in his hands. His orders were, "Drive like the wind and if you kill your horse I'll get you another one." Well, as soon as I'd driven out of sight, I slowed Diamond down to a walk. We made the depot in good time and the message went over the wires. Yes, I was pretty excited too, but still I wasn't going to kill my horse—not for Marconi, the King of England or the President of the United States.[12]

The Wellfleet station subsequently played an important role in marine communication, serving as Marconi's main U.S. ship-to-shore station until it was finally shut down in 1917 during World War I. Besides relaying weather-related and other logistical information to ships, it also served various luxury liners, providing them with daily news as well as personal messages, or "Marconi-grams." The Wellfleet operation later became part of RCA Global Communications and was moved to Chatham.

The Park has built a pavilion at the site that shelters a model of the former station and includes informative plaques on its history. There is also an observation platform near the site that offers spectacular views of the area. Aside from some foundation blocks and a few bits of timber, however, little remains of the Marconi Station today. Built some 165 feet from the cliff edge, more than half of the site has since fallen victim to erosion.

*On his way to Wellfleet, Paine would have followed "Wireless Road," now part of the Cape Cod National Seashore's White Cedar Swamp Trail and **The Great Thoreau Hike, Part III** in this guide.

Coincidentally, the station was constructed on the cliff directly above the shore where the famous pirate ship *Whydah* sunk in 1717.●

#25
The *Whydah*
(Map #18)

Location

The remains of the wreck of the 18th-century pirate ship *Whydah* were found just offshore from the **Marconi Station Site** in Wellfleet. Although this location is considered to be the approximate site of the wreck, artifacts from the *Whydah* have also been discovered up and down the coast between **Marconi Beach** and **LeCount Hollow Beach**.

Thoreau

Thoreau's scholarship on the topics that interested him was scrupulous. In *Cape Cod*, he seems to make note of every interesting historical incident that occurred prior to his visits, the wreck of the *Whydah* being no exception. He writes:

> In the year 1717, a noted pirate named Bellamy was led on to the bar off Wellfleet by the captain of a snow [ship] which he had taken, to whom he had offered his vessel again if he would pilot him into Provincetown Harbor. Tradition says that the latter threw over a tar-barrel in the night, which drifted ashore, and the pirates followed it. A storm coming on, their whole fleet was wrecked, and more than a hundred dead bodies lay along the shore. Six who escaped shipwreck were executed. "At times to this day" (1793), says the historian of Wellfleet, "there are King William and Queen Mary's coppers picked up, and pieces of silver called cob-money. The violence of the seas moves the sands on the outer bar, so that at times the iron caboose of the ship (that is, Bellamy's) at low ebbs has been seen." Another tells us that, "For many years after this ship wreck, a man of a very singular and frightful aspect used every spring and autumn to be seen travelling on the Cape, who was supposed to have been one of Bellamy's crew. The presumption is that he went to some place where money had been secreted by the pirates, to get such a supply as his exigencies required. When he died, many pieces of gold were found in a girdle which he constantly wore. As I was walking on the beach here in my last visit, looking for shells and pebbles, just after that storm which I have mentioned as moving the sand to a great depth, not knowing but I might find some cob-money, I did actually pick up a French crown piece, worth about a dollar and six cents, near high-water mark, on the still moist sand, just under the abrupt, caving base of the bank.

The coin that Thoreau found was not from the *Whydah*, however, as it was dated 1741 and was minted after the ship's demise.

The Site

277 years after its sinking, the **Whydah** was discovered near the shore in South Wellfleet under 20 feet of water and about 10 feet of sand. Given the amount of time that it had been submerged, it is amazing how many items were salvaged from the wreck, including clothing, weapons, the ship's bell, and a fortune in treasure.

The story goes that the notable pirate Sam "Black" Bellamy—known for his jet-black hair and "swarthy good looks"—had spent time in Orleans in the early 1700's where he fell in love with a 15-year-old local girl named Maria Hallet. Leaving Hallet on Cape Cod, Bellamy went in search of his fortune in the Caribbean, promising to return a rich man. Bellamy gained a large following of men and went on to plunder a number of ships before returning to Cape Cod for Hallet in 1717. Unfortunately for the couple, a ferocious storm wrecked the *Whydah* before they could be reunited. Many declared it "divine retribution" for Bellamy's sinful lifestyle that he and 144 of his men perished on the outer beach. The seven pirates who managed to escape the storm did not escape the law, however, and were all hung soon after on Boston Common.

After a great deal of scholarship (that included a detailed reading of Thoreau) and a prolonged and difficult search, treasure hunter Barry Clifford located the remains of the *Whydah* in 1984. The event provided many clues to the way pirates actually lived and marked the first-ever discovery of sunken pirate treasure in history. Since then Clifford has established the Expedition *Whydah* Sea Lab & Learning Center at the end of MacMillan Wharf in Provincetown, where visitors can view many of the objects from the *Whydah*. (See **Provincetown Center Walk.**)

But the story is still not completely over. As this book goes to press, Clifford and his team continue to search for more artifacts. Who knows what remains to be found? For information on the Expedition Sea Lab and Learning Center call (508) 487-7955.●

#26
LeCount Hollow Beach
(Map #18 & #19)

Location

LeCount Hollow Beach is located on the eastern shore of Wellfleet, 2.3 miles north of **Marconi Beach**; 0.8 miles south of **White Crest Beach**; 1.5 miles south of **Cahoon Hollow Beach**; and 3 miles south of **Newcomb Hollow Beach**. Follow Route 6 to the Wellfleet/Eastham town line and proceed north 2.7 miles to LeCount Hollow Road on the right. Turn right onto LeCount Hollow Road and follow it east 0.8 miles to the beach parking lot. Unfortunately, no parking is permitted at the beach from 9 a.m. to 5 p.m. July through Labor Day, except for Town of Wellfleet resident sticker-holders. Free summer parking is allowed, however, 0.6 miles west on LeCount Hollow Road at the Rail Trail Bike Path parking lot. Summer parking is also available without a sticker (but for a fee) at White Crest Beach, 1 mile north on Ocean View Drive.

Thoreau

On his first day's walk on Cape Cod Thoreau stopped at LeCount Hollow for a unique lunch:

> We took our nooning under a sand-hill, covered with beach grass, in a dreary little hollow, on the top of the bank, while it alternately rained and shined. There, having reduced some damp drift-wood, which I had picked up on the shore, to shavings with my knife, I kindled a fire with a match and some paper, and cooked my clam on the embers for my dinner; for breakfast was commonly the only meal which I took in a house on this excursion. When the clam was done one valve held the meat and the other the liquor. Though it was very tough, I found it sweet and savory, and ate the whole with a relish. Indeed with the addition of a cracker or two it would have been a bountiful dinner.

Unfortunately for Thoreau, his clam lunch did not sit well with him and he became ill at the Wellfleet Oysterman's house:

> In the course of the evening I began to feel the potency of the clam which I had eaten, and I was obliged to confess to our host that I was no tougher than the cat he told of; but he answered, that he was a plain-spoken man, and he could tell me that it was all imagination. At any rate, it proved an emetic in my case, and I was made quite sick by it for a short time, while he laughed at my expense.

The Site

LeCount Hollow Beach is administered by the Town of Wellfleet and has seasonal rest rooms but no public telephones.●

#27
White Crest Beach

(Map #19)

Location

White Crest Beach is located 0.8 miles north of **LeCount Hollow Beach**; 0.7 miles south of **Cahoon Hollow Beach**; and 2.2 miles south of **Newcomb Hollow Beach**. Follow Route 6 to the Wellfleet/Eastham town line and proceed north 2.7 miles to LeCount Hollow Road on the right. Follow LeCount Hollow Road 0.8 miles west and turn left onto Ocean View Drive. Follow Ocean View Drive north 1 mile, to where the White Crest Beach parking lots are located on both sides of the road. The Town of Wellfleet currently charges a $10 parking fee at White Crest Beach in the summer.

The Site

White Crest Beach is administered by the Town of Wellfleet. Although there are seasonal restrooms at the parking lots, there are no public telephones.●

#28
Cahoon Hollow Beach,
the Wellfleet Beachcomber
& the Humane House

(Map #19)

Location

Cahoon Hollow Beach, home of the **Wellfleet Beachcomber** and the former site of the **Humane House** Thoreau wrote of in *Cape Cod*, is located on the eastern shore of Wellfleet 0.7 miles north of **White Crest Beach**; 1.5 miles north of **LeCount Hollow Beach**; and 1.5 miles south of **Newcomb Hollow Beach**. Follow Route 6 to the Wellfleet/Eastham town line and proceed north 2.7 miles to LeCount Hollow Road on the right. Follow LeCount Hollow Road 0.8 miles east, turn left onto Ocean View Drive, and follow it 1.7 miles north to Cahoon Hollow Road on the right, which is marked with a sign for the Beachcomber.

Thoreau

In the early to mid-19th century, a **Humane House** was built at **Cahoon Hollow Beach** as an emergency shelter for shipwreck survivors.[13] This so-called Humane House–also referred to as a "Humane Hut" and a "Charity House"–was one of many such structures established on remote sections of beach by the Massachusetts Humane Society. While Humane Houses were nevertheless better than no shelters at all, they were few in number and were really little more than small sheds with fireplaces. (See **The Great Thoreau Hike, Part IV**.) These shelters were maintained by the Humane Society with the help of certain "benevolent persons" who usually lived nearby and volunteered to inspect them and keep them stocked with a few basic provisions such as matches, fuel, etc. Although a guide* had been printed and distributed with the locations of these huts, and a high pole was usually attached to their roofs for easier identification, they were all but impossible to locate by shipwreck survivors in a storm or at night, when they were most needed.

Thoreau was particularly unimpressed by the Humane House he found in Wellfleet, as it was not only bereft of basic supplies but nailed shut–and this just two days after the tragic wreck of the *St. John* to the north in Cohasset, where Thoreau had met one of the survivors and saw the corpses of numerous victims.

In the following passage Thoreau satirically follows the doctrine of "looking inward" for the truth; only instead of looking into himself, he looks into the Humane House:

> However, as we wished to get an idea of a humane house, and we hoped that we should never have a better opportunity, we put our eyes, by turns, to a knot-hole in the door, and, after long looking, without seeing, into the dark–not knowing how many shipwrecked men's bones we might see at last, looking with the eye of faith, knowing that, though to him that knocketh it may not always be opened, yet to him that looketh long enough through a knot-hole the inside shall be visible–for we had had some practice at looking inward.... Turning our backs on the outward world, we thus looked through the knot-hole into the humane house, into the very bowels of mercy; and for bread we found a stone.

*This guide was entitled *A Description of the Eastern Coast of the County of Barnstable* and was published in 1803. Thoreau carried a copy of it with him on Cape Cod in 1849.

It was literally a great cry (of sea-mews outside), and little wool. However, we were glad to sit outside, under the lee of the humane house to escape the piercing wind; and there we thought how cold is charity! how inhuman humanity! This then, is what charity hides! Virtues antique and far away with ever a rusty nail over the latch; and very difficult to keep in repair, withal, it is so uncertain whether any will ever gain the beach near you. So we shivered round about not being able to get into it, ever and anon looking through the knot-hole into that night without a star, until we concluded that it was not a humane house at all, but a sea-side box, now shut up, belonging to some of the family of night or chaos, where they spent their summers by the sea, for the sake of the sea-breeze, and that it was not proper for us to be prying into their concerns.

The Site

Fortunately, it was just nine years after the publication of *Cape Cod* that public sympathy for shipwreck victims had grown great enough that Humane Houses were replaced with lifesaving stations built along the **Great Beach** from Provincetown to Monomoy Island, including one at **Cahoon Hollow Beach**.

The first Cahoon Hollow Life-Saving Station was built in 1872 and lasted until 1893 when it was destroyed by fire. At that time, the present structure, now called the **Wellfleet Beachcomber**, was constructed. For decades lifesavers at the station patrolled the beach and launched countless rescue efforts using lifeboats and breeches buoys. (See **Old Harbor Life-Saving Station Museum** for further information on the U.S. Life-Saving Service.) The building played an important role in maintaining safety along the coast until the 1930's when it was deemed no longer necessary by the U.S. Coast Guard and decommissioned. At that time, the building was sold into private hands and eventually became a restaurant. Although it has changed ownership and has been remodelled a number of times, the building still retains much of its original appearance.

The Wellfleet Beachcomber was a disco for several years in the 70's, but as times changed, it was turned into a restaurant. In the early 90's a rock club was added to the restaurant, and the club has since developed into one of the most popular summer attractions on Cape Cod. Currently open from Memorial Day through Labor Day, the Beachcomber boasts that it regularly serves 80,000 patrons in its roughly 83-day season!

Summer beach walkers will find the Beachcomber a great place to stop for lunch, dinner or refreshments. But during the off-season there are no public facilities available.●

#29
Newcomb Hollow Beach
(Map #19 & #20)

Location

Newcomb Hollow Beach is located on the eastern shore of Wellfleet 2.8 miles south of **Ballston Beach**; 1.5 miles north of **Cahoon Hollow Beach**; 2.2 miles north of **White Crest Beach**; and 3 miles north of **LeCount Hollow Beach**. Follow Route 6 to the Wellfleet/Eastham town line and proceed north 2.7 miles to LeCount Hollow Road on the right. Follow LeCount Hollow Road east 0.8 miles to the intersection with Ocean View Drive. Turn left onto Ocean View Drive and proceed 3.3 miles north, past White Crest Beach and Cahoon Hollow Beach, to the Newcomb Hollow Beach parking lot. Unfortunately, no parking is permitted at the beach from 9 a.m. to 5 p.m. July through Labor Day, except for Town of Wellfleet resident sticker-holders. The nearest public parking lot is located 1.5 miles south on Ocean View Drive at Cahoon Hollow Beach, where a $10 fee is currently charged for summer parking.

Thoreau

When Thoreau first came to Cape Cod in the autumn of 1849, he encountered a number of signs of the tragic wreck of the *Franklin*, which had occurred near **Newcomb Hollow Beach** the previous spring. The shipwreck was particularly infamous at the time, as it was discovered that the captain and some of his crew had conspired to run the vessel aground, presumably to profit from an insurance scam or similar ploy; and ironically the captain was killed in the wreck. Thoreau observed vegetables growing at the Wellfleet Oysterman's house that were planted from seeds that had washed ashore from the *Franklin*'s cargo, and also met beachcombers who still searched for wreckage from the ship. He even saw tow cloth salvaged from the surf that was said to have been from the *Franklin*. Most moving, however, is the Wellfleet Oysterman's eyewitness account of the wreck, as recounted by Thoreau:

> She was on the bar, only a quarter of a mile from him, and still nearer to the men on the beach, who had got a boat ready, but could render no assistance on account of the breakers, for there was a pretty high sea running. There were the passengers all crowded together in the forward part of the ship, and some were getting out of the cabin windows and were drawn on deck by the others. "I saw the captain get out of his boat," said he, "he had one little one; and then they jumped into it one after another, down as straight as an arrow. I counted them. There were nine. One was a woman, and she jumped as straight as any of them.

In the Footsteps of Thoreau

Then they shoved off. The sea took them back, one wave went over them, and when they came up there were six still clinging to the boat; I counted them. The next wave turned the boat bottom upward, and emp tied them all out. None of them ever came ashore alive. There were the rest of them all crowded together on the forecastle, the other parts of the ship being under water. They had seen all that happened to the boat. At length a heavy sea separated the forecastle from the rest of the wreck, and set it inside of the worst breaker, and the boat was able to reach them, and it saved all that were left but one woman."

The Site

Newcomb Hollow Beach is managed by the Town of Wellfleet. There are restrooms operated on a seasonal basis at the beach parking lot, but there are no public telephones.●

#30
Williams Pond

(Map #19 & #20)

Location

The Wellfleet Oystyerman's house that Thoreau stayed at in 1849 was located on **Williams Pond** in north Wellfleet. Williams Pond can be seen from the road described in **The Great Thoreau Hike, Part V.**

Thoreau

Thoreau's *Cape Cod* was originally scheduled to be serialized in the literary magazine *Putnam's Monthly* in 1855. However, as explained in the "Thoreau on Cape Cod" section at the beginning of this book, only the first four chapters of *Cape Cod* were printed by *Putnam's* before it was abruptly dropped by the magazine without explanation. Scholars have speculated as to why the magazine dropped the series, but *Cape Cod* editor Joseph J. Moldenhauer has successfully argued the case that its editors found parts of *Cape Cod*, especially "The Wellfleet Oysterman" chapter, too crude, bawdy and indecent for the magazine's readership!

"The Wellfleet Oysterman" chapter had been scheduled to be printed the very month that Putnam's discontinued the series, and it is certainly one of the most irreverent in the book. The rough character of the Oysterman (for instance the fact that he referred to his wife and daughter as "poor good-for-nothing critturs"), the presence of his grandson ("a fool" who muttered about murdering "damn book peddlers"), and the description of the old man's bare legs ("fair and plump like a child's, and we thought he took a pride in exhibiting them"), are all examples found in the chapter that *Putnam's* probably deemed inappropriate.

Thoreau's account of his breakfast at the house, one of the most famous scenes in *Cape Cod*, serves as yet another example of the kind of narrative the magazine may well have considered unfit for print:

> She got the breakfast with dispatch, and without noise or bustle; and meanwhile the old man resumed his stories, standing before us, who were sitting, with his back to the chimney, and ejecting his tobacco-juice right and left into the fire behind him, without regard to the various dishes which were there preparing. At breakfast we had eels, buttermilk cake, cold bread, green beans, doughnuts, and tea. The old man talked a steady stream; and when his wife told him he had better eat his breakfast, he said: "Don't hurry me; I have lived too long to be hurried." I ate of the apple-sauce and the doughnuts, which I thought had sustained the least detriment from the old man's shots, but my companion refused the apple-sauce, and ate of the hot cake and green beans, which had appeared to him to occupy the safest part of the hearth. But on comparing notes afterward, I told him that the buttermilk cake was particularly exposed, and I saw how it suffered repeatedly, and therefore I avoided it; but he declared that, however that might be, he witnessed that the apple-sauce was seriously injured, and had therefore declined that.

The historical character referred to by Thoreau as "The Wellfleet Oysterman" was John Young Newcomb.[14] Thoreau's portrayal of Newcomb is accepted by many as the most interesting character sketch in all of his work, and the chapter his most humorous.

The Site

Although the area around **Williams Pond** is currently heavily wooded, it was, like much of the Cape in Thoreau's day, largely deforested. In fact, the land was so barren and wide-open that Thoreau was able to see most of the neighboring ponds from the windows of the Wellfleet Oysterman's house. And while the Atlantic is seldom audible from the pond today, the effects of deforestation were formerly such that Thoreau "could not distinguish the roar which was proper to the ocean from that which was due to the wind alone." ●

#31
Ballston Beach

(Map #11, #20 & 21)

Location

Ballston Beach is located on the eastern shore of Truro, 2.8 miles north of **Newcomb Hollow Beach** and 4.3 miles south of **Highland Beach**. Follow Route 6 to the Truro/Wellfleet town line and proceed north 2.5 miles to the well-marked "Pamet Roads" exit on the right. At the bottom of the off-ramp turn right. After 0.1 miles, you will arrive at a t-junction. Turn left at this t-junction onto South Pamet Road and follow it 1.7 miles to the beach parking lot. Unfortunately, no parking is permitted at Ballston Beach from 9 a.m. to 5 p.m. July through Labor Day, except for Town of Truro resident sticker-holders. Parking is permitted year-round, however, at the small parking area at the trailhead to the **Pamet Cranberry & Dune Walk**, located next to the **Truro Youth Hostel/NEED Center** off North Pamet Road.

Thoreau

Ballston Beach is located at the western end of the Pamet River, of which Thoreau wrote:

> To-day we were walking through Truro, a town of about eighteen hundred inhabitants. We had already come to Pamet River, which empties into the Bay. This was the limit of the Pilgrims' journey up the Cape from Provincetown, when seeking a place for settlement. It rises in a hollow within a few rods of the Atlantic, and one who lives near its source told us that in high tides the sea leaked through, yet the wind and waves preserve intact the barrier between them, and thus the whole river is steadily driven westward butt-end foremost—fountain-head, channel, and light-house at the mouth, all together.

The Pamet River continues to suffer the effects of erosion at its eastern end, or "butt-end," as Thoreau described it, with the ocean still "leaking" through during severe storms and high tides. However, the dunes that separate the river from the ocean have not always been as thin and low as they appear today. Not long ago, for instance, North Pamet Road and South Pamet Road were connected, with a substantial row of dunes separating them from the beach. But in both 1978 and 1991, the ocean punched through the dunes and buried the road behind them beneath tons of sand.

Fortunately, a force known as the "along-shore current" helps to keep

the Atlantic from running permanently into the river and completely eroding the beach away. As ocean water is continuously pushed directly up against the beach in a more or less perpendicular fashion, it also continuously rolls off to the sides and runs parallel to the beach. This parallel-moving water forms along-shore currents, which in turn carry sand and other sediments up and down the **Great Beach** and deposit it in the mouths of various openings such as the Pamet River.

Thoreau, a dedicated chronicler, did not fail to make note of these currents, which he refers to as "inshore drift":

> You would be surprised if you were on the beach when a hurricane directly blew on to it, to see that none of the drift-wood came ashore, but all was carried directly northward and parallel with the shore as fast as a man can walk, by the inshore current, which sets strongly in that direction at flood tide. The strongest swimmers also are carried along with it, and never gain an inch toward the beach. Even a large rock has been moved half a mile northward along the beach.

The Site

Ballston Beach was named for the Ozzie Ball Summer Resort. Built at the turn of the century, this popular vacation spot consisted of a large colony of buildings that included cottages, a dining hall, a community center and even a bowling alley.

Unfortunately, Ballston Beach has not always been the site of pleasant recreation. Like the rest of the **Great Beach**, it too has seen its share of tragedy. One of the worst wrecks at Ballston Beach was that of the *Jason*, a full-rigged iron ship that wrecked in 1893. Despite the efforts of the crew of the Pamet Life-Saving Station (which was established in 1872) 24 of the 25 crewmen on board died in the disaster. A sad testament to the event, the rotting hull of the *Jason* still lies under 35 feet of water just off **Ballston Beach**.[15] (See **Old Harbor Life-Saving Station Museum** for further information on the U.S. Life-Saving Service.)

In 1932, the U.S. Coast Guard also built a station here. Located at the end of North Pamet Road, this building presently serves dual uses as the **Truro Youth Hostel/NEED Center**, a youth hostel in the summer and an environmental education center in the winter. Adjacent to the building is the trailhead for the **Pamet Cranberry & Dune Walk**, as described in this book.

The Town of Truro stations chemical toilets at Ballston Beach.●

#32
Truro Youth Hostel/NEED Center

(Map #11, 20 & 21)

Location

The **Truro Youth Hostel/NEED Center** is located near the eastern shore of Truro, just across the Pamet River from the **Ballston Beach** parking lot. Follow Route 6 to the Truro/Wellfleet town line and proceed north 2.5 miles to the well-marked "Pamet Roads" exit on the right. At the bottom of the off-ramp, turn left and follow North Pamet Road 1.6 miles to the red-roofed Truro Youth Hostel/NEED Center building on the right.

The Site

A former Coast Guard Station that was constructed in 1932, this handsome building now serves a dual purpose. From the end of June until the beginning of September each year, it is a youth hostel run by Hosteling International. The rest of the year, it is as an environmental education center for the National Environmental Education Development (NEED) program.

As an education center, the building houses groups of area school children who stay at the center and study the Cape's environment and history.

As a youth hostel, it is an excellent place for walkers on **The Great Thoreau Hike** to stay in summer, especially given its proximity to the beach and central location between Eastham and Provincetown. What's more, the building boasts beautiful views from most of its windows. **Ballston Beach** is currently visible to the east through a break in the dunes, and the Pamet River can be seen to the south and west. The trailhead to the **Pamet Cranberry & Dune Walk**, described in this guide, is also located directly adjacent to the building. Advance reservations for the hostel are recommended at all times. The current fee is $12 per night for Hosteling International members and $15 per night for non-members. Youths under 14 stay for just $6 per night. Check-in is from 5 p.m. to 10 p.m., and check-out is by 9:30 a.m. The hostel closes every day from 10 a.m. to 5 p.m., and there is an 11 p.m. curfew. For further information call the hostel at (508) 349-3889.●

#33
Jenny Lind Tower
(Map #21)

Location

The **Jenny Lind Tower** is located near the northeast corner of the former North Truro Air Force Base that recently became part of the **Cape Cod National Seashore**. The tower can be viewed from Highland Light Road near the **Highland House** and **Highland Light**. A pair of geodesic radar domes near the tower can also be seen about 0.5 miles to the southeast of the road. Follow Route 6 to the Truro/Wellfleet town line and proceed north 4.8 miles to South Highland Road on the right. Turn onto South Highland Road, and Highland Light Road is 1.3 miles on the right.

The Site

The **Jenny Lind Tower** was one of a pair of medieval-style towers which were once part of the Fitchburg Railroad Depot in Boston. When the depot was slated for demolition in 1927, the tower was purchased by Henry Aldrich and moved to its present location in North Truro. The story behind the purchase of such an odd piece of architecture by Aldrich is one of true romance.

Apparently Aldrich was a dedicated fan of the wildly-popular 19th-century singer Jenny Lind*, who was known world-wide as the "Swedish Nightingale." As a young man, Aldrich purchased tickets to attend a concert in Boston featuring Lind. However, on arriving at the concert, he–along with hundreds of others–was sorely disappointed to be turned away at the door. Apparently a greedy promoter had sold twice as many tickets as the venue could accommodate!

Although the crowd demanded to see the celebrated vocalist, there was nothing the theater managers could do. A riot seemed destined to break out in Boston, when suddenly Lind's melodious voice was heard coming down from the sky above the building. Lind had climbed up one of the towers of the Fitchburg Railroad Depot, where she then sang to appease the mob. Lind crooned so well that she not only tamed the crowd but won the young Aldrich's heart forever.

Many years later, when Aldrich heard that the depot was to be demolished, he approached the owners and purchased the very tower from which Lind had sung. He then moved it to his property in Truro, where he kept it in her memory.

---

*Lind was, in fact, so popular that even the somewhat aloof Thoreau knew of her and made brief mention of her in one of his journal entries. See the **Wellfleet Bay Wildlife Sanctuary Trails** to read that entry.

#34
Highland House &
Highland Golf Links

(Map #21)

Location

The **Highland House**, home of the Truro Historical Society Museum, and the **Highland Golf Links** are located on the eastern side of North Truro near **Highland Light**. Follow Route 6 to the Truro/Wellfleet town line and proceed north 4.8 miles to South Highland Road on the right. Turn right onto South Highland Road and follow it 1.3 miles to Highland Light Road on the right. The museum and the golf course clubhouse are both located on Highland Light Road.

Thoreau

Thoreau stayed on the Highlands of North Truro during all four of his visits to Cape Cod. During his first two visits he stayed at **Highland Light**; and during his second two visits he stayed at the Highland House Hotel, a precursor to the building that currently houses the historical museum. An entry from Thoreau's 1857 journal recounts an interesting conversation he overheard at the hotel which was owned by the Small Family of North Truro:

> A youngish man came into Small's with a thick outside coat, when a girl asked where he got that coat. He answered that it was taken off a man that came ashore dead, and he had worn it a year or more. The girls, or young ladies, expressed surprise that he should be willing to wear it and said, "You'd not dare to go to sea with that coat on." But he answered that he might just as well embark in that coat as any other!

The Site

Built in 1907, the present **Highland House** is an excellent example of a turn-of-the-century Cape Cod hotel. The building houses the Truro Historical Society's superb collection of local artifacts, including 17th-century firearms, a pirate's chest, early fishing and farming tools, antique toys, intricate glasswork, fine art, historic maps, models and more. The windows along the front stairway to the second floor offer a good view of the **Jenny Lind Tower**, which is located to the southwest at the former North Truro Air Force Base. The museum also has a gift shop which carries a number of historical and local books. Admission to the Highland House is currently $3, and it is open seven days a week from 10 a.m. to 5 p.m. during summer months. Hours vary during the fall and spring, so call ahead at (508) 487-3397. The museum is closed during the winter.

The **Highland Golf Links** is the oldest golf course on Cape Cod and is celebrated for its "Scottish atmosphere," with brisk winds and stunning views in every direction. The 9-hole course runs around **Highland Light** and the Highland House. It is administered by the town of Truro, and greens fees are currently $16.●

#35
Highland Light
(Map #21)

Location

Highland Light, also known as Cape Cod Light, is located on the eastern shore of North Truro. Follow Route 6 to the Truro/Wellfleet town line and proceed north 4.8 miles to South Highland Road on the right. Turn right onto South Highland Road and follow it 1.3 miles to Highland Light Road on the right, where the lighthouse is located.

Thoreau

Thoreau actually visited **Highland Light** during all four of his Cape Cod visits. In October of 1849, as outlined in *Cape Cod*, he spent one night at the keeper's house. In June of 1850 he spent two more nights there, this time on his walk south from Provincetown. Then, five years later, during his third visit in July of 1855, he stayed the better part of 12 nights at the **Highland House**, a hotel located adjacent to the lighthouse. And during his final visit in 1857 he spent two more nights at the same hotel, on June 18 and 19. It should be noted, however, that the Highland Light Thoreau was acquainted with was not the same lighthouse that stands today. In fact, the former lighthouse was in the process of being replaced by the current structure during Thoreau's 1857 visit.

Having referred to it as "a place of wonders," Thoreau recounted his first night at the lighthouse in *Cape Cod*:

> The keeper entertained us handsomely in his solitary little ocean house. He was a man of singular patience and intelligence, who, when our queries struck him, rung as clear as a bell in response. The light-house lamps a few feet distant shone full into my chamber, and made it as bright as day, so I knew exactly how the Highland Light bore all that night and I was in no danger of being wrecked. Unlike the last, this was as still as a summer night. I thought as I lay there, half awake and half asleep, looking upward through the window at the lights above my head,

how many sleepless eyes from far out on the Ocean stream—mariners of all nations spinning their yarns through the various watches of the night —were directed toward my couch.

The Site

Established in 1797, **Highland Light** was the first lighthouse constructed on Cape Cod. As stated above, its aging original tower was replaced with the current tower in 1857. Aside from this change, however, the station's two-century history remained relatively consistent until very recently. By the summer of 1996, the 140-foot-high bluffs to the northeast had eroded to within a mere 100 feet of the base of the lighthouse and threatened to topple it into the sea. Fortunately, with the fund-raising efforts of the Truro Historical Society, and the contributions of citizens from around the world, the lighthouse was moved to safety 450 feet further inland.

The lighthouse was relocated through a complicated process that entailed reinforcing its walls, jacking it up 10 feet, mounting it onto a system of steel girders, and then rolling it carefully along tracks five feet at a time to its present site. The move combined the expertise of two unique companies: the International Chimney Corporation of Buffalo, NY and Expert Housemovers, Inc. of Sharptown, MD—the same companies that moved **Nauset Lighthouse** in the fall of 1996.

The lighthouse stands 66 feet tall. Its white light rotates every five seconds and can be seen 23 miles away. Owned by the Department of the Interior and operated by the Coast Guard, it is listed with the National Register of Historic Places. At its current distance from the cliff edge, Highland Light is expected to remain safe from erosion for the next two centuries.●

#36
Highland Beach
(Map #21 & #22)

Location

Highland Beach is located on the eastern shore of North Truro, 4.3 miles north of **Ballston Beach**, 0.5 miles south of **Head of the Meadow Beach**, and 2.4 miles south of the jeep trail from the **High Head Parking Area**. Follow Route 6 to the Truro/Wellfleet town line and proceed 5.8 miles north to the well-marked Highland Road exit on the right. At the bottom of the off-ramp, turn right onto Highland Road and proceed 0.7 miles to the t-junction. Turn left and follow Coast Guard Road 0.8 miles to the Highland Beach parking lot. Unfortunately, no parking is permitted at the beach from 9 a.m. to 5 p.m. July through Labor Day, except for Town of Truro resident sticker-holders. The nearest year-round public parking lots are at **Highland Light** to the south and at the **Cape Cod National Seashore** parking lot at Head of the Meadow Beach to the north.

Thoreau

After his 1849 stay at **Highland Light**, Thoreau returned to the **Great Beach** near today's **Highland Beach**:

> Again we took to the beach for another day (October 13), walking along the shore of the resounding sea, determined to get it into us. We wished to associate with the Ocean until it lost the pond-like look which it wears to a country man. We still thought that we could see the other side. Its surface was still more sparkling than the day before, and we beheld "the countless smilings of the ocean waves"; though some of them wore pretty broad grins, for still the wind blew and the billows broke in foam along the beach. The nearest beach to us was on the other side, whither we looked, due east, was on the coast of Galicia in Spain, whose capital is Santiago, though by old poets' reckoning it should have been Atlantis or the Hesperides; but heaven is found to be farther west now.

The Site

Highland Beach was the former site of the Highland Life-Saving Station which was built in 1872. (See **Old Harbor Life-Saving Station Museum** for further information on the U.S. Life-Saving Service.)

The Town of Truro stations chemical toilets at the beach, but there are no public telephones or other services there.●

#37
Head of the Meadow Beach
(Map #22)

Location

Head of the Meadow Beach is located on the eastern shore of Truro, 0.5 miles north of **Highland Beach** and 1.8 miles south of the High Head jeep trail. Follow Route 6 to the Truro/Wellfleet town line, and proceed north 6.2 miles to Head of the Meadow Beach Road on the right. Turn right onto Head of the Meadow Beach Road and follow it 0.9 miles to the beach parking lots. The lot on the left (north) is administered by the **Cape Cod National Seashore**, while the lot on the right (south) is run by the Town of Truro. A $7 daily fee or a $20 seasonal fee is charged for daytime summer parking at Head of the Meadow Beach and all Cape Cod National Seashore managed beaches. Summer parking at the Town of Truro lot is limited to Truro resident sticker-holders.

Thoreau

Head of the Meadow Beach is named for the nearby marsh which runs between it and **Pilgrim Lake** to the northwest. In Thoreau's day, this marsh was known as East Harbor Creek and was connected with Cape Cod Bay via Pilgrim Lake, which was then known as **Provincetown's East Harbor.**

Provincetown's **East Harbor** was transformed into Pilgrim Lake with the 1869 construction of a dike across its mouth that cut it off from Cape Cod Bay.[16] Of course, this dike also cut East Harbor Creek off from the Bay, and thus transformed it from a tidal creek into a marsh, or "salt meadow." The dike was built to address fears that the Atlantic Ocean might break through the thin line of dunes near today's Head of the Meadow Beach and wash sand into the East Harbor and perhaps even into the rest of Provincetown Harbor. Apparently, those fears were justified, for even Thoreau noted the narrowness of this line of dunes near the present location of Head of the Meadow Beach. He writes in *Cape Cod*:

> The Cape became narrower and narrower as we approached its wrist between Truro and Provincetown, and the shore inclined more decidedly to the west. At the head of East Harbor Creek, the Atlantic is separated but by half a dozen rods* of sand from the tide-waters of the Bay."

The Site

During low tide at **Head of the Meadow Beach**, one can still sometimes see the remains of the *Frances*, a three-masted iron-hulled ship that was wrecked in 1872.[17] The ship's crew of 14 were saved thanks to the heroic efforts of the keeper of **Highland Light**. Having spotted the wreck, he managed to round up volunteers and drag a whaleboat all the way from the bay-side of town to Head of the Meadow Beach, where it was launched and the crew rescued. Unfortunately, the captain of the *Frances* died of exposure several days later.

There are chemical toilets at the Head of the Meadow Beach town parking lot and seasonally operated restrooms at the **Cape Cod National Seashore** parking lot.●

* One rod equals 5.5 yards.

#38
Pilgrim Spring
(Map #12 & #22)

Location
Pilgrim Spring is a natural spring located within the boundaries of the **Cape Cod National Seashore** in North Truro and is celebrated as the first spring discovered by the Pilgrims in North America. Follow Route 6 to the Truro/Wellfleet town line and proceed north 7.4 miles to the well-marked Pilgrim Heights Area on the right. Turn right into the area and proceed 0.5 miles to the first parking lot. The spring is located at the junction of the **Pilgrim Spring Trail** (which begins at the pavilion adjacent to the parking lot) and the Head of the Meadow Bike Path.

The Site
After the Pilgrims first set foot on dry land in the New World, in what is now Provincetown, they sent out a search party to look for fresh water and other supplies. The most widely known version of the story of that search is found in *Mourt's Relation*, an account of the Pilgrim's adventures that is credited to William Bradford and Edward Winslow. (See **Pilgrim Spring Trail** for part of that account.) However, Captain Miles Standish, the Pilgrim's military leader, also provided a version of the search in his journal. Standish's perspective is particularly fascinating, not only because of his impressive writing style but because of the unique insight he offers into the group's dynamics, as well as the perils of their situation:

> Presently we came to an huge inland sweep of the harbor [Pilgrim Lake/Provincetown's East Harbor], at the end of which was a long marsh [today's Salt Meadow]. All the while, we were upon the stretch of sand hills, and eagerly sought the firm high ground across the marsh for which our aching ankles were constructed. Some of our party, to save time, wanted to wade the marsh, but our clothes are already wet from wading ashore, and there are signs of affliction in a few noses. So I forced us farther upon the sand, and when we had finally circumvented the marsh to higher ground, I thought: here we are all the same and does it matter if we are an hour later in a course that is a thousand leagues from yesterday, and knows not one foot of tomorrow? Other than myself, there is hardly a soldier among us. This is a great wonder to me, and gnaws at the edge of my sleep. For we have fled half a world - more, from one to another—without notion of conquest or compel of the unknown, with guessed-at charts, and only tales for experience. I fear it is our ignorance has got us here as much as our courage. On our way to higher ground we found a spring welling with fresh water. Two

In the Footsteps of Thoreau

months' deprivation was not only ended, but nearly justified by the sudden pleasure. Even so, a few restrained themselves, afraid of a suspected vileness, as if the elements might differ here. But upon the hungry gulpings by most, the few fell to it.[18]

It should be noted that there is no proof that **Pilgrim Spring** is the same one that the Pilgrims discovered. Although it is in the general area of that spring, it was not identified until relatively recently and there is no conclusive evidence that it is the same.●

#39
High Head Parking Area
(Map #22 & #23B)

Location

The **High Head Parking Area** is managed by the **Cape Cod National Seashore** and is the northern terminus of the Head of the Meadow Bike Path, as well as a major stopping-off point for four-wheel-drive vehicles on their way to the beach between High Head and Race Point. Follow Route 6 to the Truro/Wellfleet town line and proceed north 8.3 miles to High Head Road on the right, located just before **Pilgrim Lake**. Turn right onto High Head Road and proceed 0.4 miles to the fork. Bear left onto the unpaved road and continue another 0.3 miles to the parking area.

For those walking along the shore, the High Head jeep trail (which runs from the parking area to the beach) is located 1.9 miles north of **Head of the Meadow Beach** and 5.5 miles west of **Race Point Beach**.

Thoreau

For the beach walker on his or her way from Truro to Provincetown, the High Head jeep trail is the last "road to civilization" from the beach before **Race Point Beach,** which is located nearly 6 miles away. In his narrative of *Cape Cod*, while walking along this stretch of the shore, Thoreau comments on the timeless wildness he found here:

> Though once there were more whales cast up here, I think that it was never more wild than now. We do not associate the idea of antiquity with the ocean, or wonder how it looked a thousand years ago, as we do of the land, for it was equally wild and unfathomable always. The Indians have left no traces on its surface, but it is the same to the civilized man and the savage. The aspect of the shore only has changed. The ocean is a wilderness reaching round the globe, wilder, than a Bengal jungle, and fuller of monsters, washing the very wharves of our cities and the gardens of our sea-side residences. Serpents, bears,

hyenas, tigers, rapidly vanish as civilization advances, but the most populous and civilized city cannot scare a shark far from its wharves.

The Site
"High Head" is actually the name of the high ground located just above and south of the **High Head Parking Area**. The **Cape Cod National Seashore** discourages driving up to the private neighborhood at High Head; however, walking is not discouraged and yields a magnificent view of Pilgrim Lake, the **Province Lands**, Provincetown, Cape Cod Bay and the Atlantic.

High Head is the northernmost part of Cape Cod to have been deposited by the glaciers that formed Cape Cod during the last Ice Age. Amazingly enough, all of the land north and west of High Head (the Province Lands and Provincetown) has been established only in the last 5,000 years, transferred there by forces of erosion that have steadily washed earth off the eastern shore of Cape Cod.

Visitors to the High Head Parking Area will find chemical toilets that are maintained seasonally by the Cape Cod National Seashore, but there are no public telephones or other services available.●

#40
Pilgrim Lake/Provincetown's East Harbor
(Map #22 & 23B)

Location
Pilgrim Lake, formerly **Provincetown's East Harbor**, is located on the Truro/Provincetown town line, on the eastern side of Route 6.

Thoreau
During Thoreau's first two visits to Cape Cod in 1849 and 1850, the only road leading into Provincetown ran along the northern shoreline of what was then known as **Provincetown's East Harbor**, between it and the Atlantic Ocean to the north. It wasn't until Thoreau's third visit in 1855 that the construction of a bridge across the mouth of the East Harbor established a new road into Provincetown, roughly where today's Route 6 and Route 6A now run. In his 1857 journal, Thoreau describes this "new road":

> The skulls and backbones of blackfish, their vertebrae and spinal processes, and disk-shaped bones, five inches in diameter, from the

spine were strewn all along. These looked like rough crackers. Also the ribs of whales (probably humpbacked)–they get humpback and finback and right whales, I heard–six feet long, lay under the bank, hardly to be distinguished from their gray rails. Some of those whale ribs, ten inches wide, were from time to time set up in the sand, like milestones (or bones); they seemed to answer that purpose along the new road.

The Site

As stated above, the main road into Provincetown formerly lay to the north of **Provincetown's East Harbor** (today's **Pilgrim Lake**), along the narrow row of dunes that separated the harbor from the Atlantic. In places, this row of dunes was just 15 or 20 feet wide at high tide, and many citizens were concerned that the traffic along the road was causing erosion. They feared that if these dunes continued to erode, the Atlantic might break through into the East Harbor. Not only might such a break separate Provincetown from the rest of the Cape and transform it into an island, it could potentially sweep sand through the East Harbor and into the rest of Provincetown Harbor proper, possibly ruining the latter.

Thus, in 1854, the new road described above by Thoreau was constructed along the southern shore of the East Harbor, with a bridge built across its mouth. Unfortunately, this bridge did not solve the problem, as it was frequently washed out by storms. Plus, the dunes to the north continued to erode anyway. In fact, the ocean is even said to have leaked through on occasion.

Thus, in 1868 and 1869, with fears mounting that a major break was imminent, a dike was constructed along the southern side of Provincetown's East Harbor, right across its mouth. With this dike, Provincetown's East Harbor was transformed into Pilgrim Lake, and a reliable roadway was established between Provincetown and the rest of the Cape.[19]

Just a few years later in 1873, the railroad was extended to Provincetown and built along this route. Subsequently, the present roadways, Route 6 & 6A, developed.●

#41
The *Somerset*
(Map #23B)

Location
The *Somerset*, a 64-gun British man-of-war which served in the Revolutionary War, was wrecked in 1778 on the northern shore of Truro, about 0.5 miles west of the Truro/Provincetown town line.

Thoreau
Thoreau writes in *Cape Cod*:

> In the Revolution, a British ship of war called the Somerset was wrecked near the Clay Pounds, and all on board, some hundreds in number, were taken prisoner. My informant said that he had never seen any mention of this in the histories, but that at any rate he knew of a silver watch, which one of those prisoners by accident left there, which was still going to tell the story.

Although little is known of the silver watch that Thoreau mentions, a cannon taken off the *Somerset* is currently on display at the **Provincetown Museum**. The ship also lives on in American lore as part of Henry Wadsworth Longfellow's famous poem, *Paul Revere's Ride*. In the lines below, Longfellow describes the ominous presence of the warship in the waters off Colonial Boston:

> Just as the moon rose over the bay,
> Where swinging wide at her moorings lay
> The Somerset, British Man-o-War
> A phantom ship, with each mast and spar,
> Across the moon like a prison bar,
> A huge black hulk, that was magnified
> By its own reflection in the tide.

The Site
In her thorough and fascinating history, *The H.M.S. Somerset*, Marjorie Hubbell Gibson rightly asserts that the ship "was instrumental in changing the history of North America." Not only did the *Somerset* play a major role in the bombardment of Charlestown during the Revolutionary War, but she was also a key contributor to the landing of the British at Bunker Hill. Still, it would not be exaggerating to say that the *Somerset* made her most lasting impression on Cape Cod.

Having become lost in a northeast storm, the ship was run aground on the infamous Peaked Hill Bars shoals off North Truro on November 2,

1778, where she was eventually lifted up by the surf and flung onto the beach. Although 21 British crewmen drowned in the wreck, the better part of 500 survived and were taken prisoner by patriots from Truro and Provincetown. These prisoners were then marched to Boston where they were jailed.

Meanwhile, locals from Provincetown and Truro salvaged much of the *Somerset* and claimed what they could as repayment for the injustices done to them by the British Navy during the war. Afterward, the upper potion of the *Somerset* was burned, presumably by zealous patriots, but the remaining hulk was soon enough buried by the shifting sands of the **Great Beach**.

The wreck disappeared into history for more than a century until, amazingly enough, an 1885/1886 storm exposed its remains on the beach. These remains became a local attraction, with many 19th-century beach-combers taking chunks of wood as souvenirs.* But, before her 19th-century admirers could completely dismantle her, the *Somerset* was once again swallowed by the beach.

The saga did not end there, however. In June of 1973—nearly two centuries after the ship had originally run aground!—the *Somerset's* remains were revealed once more, causing yet another generation of tourists and history buffs to flock to the shore to view them. The National Park Service removed some of the timbers and placed them in storage; but many of the *Somerset's* "bones" remain buried under the beach. Who knows when the actions of wind and waves will "disinter" them next?●

* Occasionally, various items claimed to have been carved or otherwise made out of wood from the *Somerset* still show up at Cape Cod antique markets.

#42
Province Lands Dune Shacks
(Map #23B)

Location

The **Province Lands Dune Shacks** consist of 18 separate dwellings on approximately 1500 acres of sand dunes located in Provincetown and in North Truro. All of the shacks are within the boundaries of the **Cape Cod National Seashore**.

Four-wheel-drive access to the shacks is limited to authorized vehicles only; however, most are clearly visible from the jeep trails and walking paths that cross the dunes. All of the dwellings are private property. **Please respect owners' rights.**

Thoreau

The best-known dwellings in this area that might have been described as "dune shacks" at the time of Thoreau's visits were the fishermen's huts of **Helltown** at **Race Point** and a few Humane Houses and lifeboat stations along the Atlantic shore Nevertheless, Thoreau is recognized as a major figure in the history and preservation of today's shacks and has been identified by the National Registrar of Historic Places as an important influence on the area's 1989 designation as a U.S. National Historic District. In making its declaration, the Registrar asserted that the shacks represent the same "celebration of the Cape's natural environmental qualities [as is] eloquently embodied in Thoreau's *Cape Cod*."[20]

The Site

By 1803 the Massachusetts Humane Society had constructed survival huts for the benefit of shipwreck victims along unpopulated sections of the Cape's coast. (See **Cahoon Hollow** for more information.) Still, "dune shacks," as they are thought of today, did not really become common in the region until the establishment of manned U.S. Life-Saving Stations on Cape Cod in 1872 (See **Old Harbor Life-Saving Station Museum** for more information on the service.) With lifesavers residing in stations up and down the Cape's shore, shacks were soon built near the stations for family members to stay in while visiting Thus, some of Provincetown's first dune shacks were built near the Peaked Hill Bars Life-Saving Station, which eventually became the dune domicile of Nobel Prize-winning playwright Eugene O'Neill who owned it after it was decommissioned by the U.S. Life-Saving Service.

Many of today's shacks were built between the 1920's and the 1940's, a time when Provincetown grew substantially as an art colony and vacation destination. Famous artists and writers associated with the shacks include John Dos Passos, E. E. Cummings, Franz Kline, Jackson Pollock, Jack Kerouac, Hazel Hawthorne Werner, Edmund Wilson and Eugene O'Neill.

But perhaps the most noteworthy Provincetown dune-dweller was Harry Kemp, "Poet of the Dunes." Kemp wrote many ballads exalting the unique dune environment which he was associated with from the 1920's until his death in 1960. Kemp's simple life in the dunes, his love of nature and passion for literature, place him squarely in Thoreau's Cape Cod literary tradition which includes the likes of Henry Beston, John Hay and many others. Kemp writes to future dune visitors in his poem *Dune Revenant*:

> I said "When I'm alive no more
> And my soul at last goes free,
> You'll find me walking on the dunes
> And down beside the sea.

So, if you glimpse a wavering form,
Or front a vanishing face,
You'll know that I've come back once more
To my accustomed place!"[21]

A replica of Kemp's dune shack is currently on display in the Provincetown Heritage Museum which is included in the **Provincetown Center Walk** as described in this guide.

Many of the dune shacks are owned privately or leased from the Park, but two are managed by "artists in residency" programs which aim to keep the historic connection between the shacks and the arts alive. Call the **Park Headquarters** at (508) 349-3785 for further information.●

#43
Mount Ararat
(Map #23B)

Location
Mount Ararat is located 0.2 miles west of the Provincetown/Truro town line, on the north side of Route 6, just past **Pilgrim Lake**. Of the two largest dunes visible from Route 6, Mount Ararat is the farthest from the road and the highest. No parking is allowed along Route 6 here or at the trail gate next to Mount Ararat. **NOTE: Police and Park officials take notice and are quick to tow vehicles.** The nearest public parking areas to Mount Ararat are at Snail Road to the north and at the **High Head Parking Area** to the south. You'll find the small Snail Road parking area 0.8 miles west of Mount Ararat on the northern edge of Route 6. See **The Great Thoreau Hike, Part VIII** for a description of the route to Mount Ararat from the High Head Parking Area.

Thoreau
In 1849 Thoreau climbed **Mount Ararat** in order to "spend the noon" on its summit, a visit which he describes in *Cape Cod*. In 1857, during his last trip to the Cape, he returned to the "shrubby sand-hill" and wrote the following words in his journal:

> Soon after crossing the bridge, I turned off and ascended Mt. Ararat. It exhibited a remarkable landscape: on the one side the desert, of smooth and spotless palest fawn-colored sand, slightly undulating, and beyond, the Atlantic; on the other, the west side, a few valleys and hills, densely clothed with a short, almost moss-like (to look at it) growth of huckleberry, blueberry, bear-berry, josh-pear (which is so abundant in Provincetown), bayberry, rose, checkerberry, and other bushes, and

beyond, the Bay. All these bushes formed an even and dense covering on the sand-hills, much as bear-berry alone might. It was a very strange scenery. You would think you might be in Labrador, or some other place you have imagined. The shrubbery at the very summit was swarming with mosquitoes, which troubled me when I sat down, but they did not rise above the level of the bushes.

The view from Mount Ararat is as satisfying today as it was in Thoreau's time. In addition to many of the plants noted by Thoreau, notice the beach grass to the north, planted in rows by the **Cape Cod National Seashore** to stabilize the dunes. Of course, beyond the unique **Province Lands** landscape are Cape Cod Bay to the south, Provincetown Harbor to the southwest, the Atlantic to the north, and **Pilgrim Lake** to the east.

The Site
Mount Ararat is the namesake of the Biblical mountain on which Noah's Ark is said to have come to rest after the flood. Although it may seem hyperbolic to have named a mere sand dune after such a Biblical peak, it is not surprising; after all, Mount Ararat is the tallest sand dune in the **Province Lands**. What may be most surprising about Mount Ararat, however, is that it shows up on maps as far back as the early 19th-century—a testimony to its long-term stability and importance as a regional landmark.

A visitor parking lot was previously maintained at the foot of Mount Ararat but was closed some years ago in order to discourage large numbers of people from climbing on it and other dunes, an activity that destroyed many of the plants that hold the dunes in place. Although there are no rules against climbing Mount Ararat today, walkers are strongly urged to avoid trampling on or disturbing vegetation. (See **Safe Walking.**)●

#44
Peaked Hill Bars
Life-Saving Station Remains
(Map #23A & #23B)

Location
The stone-block foundation of the historic **Peaked Hill Bars Life-Saving Station** is located along a jeep trail within the **Cape Cod National Seashore's Province Lands**, approximately 0.6 miles north of Route 6, 0.2 miles south of the Atlantic shore, and 0.3 miles west of the Provincetown/Truro town line. Walkers of **The Great Thoreau Hike, Part VIII** will encounter the foundation 3.7 miles from the start of that hike.

But for more direct access to the site, walkers can follow the paths through the dunes from the small Snail Road parking area, which is located on the north side of Route 6 about 0.8 miles west of the Provincetown/Truro town line. Expect approximately 1.5 hours for the round-trip walk to the site from the Snail Road parking area.

The Site

The Peaked Hill area has long been identified with shipwrecks, as the constantly shifting Peaked Hill Bars just off-shore make the waters some of the most treacherous on the eastern seaboard. Since the famous wreck of the British man-of-war *Somerset* in 1778, scores of vessels and hundreds of lives have been lost here. In fact, by 1803 the Massachusetts Humane Society had already built a Humane House near Peaked Hill as an emergency shelter for shipwreck victims. (See **Cahoon Hollow Beach** for more information on Humane Houses.) More contemporary with Thoreau's visits, an 1858 map places a "Wreck House" and a lifeboat station near Peaked Hill.[22] Thus, it is no surprise that at the inception of the U.S. Life-Saving Service in 1872, a station was built here too. Like the other Provincetown stations at **Race Point** and **Wood End**, the **Peaked Hill Bars Life-Saving Station** was manned primarily by local men, "lifesavers" who patrolled the beaches diligently and who risked their lives in countless rescue operations. (See **Old Harbor Life-Saving Station Museum** for further information regarding the Life-Saving Service.)

The original Peaked Hill Station remained active until 1914 when it was deemed unsafe due to fears that it was too close to the ocean, and that it would soon succumb to erosion. In fact, the high-water mark had come to within 13 feet of the station! Thus, a new Peaked Hill Bars Station was constructed a quarter of a mile away inland.

When the second station was built, the original was purchased by a millionaire named Sam Lewisohn, apparently at the request of socialite Mabel Dodge who wished to decorate and remodel it as a summer house for him. But when Dodge and Lewisohn grew tired of the station a few years later, it was sold to one James O'Neill who gave it as a wedding gift to his son, the young playwright Eugene O'Neill. O'Neill moved into the station in 1919 and for the next six years made it his home and workplace.[23] Here the future Nobel Prize-winner wrote some of his best early works and socialized with some of the most notable writers, artists and actors of his day. In fact, it was at the station that O'Neill was notified that he had won his first Pulitzer Prize for *Beyond the Horizon*. Despite the 1914 prediction that the station would soon be washed away, it was retained by O'Neill until 1931 when it was finally destroyed by a hurricane.

But what of the second Peaked Hill Bars Station? Originally built on wooden posts, the second station was moved onto a stone block foundation, due to concerns that it too might fall victim to erosion. This foundation (which still exists) served as the station's ground floor, with the main floor set on top of it, a small third floor above the main floor, and a lookout tower reaching still higher up. In 1937, just six years after its predecessor had toppled into the sea, technological advances had increased marine safety to such an extent that the second Peaked Hill Station was deemed no longer necessary to the safety of the coast and was decommissioned. At that time, it too was sold into private hands. Unfortunately, the new owners left the building unattended to and, some time later, all but its foundation was consumed in a fire.●

#45
Province Lands Visitor Center
& the Province Lands
(Map #23A & #25)

Location
The **Province Lands** area, which falls under the auspices of the **Cape Cod National Seashore**, consists of roughly 1,200 acres of essentially undeveloped land stretching along the Atlantic from **Herring Cove Beach** in Provincetown to High Head in North Truro. To get to the **Province Lands Visitor Center**, follow Route 6 to the Provincetown/Truro town line and proceed 2.25 miles west into Provincetown to the traffic lights. Turn right at the traffic lights and follow Race Point Road 1.5 miles north to the Visitor Center on the right.

Thoreau
Thoreau spent most of his second day in Provincetown exploring the **Province Lands**, of which he writes:

> We travelled five or six miles after we got out there, on a curving line, and might have gone nine or ten, over the vast platters of pure sand, from the midst of which we could not see a particle of vegetation, excepting the distant thin fields of Beach-grass, which crowned and made the ridges toward which the sand sloped upward on each side—all the while in the face of a cutting wind as cold as January; indeed, we experienced no weather so cold as this for nearly two months afterward. This desert extends from the extremity of the Cape through Provincetown into Truro, and many a time as we were traversing it we were reminded of "Riley's narrative" of his captivity in the sands of Arabia, notwithstanding the cold. It was the dreariest scenery imaginable.

The Site

The **Province Lands Visitor Center** is open seven days a week from the Saturday prior to Patriots Day until the Sunday following Thanksgiving. The Center's hours are 9 a.m. to 4:30 p.m., except in July and August when it is open from 9 a.m. to 6 p.m. Like the **Salt Pond Visitor Center** in Eastham, the Province Lands Visitor Center offers a variety of resources. In addition to restrooms and public telephones, there are movies and exhibits, an observation deck, and a book store. A number of pamphlets and maps are also available free of charge. Inquire about Ranger-guided activities, lectures and walks. The telephone number at the Center is (508) 487-1256, or call the **Park Headquarters** at (508) 349-3785 during the off-season.

Before Provincetown was incorporated as a town in 1727, the entire tip of Cape Cod was known simply as **"The Province Lands,"** with rights to it belonging to English Colonial powers. When the town became incorporated, it was endowed with all the rights and privileges granted to other towns, except for the key fact that the Colony did not officially renounce its claim to the **Province Lands**! Indeed, it wasn't until 1893 that the Commonwealth of Massachusetts officially ceded its claim to the small strip of land on which Provincetown is laid out, mainly to the south of today's Route 6.[24] The State retained its rights to the Province Lands until 1961 when the U.S. Department of the Interior took control of the area and made it part of the **Cape Cod National Seashore.**

Interestingly, all of Provincetown, including the Province Lands, is a post-glacial formation, the creation of which did not even begin until about 6,000 years ago–a mere blink of the eye, geologically speaking. During the last Ice Age, massive quantities of earth were deposited by glaciers to form the land masses that now comprise Cape Cod, Martha's Vineyard and Nantucket. Interestingly, these glaciers did not deposit land north of the present location of High Head in North Truro.

Only with the melting of the glaciers did the earth's sea levels rise to their present heights, allowing the Atlantic to begin eroding or "sculpting" the shores of Cape Cod, as it still does today. As this sculpting occurred, earth was swept from the outer shores of the Cape and was deposited northward to form today's Provincetown and the Province Lands. Thus, over the past 6,000 years, the Atlantic has steadily made the Outer Cape thinner while simultaneously lengthening it.

As the continuing forces of erosion and ocean movement transformed Cape Cod into its current shape, grasses and other vegetation took root; so that by the time the Pilgrims arrived, there was an extensive hardwood forest across most of the Cape, including the Province Lands. (See the **Beech Forest Trail.**) Unfortunately, most of this forest was subsequently clear-cut by European settlers, who then proceeded to overgraze what was left. Soon bereft of any substantial vegetation, the Province Lands was fully exposed to the harsh Atlantic winds and stripped of its once rich topsoil.

The dangers of this erosion were recognized by legislators as early as 1714, when an act was passed to preserve what few trees remained. Still, a century later the problem had only worsened. In fact, some houses were literally buried by migrating dunes, while many more were put up on posts to allow sand to blow underneath them (a design that is still included in many of the **Province Lands Dune Shacks**). Furthermore, Provincetown Harbor, one of the most important harbors on the eastern seaboard, began to fill with sand.

In 1825, the State initiated a program to stem erosion by planting beach grass across the dunes of the Province Lands, and later a dike was built across the mouth of **Provincetown's East Harbor** (now **Pilgrim Lake**) to prevent sand from migrating into it. Nevertheless, the area continues to recover from its initial deforestation to this day.

Thus, the unique landscape of the Province Lands, barren but beautiful, continues to fascinate and inspire artists, writers and nature-lovers of every kind.●

#46
Old Harbor Life-Saving Station Museum

(Map #23A & #25)

Location
The **Old Harbor Life-Saving Station Museum** is located near the parking lot at **Race Point Beach**. Follow Route 6 to the Provincetown/Truro town line and proceed 2.25 miles west to the traffic lights. Turn right onto Race Point Road and follow it 2.3 miles, past the **Province Lands Visitor Center**, to the beach parking lot. A $7 daily fee or a $20 seasonal fee is charged for daytime parking at this and all other **Cape Cod National Seashore** managed beaches.

The Site
The Old Harbor Life-Saving Station itself was saved from the Atlantic in the winter of 1977/1978 when it was floated on a barge from Chatham to Provincetown, just before a series of winter storms struck the Cape that would have assured its destruction.

"I've cruised by a lot of Coast Guard stations during my lifetime, but this is the first time I've ever seen a Coast Guard station cruise by me!", declared one veteran mariner upon seeing the station being barged along the **Great Beach**.[25]

The station was one of a series of 13 such stations built along the Great Beach from Provincetown to Monomoy Island from 1872 to 1915. (Originally only nine were constructed; but four more, including Old Harbor Station, were added between 1882 and 1902.)

These Life-Saving Stations could not have been built with better cause, for in the less than 400 years of recorded Cape Cod history, there have been some 3,000 known shipwrecks along the Cape's shores. And while countless lives were saved during the 42-year duration of the U.S. Life-Saving Service on the Cape, only a pair of lifesavers ever died in duty—perhaps because they lived by such a simple and profound motto:

You have to go, but you don't have to come back.

Richard G. Ryder, grandson of a former keeper of the Old Harbor Station, provides a flavor of the life at the station in his fascinating account of its history, *Old Harbor Station*, published in 1990. He writes, "There was no running water, no electricity, no central heat, no refrigeration and no inside plumbing when the station was first occupied The crew provided their own food, uniforms, outer clothing, and, until 1917, their own toilet paper. The Life-Saving Service provided fuel, a place to live, and a respectable job in the winter when work was difficult to get."

The Service is perhaps most famous for its use of two primary rescue apparatus, the surfboat and the breeches buoy. A surfboat was a good-sized rowing dory, 16 to 26-feet long, usually manned by four to six life-savers who rowed the craft from the beach, often through treacherous surf, to ships wrecked offshore. The breeches buoy, on the other hand, was used when conditions were too treacherous to launch a surfboat. To set up the breeches buoy, surfmen shot a line from a small cannon on the beach to the deck of a wrecked ship. While surfmen secured their end of the line on the beach, those on board were responsible for attaching their end to the ship. The breeches buoy—essentially a circle buoy with leg supports sewn into its middle for a seat—was then attached to the line with a rope and pulley that allowed it to be maneuvered between the ship and the shore. If all went well, victims would then take turns riding along the breeches buoy to safety.

U.S. Life-Saving crews on Cape Cod consisted almost exclusively of local men who practiced lifesaving techniques diligently and were highly honored by their communities. In addition to his other duties, it was also the lifesaver's job to patrol the miles of beach between each station. Thus, the lifesavers can rightly be considered the greatest Cape Cod beach-walkers of all time.

The Sites

Stations were established in Provincetown at **Wood End**, Race Point and Peaked Hill; in Truro at High Head, **Highland Beach** and **Ballston Beach**; in Wellfleet at **Cahoon Hollow Beach**; in Eastham at **Coast Guard Beach**; in Orleans at Nauset Beach; and in Chatham at Nauset Beach and Monomoy Island.

The Service was combined with the U.S. Revenue Marine Service in 1915 to form the U.S. Coast Guard. Today, the **Cape Cod National Seashore** administers the **Old Harbor Life-Saving Station Museum** and conducts weekly reenactments of the breeches buoy each summer at **Race Point Beach**. Call the **Race Point Ranger Station** at (508) 487-2100 or the **Park Headquarters** (508) 349-3785, for further information.●

#47
Race Point Beach &
Race Point Ranger Station
(Map #23A & #25)

Location
Race Point Beach and the **Race Point Ranger Station** are located on the northern shore of Provincetown, 5.5 miles west of the junction between the High Head jeep trail and the **Great Beach**. Follow Route 6 to the Provincetown/Truro town line and proceed 2.25 miles west to the traffic lights. Turn right onto Race Point Road and follow it 2.3 miles, past the **Province Lands Visitor Center**, to the beach parking lot. A $7 daily fee or a $20 seasonal fee is charged for daytime parking at this and all other **Cape Cod National Seashore** managed beaches.

Thoreau
During his historic 1849 hike, Thoreau did not follow the curve of the Cape's **Great Beach** all the way to the true geographical location of Race Point, where **Race Point Lighthouse** is situated. Instead, he describes his route from the Provincetown/Truro town line and **Mount Ararat** as follows:

> As we did not wish to enter Provincetown before night, though it was cold and windy, we returned across the Desert to the Atlantic side, and walked along the beach again nearly to Race Point, being still greedy of the sea influence.

Thus, given the maps of Thoreau's time, he most likely left the **Great Beach** and turned inland very close to the location of today's **Race Point Beach**. Therefore, **The Great Thoreau Hike**, as described in this guide, concludes at **Race Point Beach**. (See **Additional Hike #2** for an extension of The Great

Thoreau Hike, between Race Point Beach and Provincetown Village.)

The Site
Race Point Beach is one of the most popular beaches within the **Cape Cod National Seashore**. In addition to offering four-wheel-drive access to the shore, it is the location of the **Race Point Ranger Station** and the **Old Harbor Life-Saving Station Museum**. The museum is a former U.S. Life-Saving Station, and provides unique insights into the legendary U.S. Life-Saving Service. The Ranger Station, on the other hand, is a former U.S. Coast Guard Station and currently serves as the administrative headquarters of the northern half of the Park. Built in 1931, the building was decommissioned in the 1980's when the Coast Guard constructed its new Provincetown Station on Commercial Street along Provincetown Harbor.

On clear days, **Race Point Lighthouse** can be seen to the west of the beach. A good place to view it is from the platform adjacent to the public telephones and restrooms. Those who wish to continue walking along the shore past Race Point Beach to the lighthouse can do so via the four-wheel-drive jeep trail that begins near the Ranger Station, or by simply following the shoreline west. Allot at least 3 hours for the almost 4-mile round trip.●

#48
Race Point Lighthouse & Helltown
(Map #23A & #25)

Location
Race Point Lighthouse and the former location of the 19th-century fishing camp, **"Helltown,"** are located 2 miles west of the **Race Point Beach** parking lot. There are no paved roads to this site, but it can be reached either by foot or four-wheel-drive vehicle. A **Cape Cod National Seashore** four-wheel-drive sticker can be obtained seasonally at the **Race Point Ranger Station**, telephone (508) 487-2100. Walkers should plan on at least 3 hours for the 4-mile round-trip walk between the parking lot and the lighthouse. To get to Race Point Beach follow Route 6 to the Provincetown/Truro town line and proceed west 2.25 miles to the traffic lights. Turn right onto Race Point Road and follow it 2.6 miles, past the **Province Lands Visitor Center**, to the beach parking lot. A $7 daily fee or a $20 seasonal fee is charged for parking at this and all other **Cape Cod National Seashore** beaches.

Thoreau
In the mid-19th century, Provincetown was one of the wealthiest and

The Sites   247 fastest growing towns in Massachusetts. Unlike today, when the horizon-line is usually dotted only with a handful of boats, the waters around the town at that time were often filled with more ships than one could easily count. Thoreau writes:

> We counted about two hundred sail of mackerel fishers within one small arc of the horizon and a nearly equal number had disappeared southward. Thus they hovered about the extremity of the Cape like moths round a candle; the lights at Race Point and Long Point being bright candles for them at night—and at this distance they looked fair and white, as if they had not yet flown into the light.

Of course, "flying" into **Race Point Lighthouse** was not nearly as dangerous as simply running aground near it—the fate of far too many a mariner. In *Cape Cod*, Thoreau recognizes the perils of Race Point:

> Of this part of the coast it is said: "A northeast storm, the most violent and fatal to seamen, as it is frequently accompanied with snow, blows directly on the land, a strong current sets along the shore, add to which that ships, during the operation of such a storm, endeavor to work northward, that they may get into the bay. Should they be unable to weather Race Point, the wind drives them on the shore, and a shipwreck is inevitable. Accordingly, the strand is everywhere covered with the fragments of vessels."

The Site

The waters off Race Point are, indeed, among the most treacherous on the eastern seaboard. Sometimes referred to as "the knuckles of the Cape," Race Point is the meeting place of Cape Cod Bay and the Atlantic Ocean. More than 100 shipwrecks have been documented off Race Point, even *after* the 1816 establishment of a lighthouse there! The present lighthouse and keeper's house were built in 1876. The tower stands 41 feet above the ocean, and its white light flashes every 15 seconds.

Despite its isolated and dangerous location, a small community of fishermen's shacks, now known as **Helltown**, developed at Race Point during the 19th century. With such a colorful name having become attached to it, Helltown has gone down in legend as the lair of gamblers, thieves, murderers and mooncussers*. Less romantically, however, Helltown was probably not particularly unseemly. Established sometime before 1803

---

*"Mooncusser" is the name given to those despicable individuals who purposely confused sailors at night by shining lanterns on the beach, thereby causing sailors to misjudge their locations and run their ships aground where they could then be raided and looted. Of course, if the moon shone brightly, it was all but impossible to confuse mariners with lanterns and the "mooncussers" were out of luck—hence the name of the profession.

In the Footsteps of Thoreau

and abandoned by 1875, it was the winter residence of poor fishermen whose small dories required closer access to winter fishing grounds than the wharves of Provincetown provided.

Author Joseph Berger offers the most plausible reasoning for Helltown's name when he writes in *In Great Waters*: "The men bunked eight or ten to a shack. They called it Helltown because it was just plain hell to live there." Despite its drawbacks, Race Point was a practical location for fishermen because of nearby Hatches Harbor, the small tidal inlet just to the south of the lighthouse, where fishermen probably kept their boats. Today, no signs of Helltown remain.●

#49
Herring Cove Beach
(Map #23A & #25)

Location

Herring Cove Beach is located on the western shore of Provincetown, south of **Race Point Lighthouse** and north of **Wood End**. Follow Route 6 to the Provincetown/Truro town line and proceed west 4 miles. Bear right onto Province Lands Road, and after just a short distance, the entrance to the beach parking lot will be on the left. A $7 daily fee or a $20 seasonal fee is charged for daytime summer parking at this and all other **Cape Cod National Seashore** managed beaches.

Thoreau

On his second day in Provincetown, October 14, 1849, Thoreau explored much of the **Province Lands**, including **Herring Cove Beach** which he referred to simply as "the shore south of Race Point."

The Site

Herring Cove Beach is one of the most popular beaches within the **Cape Cod National Seashore**. There are public telephones, public restrooms and a concession stand located there throughout the summer. It is also connected to the Province Lands Bike Path.●

#50
Wood End &
Wood End Lighthouse

Location

Wood End is the small stretch of sand in Provincetown that lies between **Herring Cove Beach** and **Long Point**. There are no roadways to Wood End and **Wood End Lighthouse**, but both can be reached on foot from the Provincetown Rotary by walking 1.1 miles along the stone breakwater that runs across the west end of the harbor. To get to the rotary follow Route 6 to the Provincetown/Truro town line and proceed west 4.1 miles. Bear left at the intersection with Province Lands Road and continue another 1.3 miles to the Provincetown Rotary. Limited parking is available along the side of the road near the rotary. **NOTE: Many people enjoy walking the breakwater, but very high tides can sometimes nearly submerge it. Walkers are advised to check a tide chart before heading out.**

Thoreau

Thoreau's *Cape Cod* is replete with tales of shipwrecks, one of the most interesting having occurred at **Wood End**. As related by Thoreau in Chapter 10 at the end of his book, it was the result of the very same storm that caused the wreck of the *St. John*, as described in Chapter 1. Thoreau writes:

> Before we left the wharf we made the acquaintance of a passenger whom we had seen at the hotel. When we asked him which way he came to Provincetown, he answered that he was cast ashore at Wood End, Saturday night, in the same storm in which the St. John was wrecked. He had been at work as a carpenter in Maine, and took passage for Boston in a schooner laden with lumber. When the storm came on, they endeavored to get into Provincetown harbor. "It was dark and misty," said he, "and as we were steering for Long Point Light we suddenly saw the land near us—for our compass was out of order—carried several degrees (a mariner always casts the blame on his compass)—but there being a mist on shore, we thought it was further off than it was, and so held on, and we immediately struck on the bar. Says the Captain, 'We are all lost.' Says I to the Captain, 'Now don't let her strike again this way; head her right on.' The sea washed completely over us, and wellnigh took the breath out of my body. I held on to the running rigging, but I have learned to hold on to the standing rigging the next time." "Well, were there any drowned?" I asked. "No; we all got safe to a house at Wood End, at midnight, wet to our skins, and half frozen to death." At that moment the Captain called to him from the

wharf. He looked like a man just from the country, with a cap made of a woodchuck's skin, and now that I had heard a part of his history, he appeared singularly destitute—a Captain without a vessel, only a great-coat! and that perhaps a borrowed one! Not even a dog followed him.... As we passed Wood End, we noticed the pile of lumber on the shore which had made the cargo of their vessel.

The Site

The twin of **Long Point Lighthouse, Wood End Lighthouse** was established in 1827. The present structure was built in 1873 and gives off a red flash every 15 seconds that can be seen 13 miles out to sea. Wood End is the former location of one of the thirteen U.S. Life-Saving Stations which dotted the Cape's shore at the turn of the century. (See **Old Harbor Life-Saving Station Museum** for further information.)

Unfortunately, **Wood End** is also the site of "The *S-4* Tragedy." The *S-4* was a U.S. Navy submarine in which 40 crewmen were drowned in 1927. The affair was particularly lamentable given that the sub was accidentally sunk in a collision with a U.S. Coast Guard Destroyer, and that at least six crewmen remained alive within the wreck for the better part of 24 hours while various rescue attempts were botched.●

#51
Long Point &
Long Point Lighthouse

Location

Long Point, the location of **Long Point Lighthouse**, is the small spit of sand which stretches from **Wood End** out into Cape Cod Bay to form the southern boundary of Provincetown Harbor. There are no roadways to Long Point, but it can be reached on foot from the Provincetown Rotary by walking along the stone breakwater that runs 1.1 miles across the harbor, and then following the beach east. To get to the rotary follow Route 6 to the Provincetown/Truro town line and proceed west 4.1 miles. Bear left at the intersection with Province Lands Road and continue another 1.3 miles. Limited parking is allowed along the road around the rotary. **NOTE: Many people enjoy walking the breakwater, but very high tides can sometimes nearly submerge it. Walkers are advised to check a tide chart before heading out.**

Thoreau
Thoreau writes of **Long Point**:

> About Long Point in the summer you commonly see them catching
> lobsters for the New York market, from small boats just off the shore, or
> rather, the lobsters catch themselves, for they cling to the netting on
> which the bait is placed of their own accord, and thus are drawn up.
> They sell them fresh for two cents apiece. Man needs to know but little
> more than a lobster in order to catch them in his traps.

The Site
Long Point has not always been as secluded as it is today. In fact, it was
the site of a small community that reached its heyday at about the time
Thoreau first came to the Cape in 1849. At that time there were some 38
dwellings and about 200 inhabitants there. As Thoreau observed, many of
the residents engaged in lobstering, but off-shore fishing was also very
popular, as was the salt-making industry.

The Long Point community was established in 1818 by fishermen
who found it more convenient to reach fishing grounds from the Point
rather than from other locations in town, and by entrepreneurs who took
advantage of the Point's long sandy flats to construct saltworks that pro-
duced sea salt. The major difficulty for the community, besides being
directly exposed to the elements, was the absence of fresh groundwater.
Rainwater was collected in cisterns for drinking.

By 1867 a decline in fish stocks near the Point, combined with a drop
in the price of salt, caused the residents to leave Long Point for better
prospects in town. The inhabitants of Long Point did not just abandon
their homes, however. Most floated their houses across the harbor on
barges and set them up in the west end of town. Many of these houses
remain in use today and can be identified by the blue historical signs posted by their front doors. Evidently, the floating of these buildings across
the harbor became so commonplace at the time that many inhabitants did
not even bother to leave their homes for the move, nevermind stop what
they were doing. One housewife, it is said, even continued baking her
bread through the entire process, with smoke coming out of her chimney
as the house was barged across the harbor!

Two other interesting historical structures at Long Point were the pair
of Civil War forts that were erected near the lighthouse. As Provincetown
had proven vulnerable during previous wars, the Union Army deemed it
wise to establish two fortifications there. But, as Provincetown was never
attacked, the forts were never needed. After years of disuse, members of
the community dubbed them "Fort Useless" and "Fort Ridiculous." The
mounds of dirt which were built for the forts are still visible today on Long

Point, next to the lighthouse. Models of the forts are also part of the permanent exhibitions at **Provincetown Museum**.

Long Point Lighthouse was established in 1826. It has a steady green light and its fog horn can be heard in town on most low- visibility days●

#52
Pilgrim Monument &
Provincetown Museum
(Map #15, #23A & #25)

Location

The **Pilgrim Monument & Provincetown Museum** are located on High Pole Hill in the center of Provincetown. Follow Route 6 to the Provincetown/Truro town line and proceed west 2.25 miles to the traffic lights. Turn left onto Conwell Street and follow it 0.4 miles to the t-junction with Bradford Street. Turn right onto Bradford and continue 0.3 miles, past the Provincetown Town Hall, to Winslow Street on the right. Follow Winslow Street 0.15 miles up the hill and bear right into the Monument and Museum parking lot.

Thoreau

Thoreau spent some time viewing Provincetown from the vantage point of High Pole Hill, the site of today's **Pilgrim Monument & Provincetown Museum**. He writes:

> This was the very day one would have chosen to sit upon a hill over looking sea and land, and muse there. The mackerel fleet was rapidly taking its departure, one schooner after another, and standing round the Cape, like fowls leaving their roosts in the morning to disperse themselves in distant fields. The turtle-like sheds of the salt-works were crowded into every nook in the hills, immediately behind the town, and their now idle windmills lined the shore.... From this elevation we could overlook the operations of the inhabitants almost as completely as if the roofs had been taken off. They were busily covering the wicker-worked flakes about their houses with salted fish, and we now saw that the back yards where one man's fish ended another's began.

The Site

While the view has certainly changed since the 1800's, the perspective of the town from High Pole Hill remains impressive—more impressive even, given the 252-feet and 7.5-inches of elevation provided by the **Pilgrim Monument**! The monument was erected by the Cape Cod Pilgrim Memorial Association which continues to own and operate it. It's cornerstone was laid in 1907 in a ceremony conducted by President Theodore Roosevelt; and its 1910 dedication included a speech by President William Howard Taft. The monument was built to commemorate the first landing of the Pilgrims in Provincetown on November 21, 1620. The monument stands 353 feet above sea level. It is open daily from April 1 to November 30 from 9 a.m. to 5 p.m., with hours extended to 7 p.m. in July and August. Admission, which includes access to the **Provincetown Museum**, is $5 for adults and $3 for children under 12. The museum shows a diverse collection of Provincetown treasures, from the MacMillan Arctic Collection to antique doll houses to a cannon taken from the famous British Revolutionary War ship, the *Somerset.*●

#53
The Old Kings Highway
(Map #17, #18, #20, #21 & #22)

Location
The **Old Kings Highway** was formerly the main stage route from Sandwich to Provincetown. It is generally considered to have followed the path of today's Route 6A, between Sandwich and Orleans; and sections of it still remain in various places from Eastham through Provincetown, both as regular paved roads and as a jeep trails.

Thoreau
Thoreau writes in *Cape Cod*:

> The single road which runs lengthwise the Cape, now winding over the plain, now through the shrubbery which scrapes the wheels of the stage, was a mere cart-track in the sand, commonly without any fences to confine it, and continually changing from this side to that, to harder ground, or sometimes to avoid the tide. But the inhabitants travel the waste here and there pilgrim-wise and staff in hand, by narrow footpaths, through which the sand flows out and reveals the nakedness of the land. We shuddered at the thought of living there and taking our afternoon walks over those barren swells.

Thoreau spent the majority of his four visits to the Cape walking, and there is no doubt that he became familiar with most of the **Old Kings Highway**, much of which still exists today. His description of the "barren swells" is a reference to the fact that much of the Cape was deforested at that time.

The Site

In 1684 a committee appointed by then Governor Hinckley had a highway laid out from Plymouth to Barnstable, along the route of old Indian trails, thus initiating the history of the **Old Kings Highway**. In 1715, the road was extended from Eastham through Truro and then to the **Province Lands**.[26]

Deyo's *History of Barnstable County*, published in 1890, states that "although [the Old Kings Highway is] only used in portions at the present day, its tortuous course is well known." Unfortunately, 100 years later, it is not easy to precisely ascertain the complete route of the Highway. It is certain to have changed and evolved over the years as local needs required, and as the Cape's dynamic geography altered it.

In this guide, the Old Kings Highway is designated as Route 6A, from Sandwich to Orleans. North of Orleans, it is considered to be those paved roads and unpaved jeep trails that have been labelled as the "Old Kings Highway" on the most recently field-checked U.S. Geological Survey topographical maps of 1972.●

#54
Cape Cod National Seashore

Location

The **Cape Cod National Seashore** is a U.S. Federal park that manages some 44,600 acres stretching 40 miles along the **Great Beach** of Cape Cod from Chatham in the south to Provincetown in the north. The Park administers various acreage inland from the beach, including one section that stretches across the Cape through the towns of Wellfleet and Truro and encompasses fourteen miles of Cape Cod Bay shoreline. The Cape Cod National Seashore can be reached by many routes. The **Salt Pond Visitor Center**, as described in this guide, is an excellent starting point from which to get to know the Park.

Thoreau

The establishment of the **Cape Cod National Seashore** did much to rescue undeveloped land on the Outer Cape from the massive demographic changes which have occurred here during the last four decades. While the Park has been resented by some as a manifestation of big government taking over public lands, it has nevertheless been credited by others for having saved many of those aspects of the Cape that have made it a mecca for tourists from around the world.

Almost a century and a half ago, Thoreau commented:

> At present, in this vicinity, the best part of the land is not private property; the landscape is not owned, and the walker enjoys comparative freedom. But possibly the day will come when it will be partitioned off into so-called pleasure-grounds, in which a few will take a narrow and exclusive pleasure only—when fences shall be multiplied, and man-traps and other engines invented to confine men to the "public" road, and walking over the surface of God's earth shall be construed to mean trespassing on some gentleman's grounds. To enjoy a thing exclusively is commonly to exclude yourself from the true enjoyment of it. Let us improve our opportunities, then, before the evil days come.

Certainly, there are plenty of places on Cape Cod where the "evil days" have already arrived. Still, the **Cape Cod National Seashore** has managed to preserve massive tracts of land that Thoreau explored in the mid-19th century. Without the presence of the Park, hiking Outer Cape Cod would certainly be a far less appealing prospect than it is today.

The Site

The **Cape Cod National Seashore** was authorized by an Act of Congress, Public Law 87-126, and approved by President John F. Kennedy on August 7, 1961. The Cape Cod National Seashore is actually a unit of the National Parks system of the Department of the Interior. It includes lands within the towns of Chatham, Orleans, Eastham, Wellfleet, Truro and Provincetown.

Much of the original core of the Park was composed of the **Province Lands**, Pilgrim Springs State Park and **Camp Wellfleet**, a former Army Training camp. Additional lands were added to these core areas through a diverse and ongoing land-acquisition program that has included land exchanges, purchases and donations.

Perhaps one of the more interesting aspects of the Park is that there are some 550 residential and ten commercial properties within its boundaries. These properties may be retained indefinitely by their owners, sold, left to their heirs, etc. Thus, unlike many other parks, the Cape Cod National Seashore includes a permanent residential human component.

There are two main visitor centers for the Park: the **Salt Pond Visitor Center** in Eastham and the **Province Lands Visitor Center** in Provincetown. Both centers offer a wealth of educational material about the Park, including pamphlets, maps, books and short movies. The visitor centers are also great places to direct questions to Park Rangers and other Seashore personnel, as are the **Race Point Ranger Station** and the **Cape Cod National Seashore Park Headquarters** in South Wellfleet.

The Park also manages a variety of other public assets including: the **Old Harbor Life-Saving Station Museum,** 6 seasonally-staffed public beaches, 25 hiking trails, 3 bicycle trails, 13 structures listed with the National Register of Historic Places, 23 parking areas, 3 picnic areas, and numerous ponds and wetlands.

The Cape Cod National Seashore hosts some 5 million visitors each year, approximately half this number visiting between mid-June and Labor Day.[27]●

#55
The Great Beach

Location

The **Great Beach** of Cape Cod is generally defined as that 40-mile stretch of shoreline running along the eastern, or Atlantic, side of the Cape from **Race Point** in Provincetown to the north, all the way to the tip of Monomoy Island in Chatham to the south. Various sections of the Great Beach are assigned individual names; directions to the following are listed in this book: **Coast Guard Beach, Nauset Light Beach, Marconi Beach, LeCount Hollow Beach, White Crest Beach, Cahoon Hollow Beach, Newcomb Hollow Beach, Ballston Beach, Highland Beach, Head of the Meadow Beach, High Head Parking Area,** and **Race Point Beach.** Other beaches include Longnook Beach in Truro (which is located between Ballston Beach and Highland Beach) and Nauset Beach in Orleans (which runs south from **Nauset Marsh** in Eastham, through Orleans to Chatham). Monomoy Island is only accessible by boat.

Thoreau

Thoreau begins *Cape Cod* with a simple explanation for his attraction to the area: "Wishing to get a better view than I had yet of the ocean, which, we are told, covers more than two thirds of the globe, but of which a man who lives a few miles inland may never see any trace, more than of another world, I made a visit to Cape Cod." And for all the importance of the rest of the Cape and its inhabitants in Thoreau's text, it is the **Great Beach** that serves as the focal point of *Cape Cod.* The author writes:

> On studying the map, I saw that there must be an uninterrupted beach on the east or outside of the fore-arm of the Cape, more than thirty miles from the general line of the coast, which would afford a good sea view; but that, on account of an opening in the beach, forming the

entrance to Nauset Harbor [Nauset Marsh], in Orleans, I must strike it in Eastham, if I approached it by land, and probably I could walk thence straight to Race Point, about twenty-eight miles, and not meet with any obstruction.

Thoreau's map proved accurate: the section of the Great Beach running from Eastham to Provincetown is indeed unobstructed, and he was able to walk its length. At the end of *Cape Cod*, Thoreau summarizes his adventures on the beach:

> Such beaches as are fashionable are here made and unmade in a day, I may almost say, by the sea shifting its sands. Lynn and Nantasket! this bare and bended arm it is that makes the bay in which they lie so snugly. What are springs and waterfalls? here is the spring of springs, the water fall of waterfalls. A storm in the fall or winter is the time to visit it; a light-house or a fisherman's hut the true hotel. A man may stand there and put all America behind him.

The Site

As stated above, the **Great Beach** is that stretch of the Cape's shoreline from Race Point to Monomoy Island. It is also referred to as the Outer Shore, the Outer Beach and the Back Side; individual sections of the beach have their own names, as listed under the "LOCATION" heading of this entry. The Great Beach is also somewhat unusual, in that a marine scarp, or cliff-face, defines its western boundary from **Nauset Light Beach** in Eastham to High Head in North Truro. This cliff ranges in height from 60 to 170 feet and is interrupted only by "hollows," or small valleys, that run east to west across the Cape, providing access points to the beach.

It must be pointed out, however, that the Great Beach of Thoreau's time is not the same beach today. It is a highly dynamic geographic entity, its shape altering with every tide, its sandbars constantly shifting, and its upper beach evolving from one week to the next. In addition to this continual movement, the cliff-face that forms the western boundary of the Great Beach is subject to constant erosion. In fact, while estimates vary, most agree that the cliff-face erodes at an average of three feet per year. Thus, the Great Beach of Thoreau's day was located approximately 444 feet east of today's!

The erosion of the cliff-face along the Great Beach is primarily the result of very high tides and storms which can wash away massive sections of the cliff in a very short period of time. (See **Safe Walking**.) Additionally, this erosion is a continuous process in that small bits of sand and earth are regularly blown loose from the cliff by the wind.

For all the people who have walked it and driven on it, flown over it, fished from it, sunbathed on it, been shipwrecked on it, written of it, and

In the Footsteps of Thoreau

otherwise known it, the Great Beach will always remain "undiscovered country"—a perpetual clean slate of sorts, on which each individual may compose his own story.

The Great Beach is administered by the **Cape Cod National Seashore**. As noted by nature writer John Hay in his classic 1963 book, *The Great Beach*, it is "not owned by individuals or the towns in which they reside, but by the people of the Untied States. It is under national protection and possession at the same time, so how we approach and treat its future is a very great responsibility, which is appropriate enough."[28]●

NOTES

Getting Started

IN THE FOOTSTEPS OF THOREAU

1. Harding, *The Days of Henry Thoreau*, p. 336.
2. Thoreau, *The Portable Thoreau*, *Walden*, p. 325.

SAFE WALKING

1. Thoreau, *The Portable Thoreau*, *Walking*, p. 609

Our Guide Thoreau

HENRY DAVID THOREAU (1817-1862)

1. Thoreau, *The Portable Thoreau*, *Life Without Principle*, p. 636
2. Myerson, ed. *The Cambridge Companion to Henry David Thoreau*, p. 1-11.
3. Thoreau, *The Portable Thoreau*, *Life Without Principle*, p. 633.
4. Harding, *The Days of Henry Thoreau*, p. vii.
5. Robert D. Richardson, *Henry Thoreau: A Life of the Mind*, p. 153.

THOREAU'S *CAPE COD*

6. Thoreau, *Cape Cod*, Parnassus Imprints Inc., p. vii.
7. Channing, *Thoreau, the Poet Naturalist*, p. 21.
8. Harding, *The Days of Henry Thoreau*, p. 361.
9. Thoreau, *The Portable Thoreau*, *The Maine Woods*, p. 95.
10. Thoreau, *The Portable Thoreau*, *Walking*, p. 611.

Individual Walks

HARDING BEACH & LIGHTHOUSE WALK

1. Clark, *Lighthouses of Cape Cod, Martha's Vineyard, Nantucket*, p. 130-135.

THE OUTERMOST WALK

2. Beston, *The Outermost House*, p. 90.

PAMET CRANBERRY & DUNE WALK

3. Willison, *Saints and Strangers*, p. 152.
4. Hicks, "Cranberries on Cape Cod."

PILGRIM SPRING TRAIL

5. Willison, *Saints and Strangers*, p. 149.

SMALL'S SWAMP TRAIL

6. Kaye, "Small's Swamp Trail."
7. Kaye, "Small's Swamp Trail."

PROVINCETOWN CENTER WALK

8. Provincetown Historical Association, "Walking Tour No. 1."
9. Provincetown Historical Association, "Walking Tour No. 1."

Additional Hikes

ADDITIONAL WALK #2

1. Provincetown Historical Association, "Walking Tour No. 1."

The Sites

"THE HOUSE ON NAUSET MARSH" & CEDAR BANKS GOLF COURSE

1. Wyman Richardson, *The House on Nauset Marsh*, p. 99.

DOANE HOMESTEAD MEMORIAL

2. Michael Whatley et al. *The Guide's Guide to the Cape Cod National Seashore*, p. 69-70.

EASTHAM COAST GUARD STATION
   3. Freeman, *A Description of the Eastern Coast of the County of Barnstable*, p. 11.
   4. Bache, "U.S. Costal Survey Map, Nauset Harbor."
NAUSET LIGHT BEACH & THE FRENCH TRANSATLANTIC CABLE
   5. Thoreau, *The Portable Thoreau, Walden*, p. 307.
THREE SISTERS LIGHTS OF NAUSET
   6. West, *Life on the Edge*, p. 17.
CAMP WELLFLEET
   7. Whatley, et. al. *The Guide's Guide to the Cape Cod National Seashore*, p. 120.
MARCONI BEACH
   8. Walling, "1858 Map of the Counties of Barnstable, Dukes & Nantucket."
   9. Freeman, *A Description of the Eastern Coast of the County of Barnstable*, p. 10.
FRESH BROOK VILLAGE
  10. Whatley, et. al. *The Guide's Guide to the Cape Cod National Seashore*, p. 120.
MARCONI STATION SITE
  11. Whatley, *Marconi Wireless on Cape Cod*, p. 17-21.
  12. Whatley, *Marconi Wireless on Cape Cod*, p. 20.
CAHOON HOLLOW BEACH
  13. Bache, "U.S. Costal Survey Map, Cape Cod Light to Nauset Light."
WILLIAMS POND
  14. Bryant, "Following Thoreau," p. 4-5.
BALLSTON BEACH
  15. Whatley et al. *The Guide's Guide to the Cape Cod National Seashore*, p. 173.
HEAD OF THE MEADOW BEACH
  16. Kittredge, *Cape Cod: It's People and Their History*, p. 162.
  17. Whatley et al. *The Guide's Guide to the Cape Cod National Seashore*, p. 201.
PILGRIM SPRING
  18. Whatley et al. *The Guide's Guide to the Cape Cod National Seashore*, p. 200.
PILGRIM LAKE/PROVINCETOWN'S EAST HARBOR
  19. Kittredge, *Cape Cod: It's People and Their History*, p. 162.
PROVINCE LANDS DUNE SHACKS
  20. United States, "Determination of Eligibility for the Dune Shacks Cape Cod National Seashore," p. 1.
  21. Kemp, *Poet of the Dunes*, p. 58.
PEAKED HILL BARS LIFE-SAVING STATION REMAINS
  22. Walling, "1858 Map of the Counties of Barnstable, Dukes & Nantucket."
  23. Egan, *Provincetown as a Stage*, p. 139-140, 144-146.
PROVINCE LANDS VISITOR CENTER & THE PROVINCE LANDS
  24. Kittredge, *Cape Cod: Its People and Their History*, p. 162.
OLD HARBOR LIFE-SAVING STATION MUSEUM
  25. Ryder, *Old Harbor Station Cape Cod*, p. 60.
THE OLD KINGS HIGHWAY
  26. Green, *Names of the Land*, p. 65.
THE CAPE COD NATIONAL SEASHORE
  27. Whatley et al. *The Guide's Guide to the Cape Cod National Seashore*, p. 319.
THE GREAT BEACH
  28. Hay, *The Great Beach*, p. 3.

BIBLIOGRAPHY

Bache, A.D. "U.S. Coastal Survey Map of the Extremity of Cape Cod, Including Provincetown and Parts of Truro," 1857.
--- "U.S. Coastal Survey Map, Cape Cod Light to Nauset Light," 1848.
--- "U.S. Coastal Survey Map, Nauset Harbor," 1856.

Beston, Henry. *The Outermost House.* New York: Henry Holt and Company, 1929.

Bryant, Gregory. "Following Thoreau." *Cape Cod Times*, August 10, 1996, "Summer Times Supplement," p. 4-5.

Burke, William Jeremiah. *Cape Cod Bibliography.* 10 vols. Unpublished manuscript: William Brewster Nickerson Room, Cape Cod Community College, 1973.

Burrows, Fredericka A. *Windmills on Cape Cod & the Islands.* Taunton, Massachusetts: William S. Sullwold Publishing, 1978.

Canby, Henry Seidel. *Thoreau.* Boston: Houghton, 1939.

Chamberlain, Barbara Blau. *These Fragile Outposts.* Yarmouth Port, Massachusetts: Parnassus Imprints, 1981.

Champlain, Samuel de. *Voyages of Samuel de Champlain, 1604-1618.* W.L. Grant, ed. New York: C. Scribner's Sons, 1907.

Channing, Jr. William Ellery. *Thoreau, the Poet Naturalist.* New York: Biblo and Tannen, 1996.

Clark, Admont G. *Lighthouses of Cape Cod, Martha's Vineyard, Nantucket: Their History and Lore.* Orleans, Massachusetts: Parnassus Imprints, 1992.

Conrad, Hawkins, et al. "A Map of Historic Eastham." Eastham, Massachusetts: The Eastham Historical Society, 1994.

Dalton, J.W. *The Life Savers of Cape Cod.* Orleans, Massachusetts: Parnassus Imprints, 1991.

Daubenspeck, Mary van Roden. *Nauset Light: A Personal History.* Lyme, New Hampshire: Blackrabbit Press, 1995.

Deyo, Simeon L. *History of Barnstable County, Massachusetts.* New York: Blake & Co., 1890.

Egan, Leona Rust. *Provincetown As a Stage.* Orleans, Massachusetts: Parnassus Imprints, 1994.

Farson. Robert H. *The Cape Cod Canal.* Middletown, Connecticut: Wesleyan University Press, 1977.

Finch, Robert. *Outlands: Journeys to the Outer Edges of Cape Cod.* Boston: David R. Godine Publisher, 1986.
--- ed. *A Place Apart: A Cape Cod Reader.* New York, London: W.W. Norton & Company, 1993.

Freeman, James. *A Description of the Eastern Coast of the County of Barnstable: From Cape Cod or Race Point, to the Sandy Point of Chatham.* Boston: The Trustees of the Humane Society, 1802.

George, Diane Hume and Malcolm A. Nelson. *Epitaph and Icon: A Field Guide to the Old Burying Grounds of Cape Cod, Martha's Vineyard, and Nantucket.* Orleans, Massachusetts: Parnassus Imprints, 1983.

Gibson, Marjorie Hubbell. *H.M.S. Somerset, 1746-1778: The Life and Times of an Eighteenth Century British Man-o-War and Her Impact on North America.* Cotuit, Massachusetts: Abbey Gate House, 1992.

Green, Eugene and William Sachse. *Names of the Land: Cape Cod, Nantucket, Martha's Vineyard, and the Elizabeth Islands.* Chester, Connecticut: The Globe Pequot Press, 1983.

Harding, Walter. *The Days of Henry Thoreau: A Biography.* New York: Alfred A. Knopf, 1965.

Hay, John. *The Great Beach.* New York, London: W.W. Norton & Company, 1963.

----*The Run.* New York: Ballantine Books, 1959.

Hicks, Margie. *Cranberries on Cape Cod.* Cape Cod National Seashore, National Park Service, U.S. Department of the Interior, 1980.

Hossfeld, Nancy and Michael Whatley. "The Nauset Marsh Trail." National Park Service, U.S. Department of the Interior, 1986.

Kaye, Glen. "Small's Swamp Trail." Cape Cod National Seashore, National Park Service, U.S. Department of the Interior, 1977.

----"Fort Hill Trail." Cape Cod National Seashore, National Park Service, U.S. Department of the Interior, 1978.

Kemp, Harry. *Poet of the Dunes.* Provincetown, Massachusetts: Cape Cod Pilgrim Memorial Association, 1988.

Kittredge, Henry C. *Cape Cod: Its People and Their History.* Orleans, Massachusetts: Parnassus Imprints, 1930.

----*Mooncussers of Cape Cod.* Hamden, Connecticut: Anchon Books, 1971.

Mourt, G. (William Bradford and Edward Winslow). *Mourt's Relation: A Journal of the Pilgrims at Plymouth.* Dwight B. Heath, ed., from the original text of 1622. Bedford, Massachusetts: Applewood Books, 1963.

Myerson, Joel, ed. *The Cambridge Companion to Henry David Thoreau.* New York: The Cambridge University Press, 1995.

Penniman, Augusta. *Journal of a Whaling Voyage.* Dorinda Partsch, ed. Eastham, Massachusetts: Eastern National Park and Monument Association, 1988.

Pratt, Rev. Enoch. *A Comprehensive History, Ecclesiastical and Civil, of Eastham, Wellfleet and Orleans.* Yarmouth, Massachusetts: W.S. Fisher & Co., 1844.

Provincetown Historical Association. "Walking Tour No. 1: The Center of Provincetown." Provincetown, Massachusetts, 1982.

Quinn, William P. *The Saltworks of Historic Cape Cod.* Orleans, Massachusetts: Parnassus Imprints, 1993.

----*Shipwrecks Around Cape Cod.* Farmington, Maine: The Knowlton & McLeary Co., 1973.

Rich, Shebnah. *Truro—Cape Cod or Land Marks and Sea Marks.* Boston: D. Lothrop and Company, 1884.

Richardson, Robert D. *Henry Thoreau: A Life of the Mind.* Berkeley, Los Angeles, London: University of California Press, 1986.

Richardson, Wyman. *The House on Nauset Marsh.* Riverside, Connecticut: The Chatham Press, Inc., 1972.

Ryder, Richard G. *Old Harbor Station Cape Cod.* North Eastham, Massachusetts: Ram Island Press, 1990.

Finishing Up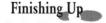

Strahler, Arthur N. *A Geologist's View of Cape Cod*. Orleans, Massachusetts: Parnassus Imprints, 1966.

Stowell, Robert F. *A Thoreau Gazetteer*. Princeton, New Jersey: The Princeton Press, 1970.

Thoreau, Henry David. *Cape Cod*. Joseph J. Moldenhauer, ed. Princeton, New Jersey: Princeton University Press, 1988.
——*Cape Cod*. Orleans, Massachusetts: Parnassus Imprints, Inc., 1984.
——*Cape Cod*. New York: Bramhall House, 1951.
——*Cape Cod: With the Early Photographs of Herbert W. Gleason*. Thea Wheelwright, ed. Barre, Massachusetts: Barre Publishers, 1971.
——*Cape Cod: Henry David Thoreau's Complete Text with the Journey Recreated in Pictures by William F. Robinson*. Boston: Little Brown and Company, 1985.
——*The Journal of Henry D. Thoreau*. Bradford Torrey and Francis H. Allen, eds. New York: Dover Publications, Inc., 1962.
——*Thoreau's Guide to Cape Cod*. Alexander B. Adams, ed. New York: Devin-Adair Company, 1962.
——*Thoreau on Birds: Notes on New England Birds from the Journals of Henry David Thoreau*. Francis H. Allen, ed. Boston: Beacon Press, 1993.
——*The Portable Thoreau*. Carl Bode, ed. New York: Penguin Books, 1947.

United States. United States Department of the Interior. "Determination of Eligibility for the Dune Shacks Cape Cod National Seashore," a memorandum from the Chief of Registration to the Regional Director of the National Register of Historic Places. Washington, D.C.: May 12, 1989.

Walling, Henry F. "1858 Map of the Counties of Barnstable, Dukes & Nantucket." Washington D.C.: D.R. Smith & Co., 1858.

Waldron, Nan Turner. *Journey to Outermost House*. Bethlehem, Connecticut: Butterfly and Wheel Pub., 1991.

West, J. Brian. *Life on the Edge: The Lighthouses of Nauset*. 1989.

Whatley, Michael A. *Marconi Wireless on Cape Cod: South Wellfleet, Massachusetts 1907-1917*, 1987.
——— et al. *The Guide's Guide to Cape Cod National Seashore*. National Park Service and National Park Foundation, 1995.

Willison, George F. *Saints and Strangers*. Orleans, Massachusetts: Parnassus Imprints, 1983.

Wood, Timothy J. *Breakthrough: The Story of Chatham's North Beach*. Chatham, Massachusetts: A Cape Cod Chronicle Publication, 1995.

INDEX

I went to the woods because I wished to live deliberately, to front only the essential facts of life, and see if I could not learn what it had to teach, and not, when I came to die, discover that I had not lived.
— Henry David Thoreau, Walden, 1854.

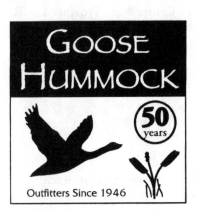

The Goose Hummock Shop has been supplying outdoor enthusiasts on Cape Cod with all they've needed to "front the essential facts" of nature since 1946. They offer the best selection of fishing, hunting, canoeing and kayaking equipment on Cape Cod, as well as a superb inventory of outdoor clothing. Hikers get your Cape Cod topographical maps here!

I wish to speak a word for Nature, for absolute freedom and wildness, as contrasted with a freedom and culture merely civil—to regard man as an inhabitant, or a part and parcel of Nature...
— Henry David Thoreau, Walking, 1862.

Chatham Nature Shoppe
637 Main Street, Chatham (508) 945-7700

Like Thoreau, the Chatham Nature Shoppe strives "to regard man as an inhabitant, or part and parcel of nature." Walkers are invited to stroll on in from Chatham's Main Street to check out the shop's walking sticks, hats, local books and Cape Cod maps. Specializing in educational and natural history products for the whole family, you'll find a great selection of nature-related products such as clothing, toys, gemstone jewelry, drums, candles, natural bath and body products, and so much more. Come in and see what's in store for you.

The Thoreau Society Shop at Walden Pond

The Thoreau Society
Founded in 1941

Society members receive a 10% discount

The Shop at Walden Pond carries an extensive selection of books by and about Henry David Thoreau, the Transcendentalists, and the environmental movement.

Other items include:

- ♠ coffee mugs
- ♠ notecards
- ♠ prints and photographs
- ♠ clothing
- ♠ children's books
- ♠ Walden Pond souvenirs

Check out our new Thoreau quote tees and embroidered Walden Pond sweatshirts and hats!

Simplify, simplify

WALDEN POND

Call, e-mail, or write for a copy of our catalog: 915 Walden Street, Concord, MA 01742, (781) 259-4770, e-mail: shop@walden.org

Consider joining the Thoreau Society.